ROUTE SUMMARY TABLES

C000146349

Stage	Start	Distance (km)				
1	Le Puy-en-Velay	16.7				
2	Montbonnet	26.1				
3	Saugues	19.3				
4	Domaine du Sauvage	28.2	7.30	480	725	60
5	Aumont-Aubrac	27.3	6:45	550	430	67
6	Nasbinals	32.7	10:00	640	1440	73
7	Saint-Côme-d'Olt	21.3	6:00	570	615	83
8	Estaing	35.3	10:00	980	1010	90
9	Conques	24.3	7:30	780	865	99
10	Livinhac-le-Haut	23.2	6:15	495	510	106
11	Figeac	30.8	8:15	620	670	113
12	Cajarc	27.5	7:00	510	340	119
13	Varaire	32.5	7:15	365	550	124
14	Cahors	23.8	6:30	475	415	136
15	Lascabanes	23.7	6:45	615	595	140
16	Lauzerte	27.8	7:30	475	605	145
17	Moissac	19.8	4:30	135	105	152
18	Auvillar	32.8	8:15	590	535	156
19	Lectoure	32.1	8:30	610	695	163
20	Condom	33.8	7:30	460	390	170
21	Éauze	21.0	4:45	250	300	177
22	Nogaro	27.6	6:15	230	255	181
23	Aire-sur-l'Adour	33.8	7:30	485	330	186
24	Arzacq-Arraziguet	30.2	7:30	460	495	191
25	Arthez-de-Béarn	31.6	8:00	475	550	196
26	Navarrenx	19.5	4:15	275	290	202
27	Aroue	24.0	7:00	645	585	206
28	Ostabat-Asme	22.2	5:00	325	310	212
	Saint-Jean-Pied-de-Port					
	TOTAL	**748.9**	**194:00**	**14,455**	**14,965**	

CÉLÉ VALLEY VARIANT

Stage	Start	Distance (km)	Time (hr:min)	Total ascent (m)	Total descent (m)	Page
C1	Figeac	25.7	6:30	475	510	220
C2	Espagnac-Sainte-Eulalie	15.9	5:00	535	555	225
C3	Marcilhac-sur-Célé	18.3	5:45	585	605	229
C4	Cabrerets	10.7	3:30	330	240	233
C5	Saint-Cirq-Lapopie	33.2	9:00	575	675	238
	Cahors					
	TOTAL	**103.8**	**29:45**	**2500**	**2585**	

ROCAMADOUR VARIANT

Stage	Start	Distance (km)	Time (hr:min)	Total ascent (m)	Total descent (m)	Page
R1	Figeac	22.8	6:00	560	375	246
R2	Lacapelle-Marival	24.0	5:30	270	380	250
R3	Gramat	12.4	3:15	185	280	255
R4	Rocamadour	25.5	7:15	745	460	259
R5	Labastide-Murat	24.2	6:00	280	580	263
R6	Vers	16.3	3:30	160	190	267
	Cahors					
	TOTAL	**125.2**	**31:30**	**2170**	**2235**	

CONNECTING TO THE CAMINO DEL NORTE

	Start	Distance (km)	Time	Total ascent (m)	Total descent (m)	Page
The GR10	Saint-Jean-Pied-de-Port	99.2	5 days	5875	6065	271
The Voie Nive Bidassoa	Saint-Jean-Pied-de-Port	77.2	3–4 days	1850	2040	279

CAMINO DE SANTIAGO - VIA PODIENSIS

LE PUY TO THE PYRENEES ON THE GR65

by Dave Whitson

JUNIPER HOUSE, MURLEY MOSS,
OXENHOLME ROAD, KENDAL, CUMBRIA LA9 7RL
www.cicerone.co.uk

© Dave Whitson 2022
First edition 2022
ISBN: 978 1 78631 102 3

Printed in China on responsibly sourced paper on behalf of Latitude Press.
A catalogue record for this book is available from the British Library.

Route mapping by Lovell Johns www.lovelljohns.com
The routes of the GR®, PR® and GRP® paths in this guide have been reproduced with the permission of the Fédération Française de la Randonnée Pédestre holder of the exclusive rights of the routes. The names GR®, PR® and GRP® are registered trademarks. © FFRP 2022 for all GR®, PR® and GRP® paths appearing in this work.

All photographs are by the author unless otherwise stated. Contains OpenStreetMap.org data © OpenStreetMap contributors, CC-BY-SA. NASA relief data courtesy of ESRI

Dedication

This book is dedicated to Alison Raju, who led the way; to all of the students who have accompanied me on pilgrimage, across many different summers; to the hosts in gîtes who have cared for us and so many others, like Sabine and Sylvain, Eden, Rom and Aideen, and Corinne; and to Bronwen Perry and Sandy Brown, for their support, encouragement, and inspiration.

Front cover: Pilgrims on the cliffside trail after Sauliac-sur-Célé (Stage C3)

Symbols used on maps

Ⓢ start point
Ⓕ finish point
Ⓢ/F start/finish point
11.1 distance marker
3.2 alt distance marker
■ building
▲ summit
= footbridge
≍ bridge

~ main route
-~- alternative route
~ main route (alternative stage)
international boundary
regional boundary
-~-- ferry route
▭━━ station/railway
woodland
urban areas

⚓ ferry
🏰 castle
☀ viewpoint
☆ point of interest
• water feature
• other feature
✈ airport
⊕ church
📍 church shown on town map

Facilities

⬛ Accommodation
  🏠 gîte d'étape
  🏠 hotel
  🏠 chambre d'hôte
  🏕 camping

  🌐 groceries
  🚻 public toilets
  🏧 ATM
  🅿 rest/picnic area
  💧 drinking water tap
  ⦿ bus station
  ⦿ rail station
  ⊕ pharmacy
  Ⓗ hospital
  ⊕ medical clinic
  ⓘ tourist/pilgrim information

🍴 Catering
  ☺ bakery
  ⓜ restaurant
  ☕ café

Relief
in metres

1000–1200	
800–1000	
600–800	
400–600	
200–400	
0–200	

SCALE: 1:100,000

0 kilometres 1   2
0 miles   1

MAP SCALES
Route maps at 1:100,000
Town maps are at 1:40,000
unless otherwise indicated
(see scale bar)

GPX files for all routes can be downloaded free at www.cicerone.co.uk/1102/GPX.

CONTENTS

Updates to this guide

While every effort is made by our authors to ensure the accuracy of guidebooks as they go to print, changes can occur during the lifetime of an edition. Any updates that we know of for this guide will be on the Cicerone website (www.cicerone.co.uk/1102/updates), so please check before planning your trip. We also advise that you check information about such things as transport, accommodation and shops locally. Even rights of way can be altered over time.

We are always grateful for information about any discrepancies between a guidebook and the facts on the ground, sent by email to updates@cicerone.co.uk or by post to Cicerone, Juniper House, Murley Moss, Oxenholme Road, Kendal, LA9 7RL.

Register your book: To sign up to receive free updates, special offers and GPX files where available, register your book at www.cicerone.co.uk.

Note on mapping

The route maps in this guide are derived from publicly available data, databases and crowd-sourced data. As such they have not been through the detailed checking procedures that would generally be applied to a published map from an official mapping agency. However, we have reviewed them closely in the light of local knowledge as part of the preparation of this guide.

Pilgrims walk through a field of sunflowers near Lascabanes (Stage 14)

(Above) Looking back from the chemin towards Monistrol-d'Allier (Stage 2)
(Opposite) Setting forth: the view on departure from Le Puy's cathedral (Stage 1)

INTRODUCTION

Be warned: if you journey forth on pilgrimage on the Via Podiensis, you will spend the rest of your days longing to return. Distinguished by delightful and historic French villages and pleasing walking through idyllic countryside, the route offers tranquility and charm in equal measure. With small bakeries churning out *pain au chocolat* in the morning, rustic cafés offering delicious lunches, and home-cooked dinners served with warm hospitality each evening, it's hard not to feel an all-encompassing *joie de vivre*. And behind it all is the sacred and profound pilgrimage tradition that has brought countless faithful along these paths over the centuries,

headed for a destination that sits some 1500km and another country away.

Santiago de Compostela, whose cathedral houses the relics of St James, or Saint-Jacques, was one of three major centers of Catholic pilgrimage in the Middle Ages, along with Rome and Jerusalem. Inspired by religious zeal – particularly the desire to connect more deeply with God through relics, such as the bones of deceased saints – pilgrims from all over the Christian world made the dangerous journey to these celebrated sites. There was no single route to Santiago; the trail began at one's doorstep. But as pilgrims approached Spain, many converged on a handful of routes

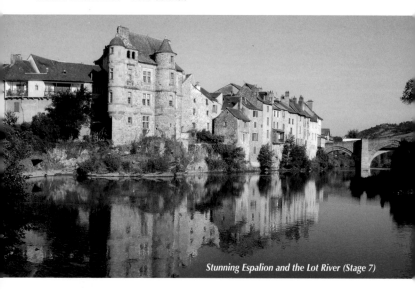

Stunning Espalion and the Lot River (Stage 7)

known historically as the Caminos de Santiago, the Ways of St James, or the Chemins de Saint-Jacques. In France, four major branches of the pilgrim road developed: the Chemin de Tours (from Paris), the Chemin de Vézelay, the Chemin d'Arles, and the Chemin du Puy, from Le Puy-en-Velay.

Those pilgrim roads have experienced a popular resurgence in modern times and are today walked not just by traditional pilgrims but by people from all manner of backgrounds and places. The most frequented branch, Spain's Camino Francés, draws hundreds of thousands of people annually, leading to it often being thought of as *the* Camino de Santiago. However, the French *chemins* are well loved by the smaller subsection of pilgrims that have branched out beyond Spain. The Via

Podiensis – also known as the Chemin du Puy and the GR65 – is specially regarded for its outstanding walking and hospitality.

The Via Podiensis spans roughly 750km through Southern France, from Le Puy-en-Velay to Saint-Jean-Pied-de-Port. The full route takes 4–6 weeks to complete. There are two optional major variants to consider – the Célé Valley and Rocamadour routes – both diverging from the Via Podiensis between Figeac and Cahors. These are described in full detail in this guide. Pilgrims continuing onward to Santiago can proceed directly from Saint-Jean on the Camino Francés. Some, however, may wish to transition over to the Camino del Norte; a skeletal outline of the routes linking Saint-Jean and Irún, Spain is also included.

THE STORIES OF ST JAMES AND ST ROCH

While countless pilgrimage shrines exist within the Catholic world, three cities stand out as major centers of pilgrimage. Two are obvious: Jerusalem is intimately associated with the life of Jesus, while Rome houses the relics of Saints Peter and Paul, not to mention St Peter's Basilica. The third center, situated in an otherwise forgotten corner of Spain, is much more surprising. Santiago de Compostela, in Spain's northwestern region of Galicia, has a history built on equal parts rumor and legend.

Of Jesus's 12 apostles, perhaps less is known about **St James** (or Santiago) than any other. The brother of John and the son of an assertive mother, James was one of Jesus's first followers – and the first to be martyred. However, mystery surrounds James's life following the crucifixion of Christ. Spanish legend asserts that he brought the good word to the Iberian peninsula, but with minimal success, winning few followers. That said, on his subsequent return to the Holy Land he fared worse; he was decapitated by Herod Agrippa in AD44.

After James's death, so the story goes, his disciples smuggled his body to the coast, where it was placed on a stone boat – lacking sails, oars, and sailors – and put to sea. Amazingly, and perhaps under the guidance of angels, this boat maneuvered westward across the Mediterranean and north into the Atlantic, before ultimately making landfall at today's Padrón on the Galician coast. Once there, two disciples met the boat, took James's body, and eventually buried him in present-day Santiago de Compostela.

Saint James and St Roch, as portrayed in Éauze's Cathédrale Saint-Luperc

Almost eight centuries later, in 813, the hermit Pelayo had a vision in which a star shined brightly on a nearby field. Digging there, Pelayo made a stunning discovery: the very bones of St James, buried and forgotten so many years earlier. The timing couldn't have been better for local Christians. With the Moorish conquest of the Iberian peninsula nearly complete, their armies enjoying victory after victory behind the 'arm of Mohammed,' the Christian kingdom of Asturias in northern Spain was in dire straits. However, according to legend, the tide turned at the pivotal (and fictional) Battle of Clavijo. As the Asturian army prepared to face the much larger Muslim force, St James appeared on his white horse and led them into battle, and so began the legend of Santiago Matamoros ('St James the Moor-killer') – one of the saint's two faces along the *camino*, along with Santiago Peregrino ('pilgrim').

The cult of Santiago grew gradually over the next two centuries, before two major developments in the 12th century propelled Compostela to the forefront of the Christian world. First, Diego Gelmírez became the bishop of Santiago in 1101 (and archbishop in 1120), and quickly devoted his life to the aggrandizement of Compostela. Second, the *Codex Calixtinus* emerged sometime in the 1130s or 1140s. The first 'guidebook' to the Camino de Santiago, it included, among other things, a list of miracles attributed to St James, the history of the route, and a collection of practical advice for travelers, including warnings about 'evil toll gatherers' and 'barbarous' locals.

In France, most representations of St James feature him in pilgrim garb, complete with a brown cloak, a broad hat adorned with a scallop shell, and a staff with attached gourd. However, he is not the only saint dressed in this manner. Indeed, along the Via Podiensis, St James might be outshone by **St Roch**. Born to a noble family around 1295 in Montpellier, France, Roch was a blessing to his otherwise childless, older parents. After both parents died, Roch gave his inheritance to the poor, keeping nothing but a pilgrim's garb and the minimal means necessary for survival. He journeyed on pilgrimage to Rome. When he reached Acquapendente, still a stop on today's Via Francigena, he found the town ravaged by plague and offered to treat the ill. While he later reached Rome, plague was a recurring companion, and he continued serving those in need.

Inevitably, Roch too fell ill with the plague. When that happened, in Piacenza, he was chased from town by those he had healed. Taking shelter in a riverside hut, he suffered through privation, until God miraculously intervened, with rainfall to refresh his thirst and a dutiful dog delivering bread. Eventually he recovered and, at age 27, decided to return home. After many years and extended illness, he was now unrecognizable, and was swiftly imprisoned as a suspected spy. He spent five years in jail, only to pass away upon release, at which point he was recognized. In the succeeding decades, miracles followed Roch's name, as he was invoked in defense against the plague.

While Roch is easily confused with James in church statuary and paintings, there are two distinct elements. First, Roch's loyal dog typically appears at his side, bread roll readily accessible. Second, Roch often has his robe lifted,

*Entrance to the village
of Saint-Antoine is
via the medieval gate
(Stage 18)*

exposing one bare leg, to highlight (depending upon the story) a birthmark or plague sore.

In the Middle Ages, hundreds of thousands of pilgrims made the journey to Santiago de Compostela. After a decline following the Reformation and a near-total collapse during the Enlightenment, the Camino de Santiago returned to prominence in the late 20th century.

THE VIA PODIENSIS: YESTERDAY AND TODAY

As Edwin Mullins explains in his excellent overview of the four French pilgrimage routes, *The Four Roads to Heaven*, the Via Podiensis is historically the least documented. However, today's pilgrims benefit from its relative isolation and lack of modern development, with well-preserved medieval villages and towns lining the route.

That said, Le Puy-en-Velay was a sacred destination even before St James's relics were rediscovered. Indeed, Charlemagne, the Holy Roman Emperor, celebrated mass here on two separate occasions. By the 10th century, Le Puy was a pilgrimage destination in its own right. The town's link to Compostela was secured, though, by Bishop Godescalc, who in 950 journeyed on pilgrimage from Le Puy to Santiago. Mullins observes that this may have been the first 'official' visit to Compostela by such a high-ranking church official. Upon returning to Le Puy, Godescalc ordered the construction of the chapel of Saint-Michel-d'Aiguilhe, the town's most distinctive sight, perched atop a tall volcanic spire.

While Le Puy drew many pilgrims in the Middle Ages, with three hospitals serving pilgrims in the 13th century, and it was acknowledged in the *Codex Calixtinus* as one of the primary French routes to Compostela, it rapidly receded from the spotlight. Indeed, by the 19th century its connection to Santiago was largely forgotten. Only when the archives of Haute-Loire were reopened did its once-prominent role resurface. It wasn't until the late 20th century, though, that walkers returned in any real numbers. The key event was not the resurgence of interest in Santiago, but rather the growing phenomenon of walking holidays, which spurred the development of Grande Randonnée (GR) routes in Europe. The first GR route was established in 1947; the GR65, as the Via Podiensis became numbered, followed in the early 1970s. Today, the Via Podiensis is as popular as any of the four major *Chemins de Saint-Jacques*.

REGIONS ENCOUNTERED ALONG THE ROUTE

The French nation-building project that unfolded following the 18th-century French Revolution should also be viewed as a regional-identity-destroying initiative. This process is wonderfully described by Graham Robb in *The Discovery of France*. At the time of the Revolution, four-fifths of the population was rural, and most people rarely travelled more than a day's journey beyond their birthplace over their lives. French towns were isolated and confined, and linguistic differences were profound. The Abbé Gregoire, who assumed responsibility for language in the 1790s, determined that no more than 3 million Frenchmen (roughly 11% of the population) were 'pure' French speakers. Once outside of the greater Paris region, France was marked by a proliferation of languages and dialects. Peasants, the Abbé concluded, were 'too ignorant to be patriotic.'

One of the first steps taken to combat regional identities was the elimination of traditional provinces in 1790. These were replaced by departments, all roughly equal in size, with the idea being that all citizens would live within a day's ride of their capital. This fragmentation placed significant power in Paris, as no individual department wielded meaningful authority. That imbalance was only remedied in 1982, with the establishment of administrative regions, each composed of multiple departments.

Setting aside the political merits of these changes, they eroded traditional identities by replacing distinct and meaningful names with more banal geographical identifiers. Gascons were a people; by contrast, Tarn et Garonne are a pair of rivers. In the regional breakdown that follows, the sections are organized around the three traditional provinces encountered.

Languedoc

The name of this historic province highlights a critical phenomenon. France was loosely divided into two linguistic regions: the *langues d'oc* and the *langues d'oïl*. These differentiate between how 'yes' was expressed, with the northern dialects saying *oïl* (or the more familiar *oui*), and the southern ones (most significantly Occitan) saying *oc*. The province became attached to the Kingdom of France following the 13th-century Albigensian Crusade against the Cathars. With its centers of power situated in Toulouse and Montpellier, the parts of Languedoc situated on the Via Podiensis enjoyed a great deal of geographic isolation, and thus a high degree of autonomy, until the Revolution.

Today, this northern portion of historic Languedoc falls within the **Auvergne-Rhône-Alpes** region. The first three stages of the *chemin*, between Le Puy-en-Velay and Domaine du Sauvage, are in the **Haute-Loire** department. These move from the historic area of **Velay**, shaped by its volcanic past, to the former province of **Gévaudan**, once a rugged and wild area. Historic Languedoc also included the Aubrac plateau, but for clarity's sake that will be discussed in the next section.

Guyenne and Gascony

The bulk of the Via Podiensis passes through this former province, which – as the name suggests – was once two separate provinces. Guyenne was part of Aquitaine, but it broke away in the 13th century, only to merge with Gascony in the 17th century. Gascony has a more resonant history, distinguished by famous characters like the Three Musketeers and Cyrano de Bergerac. The French desire to reassert control over Gascony, which had passed under English control, was a key cause of the Hundred Years' War.

The next 19 stages of the Via Podiensis, along with the Célé Valley and Rocamadour variants, fall in this historic province. Conveniently, they are also all included in the new region of **Occitanie**, which in 2016 replaced the two earlier regions of Languedoc-Roussillon and Midi-Pyrénées. Stages 4 and 5 are part

of the **Lozère** department, while Stages 6–9 are in the **Aveyron** department. All six of those stages pass through the Aubrac Plateau, a granite and volcanic plateau – and rich cattle country – that is the highest-elevation section of the Via Podiensis, before descending abruptly to the Lot River valley at the end of Stage 7.

The **Lot** department, though, doesn't begin until Stage 10, lasting through Stage 15 and also including the Célé Valley and Rocamadour variants. This overlaps in part with historic **Quercy**. The GR65 passes through the Causse de Quercy, while the Rocamadour variant climbs through the Causse de Gramat, both raised limestone plateaus, although much lower in elevation than the Aubrac. Meanwhile, the Célé Valley variant winds between the river valley and its neighboring cliffs. The routes rejoin in or near Cahors and then diverge from the Lot

The Aubrac's cattle are not always impressed by pilgrims

Pilgrims descend through rolling hills near Durfort-Lacapelette (Stage 16)

River, leaving the department just before Lauzerte. After passing briefly through the **Tarn et Garonne** department and its eponymous rivers, in Stages 16 and 17, the region concludes in the **Gers** department – the heart of historic Gascony – for Stages 18–22. Over the course of the last two departments, the frequent ups-and-downs of the river valleys yield to increasingly gentle terrain, characterized by sunflowers, orchards, and vineyards.

Béarn and Basque Country

Once again, this final section includes two distinct historical areas: proud regions with strong traditions of self-rule. The town of Arthez-de-Béarn, in Stage 24, still bears the name, while Basque cultural traditions have experienced a resurgence over the last half-century. **Béarn's** independence came to an end in the 16th-century Wars of Religion; the region's leaders had promoted Protestantism, drawing the

brunt of the French crown's pro-Catholic response. Meanwhile, the **Basque Country** enjoyed significant autonomy until the French Revolution, when it suffered terribly, with whole town populations forcibly deported to Gascony by the state, as military leaders questioned their loyalty in the border zone. Conditions improved in succeeding decades, though, and while some independence movements flickered to life in the late 20th century, those have not gained the prominence of their Spanish Basque equivalent.

The final six stages of the Via Podiensis fall into these historic provinces, all of which today comprise the **Nouvelle-Aquitaine** region. Most of Stage 23, between Aire-sur-l'Adour and Pimbo, is situated in the **Landes** department; everything else is in the **Pyrénées-Atlantiques**. This is rich agricultural terrain, with large fields, often dominated by corn. Only in the penultimate stage does the route encounter notable Pyrenean foothills – a reminder that the easy walking is over (for now at least), with mountains and the Spanish border just ahead for those continuing on the Camino Francés to Santiago de Compostela.

A TURBULENT HISTORY

The peacefulness that permeates the Via Podiensis today belies the turbulent history that has repeatedly ravaged this countryside over the past millennium. The following overview necessarily neglects ancient conflicts, like the Roman conquest of the Gauls, as well as more recent ones, like the two world wars – despite those, too, having left their mark on this route. Instead, it focuses on four pivotal conflicts that dramatically reshaped towns and villages along the way.

While the most famous crusades occurred in the Holy Land and Spain, France hosted its own. The **Albigensian Crusade** (1209–29) saw the Church turn inward to root out heresy at home. The target was the Cathars, a group of Christians based in Southern France, whose Manichean outlook – which divided the world into good and evil – rejected the Church's authority. Pope Innocent III called for the faithful to take action, promising full remission of sins and former Cathar land to those who took the field. Nobody received this call more enthusiastically than Simon de Montfort, a minor noble who gained prominence as a cruelly effective leader. While he wouldn't survive the conflict, he emerged as the dominant landowner in Occitanie before his death. And indeed, that reflects the underlying incentive for the French crown in supporting this initiative, as the crusade provided an excuse to formally colonize much of Southern France. For that reason, fighting persisted beyond the Cathars' eradication until the Toulouse nobility was appropriately cowed. Following the war, a wave of new, fortified towns was established throughout the region, further reinforcing control. Known as **bastides**, nearly 700 were built over roughly 150 years; many are encountered on the *chemin*.

Many people know that the **Hundred Years' War** (1337–1453) was neither a single war nor lasted a hundred years; few know much more. The war was partially triggered by a succession dispute, in which Philip, the Count of Valois, was raised to the French throne, over Edward III of England, who also had a claim. Philip responded to that claim by seizing Aquitaine, a sizable duchy that covered most of Southwest France, which had been under Edward's rule. In response, Edward asserted his right to the French crown. While the wars that followed were much messier than a simple French-English conflict, with many feudal commitments causing entangled loyalties, it nonetheless kindled a nascent French nationalism. Joan of Arc played a significant part in this. Believing that she was chosen by God to expel the English from France, she led troops into battle in Orléans, inspiring them to victory. Ultimately captured by the English, tried as a heretic, and burned at the stake, she nonetheless left a lasting legacy. And while she didn't live to see it, she would have appreciated the outcome: by the time hostilities ceased, the English were driven from France completely, save for Calais.

The Protestant Reformation shook the world, and in France it spawned a series of conflicts later known as the **French Wars of Religion** (1562–98). In the decades following Luther's declaration, small Huguenot (French Protestant) communities took root, while others were influenced by John Calvin, in nearby Geneva. French leaders made modest attempts at accommodation, but these failed decisively. Due to the French Crown's deep relationship with the Catholic Church, Protestantism soon became seen as a particular threat, as the questioning of Church authority would inevitably extend to its royal equivalent. The Béarn emerged as a Huguenot hotbed, with its leaders – most notably Jeanne d'Albret, the Queen of Navarre – endorsing Protestantism. While labeled as wars, these conflicts were bitterly and foully contested, and most infamously associated with mass slaughter by both sides. Ultimately, they expired when Jeanne d'Albret's grandson, Henry of Navarre, the heir to the French throne, converted to Catholicism in 1598. In conjunction with this, he published the Edict of Nantes, granting some rights to Huguenots (although this was revoked by Louis XIV in 1685, leading to the effective expulsion of the Huguenot population). While the fighting thus officially concluded, tensions would long linger on these fault lines.

The **French Revolution**, of course, had a profound series of impacts. For our immediate purposes, though, the religious impact was particularly notable. The revolutionary leaders tapped into popular resentment towards the nobility and clergy, a consequence of the great wealth and power both enjoyed. This inspired a wave of anti-clerical violence in the revolution's initial years. At the same time, France moved through a process of de-Christianization, with freedom of religion declared as the Church hierarchy was moved beneath civil authority. As part of this, Church property was nationalized – and then it was ravaged. Revolutionary leaders called for the destruction of statues, crosses, and bells; churches were shuttered, sold off, repurposed, and destroyed. While the Concordat of 1801 ended the most disruptive part of this transition, former Church properties were not restored to their ownership. The scars of these years remain evident on many of the country's surviving churches.

Joan of Arc, as portrayed in stained glass in Issendolus's church (Rocamadour variant, Stage R2)

Pilgrim routes to Santiago through France and Spain

CHOOSING YOUR ROUTE

Completing the full Via Podiensis, walking from Le Puy-en-Velay to Saint-Jean-Pied-de-Port, typically requires 4–5 weeks, not counting rest days – although some take longer and enjoy every minute. A four-week approach operates at a 26km daily average, while a five-week schedule drops that pace to 21km per day.

While there are many smaller route choices to make, the biggest decision involves Stages 11–13 on the Via Podiensis between Figeac and Cahors. There are three options. The Via Podiensis (GR65) loops south of the Lot River, through the Causse du Quercy. It's the shortest option and the easiest walking. The Célé Valley variant (GR651) follows the Célé River from Figeac through a narrow valley with limestone cliffs flanking each side. It's much more strenuous than the GR65, but also quite scenic and much loved by walkers. Finally, the Rocamadour variant follows the GR6 and GR46, leading north from Figeac to the famous pilgrimage shrine, and then looping back to the southwest. This is the longest option and middle-of-the-pack in terms of challenge. The latter two variants converge near Vers and then rejoin the GR65 in Cahors. If following either variant, add 2–3 days to your schedule. Don't simply default to the GR65 because it seems 'official;' the other two routes have notable advantages to consider.

Many pilgrims, due to time constraints, complete the route in sections. The larger towns – Le Puy-en-Velay, Figeac, Cahors, Moissac, and Condom – offer the best transportation connections. Figeac and Condom are particularly well positioned to break the walk into three equivalent chunks.

While the Camino Francés in Spain sees a significant increase in pilgrim traffic as it proceeds westward, the Chemin du Puy is quite different. Indeed, the opening section, between Le Puy-en-Velay and Conques, is the busiest, as it's very popular among French walking

The cliff-side trail leading into Cabrerets (Célé Valley variant, Stage C3)

groups. It's also the most strenuous part of the walk, aside from the Célé Valley variant. The next section, between Conques and Cahors, is also quite popular, but the three route options after Figeac disperse traffic quite well. After Cahors, many of the holiday walkers return home, leaving mostly pilgrims on the trail. From that point on, the route has much less foot traffic – and much easier walking – right up until Saint-Jean-Pied-de-Port, when the Camino Francés crowds arrive.

WHEN TO GO

Spring and fall are the most popular seasons on the Via Podiensis, with May and September standing out as periods of peak traffic – and, perhaps, peak beauty. Temperatures are generally comfortable, rainfall is moderate, and all services are on offer. By contrast, summer is less crowded, due to hot conditions, particularly as you move further south (although Le Puy to Conques in August still draws many holiday walkers).

The areas exposed to the worst weather come early on the route. Snow is possible in the Aubrac Plateau in April and conditions can still be quite cold and wet in May and June. Indeed, at that elevation, a nasty storm can hit any time. So, warmer layers may be required for the first week of your pilgrimage, but rarely after that.

While the Via Podiensis can technically be walked all year, the offseason (November to Holy Week) is very challenging. Many *gîtes* and other businesses close, as pilgrim and tourist traffic dissipates almost completely. The Aubrac Plateau is a truly intimidating proposition, with snow blanketing the land (and waymarks). Dirt tracks and footpaths, always vulnerable to becoming slick and squishy following a rainstorm, can become quite a slog. Those hardy souls seeking solitude will have it, but this should only be considered by those with experience, and with careful planning.

PREPARATION AND PLANNING

The most important part of your preparation is the physical component, training for the rigors of the trail by walking. Start slowly and build as your body allows, gradually increasing the distances covered. As you become stronger, add weight to your pack until its contents mirror what you will carry in France. If possible, hike on consecutive days; what feels easy on fresh legs can be more draining on tired ones.

As you train, monitor three areas. First, track how much distance you can cover comfortably, how your body responds to breaks, and what kinds of food provide you with the energy that you need. Second, keep a close eye on your feet, watching for blisters or other hot spots, and figure out what kinds of treatment work for you. Third, test your gear and clothing, making sure that your pack fits properly, the weight is manageable, and your clothes don't chafe.

Read about the Via Podiensis and pilgrimage more generally before you go. Knowing some of the region's history and language will add meaning to your walk. Familiarity with Romanesque and Gothic architecture will help you to know where to direct your eye. Some sense of anticipated highlights will help with planning stopping points. Every gîte has its own distinct qualities, so read about other pilgrims' experiences. A selection of background reading is included in Appendix D.

That said, unless your schedule is quite restrictive, try to arrive in France without a rigid plan. Take it easy early on. Many pilgrims arrive overflowing with energy and excitement and go too far in their initial stages. It's better to stop too soon than push too far, as the consequences of over-exertion can linger in the forms of blisters, tendonitis, or other aches and pains for many days.

In addition, be wary of setting your spiritual expectations too high. Many pilgrims spend their *chemin* waiting for their epiphany, the life-changing moment of enlightenment that they feel is promised to them, only to be disappointed when it never arrives. Every pilgrim's experience is different.

BEING A PILGRIM

Simply walking a pilgrimage route does not make one a pilgrim; intention is required. However, pilgrimage can mean many things. Indeed, it always has. Some of today's pilgrims on the Via Podiensis are practicing Catholics, making the journey as an act of faith. Many bring a diverse array of other religious backgrounds and are drawn to the walk's spiritual qualities. Others have a purely secular orientation but seek growth through a physical or communal experience. Of course, some walk solely to walk, with no pilgrimage intentions at all, and there's room for them as well! All of that said, several unique elements of the pilgrim experience deserve comment:

The rising sun peeps through a pilgrim sign on the high-level variant near Boudou (Stage 17)

Pilgrim passport

Known as the *creánciale* in French, this document identifies you as a pilgrim. It's available from Le Puy-en-Velay's cathedral, major tourism offices along the route, and many Camino-related groups, such as the UK's Confraternity of St James (CSJ) (paid-up members only) and the US-based American Pilgrims on the Camino (APOC). You will get a stamp (*tampon*) each day, usually in a gîte, although also in bars, churches, and tourism offices. For most pilgrims, this becomes a treasured memento.

Hospitality

While most gîtes along the Via Podiensis are not exclusively opened to pilgrims – a notable difference from Spain – many hosts are former pilgrims or passionate about supporting walkers. They are

A pilgrim approaches the village of Pimbo (Stage 23)

attuned to the particular needs of long-distance hikers and offer the facilities necessary to support those. Perhaps most importantly, they offer a space where pilgrims can come together each day, sharing stories and making plans. Similarly, friends of the *chemin* sometimes host evening receptions, welcoming pilgrims with a drink and good company.

Pilgrim ethic

A common saying in Spanish is '*Turistas manden; peregrinos agradecen*' ('Tourists demand; pilgrims give thanks'). While challenging to remember at the end of a long day, it is an important message to internalize. Gîte hosts work long days, sometimes juggling hospitality obligations with another full-time gig. Waymarks are maintained by local organizations. It is easy to find fault, but be cognizant of how many people are giving their time, money, and energy to make your pilgrimage possible. Leave the *chemin* better than you found it.

Masses, blessings, and other services

While no pilgrims are obligated to participate in religious services, for some these are a valued part of the experience. Many attend the morning mass and pilgrim blessing in Le Puy before starting their pilgrimage. Others are drawn to hear the nuns singing vespers in Moissac, the monastic services in Vaylats, the intimate mass in Lascabanes, and the blessing and organ concert in Conques. During communion, non-Catholics can request a pilgrim blessing by crossing their arms before the priest.

25

The Compostela

Should your pilgrimage lead you to Santiago, the Archbishopric will award you the Compostela – a document acknowledging your completion of the pilgrimage – if you meet two conditions. First, you must have your *creánciale*, with stamps documenting your progress (including at least **two** stamps daily over the final 100km). Second, you must have walked the final 100km or bicycled the final 200km. Prior to that (which includes all of France!), it is acceptable to skip ahead. There is no certificate specific to completing the Via Podiensis.

GETTING THERE AND BACK

Getting to Le Puy-en-Velay

On foot

Pilgrims approaching Le Puy-en-Velay on foot do so from three different routes. The most common is from Geneva, Switzerland, also following the GR65 and spanning roughly 350km. A second option leads from the historic monastic center of Cluny, following the GR765 for roughly 320km. Finally, some walk 160km from Lyon, on the Chemin de César.

By air and train

Most pilgrims travel to Le Puy by plane and then train. The majority fly into Paris and then onwards via TGV (high-speed train) either directly from Charles du Gaulle Airport or from Gare du Lyon in the city center. The latter offers more frequent departures. The journey generally takes 4hr 30min–6hr and includes

a connection in Saint-Etienne and/or Lyon. Don't be surprised if the last leg shifts from train to bus in Saint-Etienne, as the line seems to be frequently under repair. UK pilgrims have the alternative of avoiding the plane and taking the TGV direct from London, a journey of 2hr 15min. Some opt to bypass Paris and fly into Lyon. The Rhone Express links the airport to Lyon Part-Dieu station, and then a 2hr 30min train journey, also including a connection in Saint-Etienne, brings pilgrims onward to Le Puy. Regardless of the approach, you will likely get a better price if booking train tickets early. See Appendix B for useful transport contact details.

Other likely points of departure

The other major towns on the Via Podiensis – Figeac, Cahors, Moissac, and Condom – are generally reached through a similar combination of air and rail, with most still routing through Paris. The train trip duration varies between 4hr 45min (Moissac), 5hr (Condom, includes a bus), 5hr 30min (Cahors), and 6hr 30min (Figeac). As you move further south, Toulouse-Blagnac Airport becomes an increasingly appealing alternative to Paris's airports. Indeed, train travel from Toulouse's city center to Moissac is less than an hour, while Cahors is only 1hr 30min away.

Getting back from Saint-Jean-Pied-de-Port

By train

A regular, hour-long service connects Saint-Jean-Pied-de-Port with Bayonne. From there, regular TGV service delivers travelers into Paris in 4hr.

The Pont Notre-Dame over the Nive River in Saint-Jean-Pied-de-Port

By air

Biarritz airport, near Bayonne, offers no-frills connections to Paris and London, among other major cities. On the Spanish side, Pamplona and San Sebastián have small airports with very few flights, mostly oriented towards Madrid and Barcelona.

WHERE TO STAY

Gîtes, providing dorm-style accommodation primarily (but often not exclusively) for walkers, are widely available along the Via Podiensis and its variants. Pilgrims with experience on the Camino de Santiago will be familiar with the albergues, or pilgrim hostels, located there. In comparison, gîtes tend to be smaller (most have fewer than 20 beds), with more amenities and a higher level of upkeeping. Single beds are more common than bunks. Some gîtes also offer private rooms. Of course, the price is also a bit higher, in the €12–20 range for beds and €35–60 for rooms.

Perhaps the most notable aspect of French gîtes is the availability of home-cooked meals, often produced with locally grown ingredients, following regional recipes. Many pilgrims find this to be a major highlight, with long, relaxing dinners that include multiple courses, plenty of wine, and convivial conversation (often predominantly in French). Breakfasts don't stray too far from the basic continental model, but toast is often complemented with home-made jams produced from local fruits. Many gîtes will prepare a picnic lunch (€6–8) on request. To add dinner and breakfast to your gîte stay, ask for *demi-pension* (typically €16–22). Most gîtes are willing to accommodate different dietary restrictions, but make this request in advance.

There are different kinds of gîtes, although the distinction is often indiscernible to the walker. By and large, pilgrims stay in **gîtes d'etape**, which are geared primarily towards walkers and bikers staying for a single night. Unlike in Spain, though, it is usually fine to stay multiple nights. In this guidebook, for the most part, when you read 'gîte,' think 'gîte d'etape.' Many towns along the *chemin* operate their own gîtes, generally called **gîtes communal** or **gîtes municipal**. These tend to be a little cheaper, a bit more basic, and often don't offer *demi-pension*, although there are notable exceptions. You will also see accommodations labeled as **Accueil Pèlerins** and **Accueil Chrétien**. The former tends to be a gîte-like operation offered exclusively to pilgrims, while the latter explicitly operates in the Christian spirit, and is sometimes based in larger institutions, like monasteries and convents. Either may operate on a donation-based model. Please note that 'donation' does not mean 'free;' if you can give more, it will allow your hosts to continue providing hospitality to others who cannot. You may also encounter **gîtes rural**. These are rarely relevant to walkers, as they tend to be holiday homes booked by families or groups for multi-day stays.

Of course, all pilgrims are welcome to stay in any manner of accommodation. Some find the gîtes to be a central part of the experience, while others need additional comfort to regroup for the next day's walk. A range of options is presented for each stage in this guide, but other possibilities can always be found at the local tourism office. A popular alternative to gîtes is the **chambre d'hôte**, which offers a small number of B&B-style rooms in the host's own home, thus combining the privacy of a bedroom with the hospitality of an attentive host. **Hotels** are available in most towns, organized on a five-star scale. The word **auberge** literally translates

A gîte appeals to pilgrims in Saint-Privat-d'Allier (Stage 2)

to 'hostel,' but in practice you'll see it linked to everything from youth hostels to bed and breakfasts to rural hotels. Finally, **campsites** (*campings*) can be good options. While some only offer space for RVs and tents, others have bungalows, mobile homes, or hut-style dorm accommodation. Tent-carrying pilgrims should also note that many gîtes will allow you to pitch a tent on their property.

It is customary on the Via Podiensis to make a reservation, especially if requesting demi-pension, as this helps your host prepare. While not explicitly required at many places, it may be necessary if walking in the peak months of May and September, particularly between Le Puy-en-Velay and Conques. If you don't speak French, just ask your host to call; this is quite a common request. Many hotels and chambres d'hôtes are also listed on booking.com, although this might be at a higher price than if reserved directly.

TIPS FOR MAKING THE MOST OF YOUR WALK

WHAT TO PACK

Remember that you will have to carry everything you take, every day (unless using a baggage transportation service – see below). The guiding principle is to pack light, bringing what is absolutely necessary and cutting everything else. As the *chemin* passes regularly through towns, it will be possible to restock or acquire new supplies.

Footwear

Walkers passionately debate whether shoes or boots are superior. Modern cross-trainers typically provide a great deal of support and comfort, without the weight and bulkiness of boots, and are advisable for most. If you prefer boots, it's particularly important that they are broken in prior to departure. Outside summer, it is worth considering waterproof shoes, although these have their downsides, most notably a loss of 'breathability' that tends to result in hotter feet. In addition, bring a pair of sandals suitable for post-walk strolls and emergency trail use if your primary footwear fails you.

Sleeping sheet

A sleeping bag is generally unnecessary, as gîtes are equipped with blankets. Silk or cotton sleeping bag liners weigh little and are easily washed. However, if you feel strongly compelled to bring a sleeping bag, use an ultra-lightweight +5°C bag.

Backpack

Those carrying a sleeping sheet can comfortably walk the *chemin* with a 35–40-liter pack. Look for a pack that

The first view of Rocamadour from the trail (Rocamadour variant, Stage R3)

is properly sized for your torso and distributes the weight to your hips.

Clothing

Aim for two or three sets of clothes (shirt/top, socks, underwear) – one or two in your pack and one on you – along with two pairs of shorts/pants. Avoid cotton. Synthetic clothing wicks moisture from the body, dries quickly, and packs light. Finally, bring a warm outer layer. In the offseason, a long-sleeved/legged base layer is recommended as well. Conditions can be quite cold in the Aubrac, so track the forecast in that area closely.

Poncho

A good poncho will cover both person and pack and can be donned quickly. If walking outside of summer, consider more extensive raingear.

Water

Personal preference will determine the choice of either a bottle or hydration bladder, but make sure to always have at least a liter of water with you, and more on certain stretches.

Pack towel

A synthetic, chamois-style towel packs lighter and smaller than a normal towel and dries faster.

Basic first-aid kit

Bring small amounts of most first-aid essentials. It's easy to buy more. Pack a good supply of foot-care materials, including Compeed, moleskin, or another similar product to treat blisters, and a sterilized needle.

Flashlight/headlamp

Essential for late-night bathroom runs, early-morning packing, and pre-sunrise walking, not to mention the occasional, impromptu cave exploration.

Toiletries

Limit these to the essentials (including sunscreen) – you can always resupply!

Other gear worth considering

A hat, sunglasses, neck gaiter, swimsuit, notepad/pen, bowl and utensils, digital camera, smartphone, plug adapter, and French–English dictionary. Trekking poles are commonplace in France. If you're adding these to your kit, first research how to use them most effectively – it's not entirely intuitive.

FOOD AND DRINK

More so than on many other pilgrimage routes, food is a major highlight on the Via Podiensis. Many pilgrims receive most of their breakfasts and dinners in their gîtes. This is not required, though, and other options abound.

In the morning, follow your nose to the nearest *boulangerie*, for a *croissant* or *pain au chocolat* (€1) that is still warm and flaky. Bakeries are also fantastic places to load up on trail snacks, including quiches (€2.50) and sandwiches (€4–5). Head over to a bar for *un café* (a shot of espresso, €1–2) or *café au lait* (€2.50). In the *chemin's* northern portion, you may be able to grab lunch at a farm café, where the fare includes sandwiches on thick, crusty bread (€5), fresh salads (€7), and fruit tarts (€3.50). The cheese, of course, is outstanding. In a café, it's common to see warm

A hybrid boulangerie–épicerie keeps pilgrims well stocked in Saint-Privat-d'Allier (Stage 2)

sandwiches available, like the classic *croque-monsieur* and *jambon-beurre* (€6). More formal sit-down lunches and dinners will often have multiple courses, with a soup or salad leading to a main dish, followed by a cheese plate or dessert (€12–20 and beyond).

Regional specialties are a joy to discover. Le Puy-en-Velay is famous for its green lentils. The dominant dish in the Aubrac is aligot: a cheesy, mashed potato concoction. Both are commonly served with sausages. Duck moves into the spotlight further south, often served as duck *confit*, while *pâté* is widely available throughout. Finally, fish takes a more prominent role in the Basque Country. The array of cheeses and homemade yogurts are a special part of cattle country.

Wine is, of course, *de rigueur* at every meal. Some meals also open and close with an *aperitif* and *digestif*, respectively. The former is typically a drier alcohol, to kindle the appetite, while the latter is often sweeter. Gîtes will often welcome walkers with *sirop à l'eau*, a sweet syrup (mint is popular) mixed into ice water. On the trail, water fountains are often encountered, particularly near churches, *mairies* (town halls), and cemeteries.

Some gîtes have open kitchens, where pilgrims can prepare their own meals. Groceries (*épiceries*) and supermarkets are accessible on most days, although some planning is often necessary. Most shops and supermarkets close during mid-day, so typical opening hours are from 8.30am to 12.30pm and 4–6.30pm. In addition, most are closed on at least one day (typically Sunday or Monday, sometimes both), while smaller groceries often also close on at least one weekday afternoon. Note as well that some businesses operate on seasonal schedules, and may be closed or have reduced hours in the winter. Never depend on a single grocery or café for your needs, as you may find it closed even when all indications are that it should be open!

A list of *épiceries*, bakeries, cafés, and other food services, frequently updated and including opening schedules, is available at http://davewhitson.com and www.cicerone.co.uk/1102.

POSTAL SERVICES AND BAGGAGE TRANSPORTATION

It is difficult to generalize post office (*la poste*) operating hours along the *chemin*. In larger towns, they will likely operate in both the morning (9am–12 noon) and afternoon (2–5pm) on weekdays and Saturday mornings. In smaller towns, the schedule is more erratic, perhaps only opening on three weekday mornings. Most have schedules posted on Google Maps, so check ahead. Stamps are available in post offices and tobacco shops (*tabacs*).

If you find yourself with unnecessary gear, but don't want to abandon it, consider mailing it ahead to your final destination, which will likely be considerably cheaper than sending it home. If you have a reservation already booked for that destination, your hosts may be willing to store a package. Otherwise, though, the 'poste restante' system allows you to mail the package to your destination's post office. For example, here is how you would label a package for mailing to Saint-Jean-Pied-de-Port: Bureau de Poste / A l'attention de (Your Passport Name) / Poste Restante / 1 Rue de la Poste / 64220 Saint-Jean-Pied-de-Port. Take photo identification to retrieve your package.

Two companies offer baggage transportation services along the Via Podiensis. **La Malle Postale** provides service between Le Puy-en-Velay and Moissac, and also serves the Célé Valley and Rocamadour variants, between April and October (www.lamallepostale.com/en). Meanwhile, **Transport Claudine** operates between Conques and Saint-Jean-Pied-de-Port, as well as on the Célé Valley variant (www.claudine32.com), from April through October.

As of 2022, baggage transportation on the Via Podiensis costs €7.50–8.50 per stage. Most companies pick up bags from your previous night's accommodation and deliver them directly to your next destination. It's possible to prebook your full itinerary in advance, and this may result in a discounted rate, but you can also typically phone the night before (prior to 7pm) to schedule a single day's service.

Baggage transportation can be a particularly prudent choice during the first week, if you're concerned about how your body will respond. If you anticipate shipping your pack ahead, bring a lightweight day pack as well, to carry valuables, snacks, essential medications, and water.

TELEPHONES AND INTERNET

Public access to phones and internet-connected computers is very limited on the Via Podiensis. Some gîtes have computers available, while some tourism offices provide access for a small fee.

Leaving Conques on a foggy morning (Stage 9)

It is now commonplace for pilgrims to travel with smartphones. Wifi access is abundant (note that it's pronounced *weefee*!), so it's possible to keep your phone in airplane mode and operate exclusively when connected, making calls through Skype and texting through WhatsApp, or similar apps. If you wish to have phone service, though, you have two options. First, check with your home provider; international plans are increasingly affordable. Second, consider purchasing a French SIM card, which could be used for phone calls only, or could also include a data package. Some companies have offices in Le Puy-en-Velay, like Orange, while others, like LeFrenchMobile, sell online.

OTHER LOCAL FACILITIES

Many towns along the *chemin* have **tourism offices**, which can help with booking accommodations and exploring transportation options, and usually offer wifi and a pilgrim stamp. English is usually spoken. French **banking** hours in larger towns typically run from around 9am–12.30pm and then 2–5pm, Tuesday to Friday, with many also open on Monday or Saturday. In smaller towns and villages, though, don't expect an afternoon opening. **ATMs** are generally available every 2–3 days on the GR65, although there are none in the Célé Valley. **Pharmacies** are available in most towns with populations exceeding 500 and maintain a similar schedule to supermarkets. Medications, even basic items such as ibuprofen, are only available from pharmacies. Municipal **swimming pools** can be a refreshing afternoon diversion in the summer; most offer single-day passes to visitors, but you'll need a swimsuit. **Hospitals** are rare along the way, but doctors may be available on-call in smaller places; ask your host or at the tourism office. In the event of an **emergency**, dial 112, or you can make a more targeted call: 15 (medical), 17 (police), or 18 (fire).

HOW TO USE THIS GUIDE

ROUTE DESCRIPTIONS

This guidebook breaks the pilgrimage into stages. With rare exceptions, each stage ends in a town or village with available services; all have at least one gîte d'etape. However, these stages are simply organizational aids and should not be considered the 'official' way of walking the route. Listen to your body: if you're struggling, stop earlier; if you're flying, enjoy it. Listen to your heart: if the beauty of a place strikes you, stick around. And listen to your fellow pilgrims: they may have excellent advice to offer. While it's convenient to end the day in a place with many services, part of the charm for many pilgrims on the Via Podiensis is sleeping in the country, surrounded by nothing but peace, quiet, and majestic cattle.

Each stage is laid out in the following format:

ROUTE SUMMARY INFORMATION

A summary is included at the start of each stage that provides the specific starting and ending point as well as information summarizing the walk.

Total distance: The distance corresponds to the recommended route, which isn't always the 'official' Via Podiensis; recalculate if you plan to follow alternatives. Expect the unedited tracks from your recreational GPS, smartphone app, or step counter to add 10–15% to the stage total.

Total ascent and descent: These figures record the up-and-down bumps

as you gain and lose elevation through the day. Elevation figures for GPS tracks in this book are provided through www.gpsvisualizer.com using the best of either ODP1, ASTER or NASA altitude data.

Difficulty: This is based on a five-tier scale, comprising: easy, easy-to-moderate, moderate, moderate-to-strenuous, and strenuous. An easy stage is mostly flat, often with level footing. A strenuous stage, by contrast, has significant elevation changes, likely including some particularly steep sections and/or notably rough or uneven footing. Note that the overall length of the stage is not explicitly woven into this rating, so factor that in separately.

Stage timing: These estimates use a 4km/hr pace as the baseline for an easy-to-moderate stage, with the pace accelerating on a genuinely flat and easy track, or slowing on a more strenuous one. They do not factor in time for breaks – which, of course, are advised!

Percentage paved: This shows how much of the walk is on hard surfaces like concrete, tarmac, and asphalt, rather than softer surfaces like gravel, dirt roads, and footpaths.

Gîtes: Distances from the start of the stage to all gîtes – but not other accommodation options – are included. Note that gîtes located off-route will have their distance listed in two figures (eg 12+1.2km), with the former indicating how far to walk on the official route and the latter noting how far you'll need to walk off route.

Overview: This paragraph summarizes the stage and shares any special tips, highlights, or warnings walkers should know before setting out.

WALKING DIRECTIONS AND WAYMARKING

With occasional exceptions, waymarking on the Via Podiensis is highly reliable. Red-and-white blazes painted on trees, signs, rocks, and other physical landmarks guide you through the countryside and towns. At turns, the blazes clearly indicate whether to go left or right, while red-and-white Xs will warn you away from potential wrong turns. The Célé Valley and Rocamadour variants enjoy the same markings. Occasionally, the guidebook describes other variants that have different markings, or no markings at all, and these are specifically indicated.

With this reassurance, you should not have to clutch this book tightly each step of the way, nor should you count on it for turn-by-turn directions. Indeed, the directions are often quite skeletal, intended more to help you gauge your progress.

That said, it is advisable to review each day's route before starting, as there are several potential complications. First, there are multiple stretches where the *chemin* splits, with two (or three) options available. You will want to anticipate these crossroads to ensure that you follow your desired course. Second, there are some relatively long stretches without food or water, especially as you proceed further south. Plan well to avoid unnecessary difficulties. Finally, the Via Podiensis crosses other GR routes, which are similarly marked with red-and-white blazes. You don't want to transition onto one of these by accident!

Assorted waymarks on the Via Podiensis and the Voie Nive Bidassoa (bottom right)

Figure 1: Example of stage description and municipal information

total distance from previous municipality

elevation population infrastructure

distance remaining

6.6KM SAINT-PRIVAT-D'ALLIER (ELEV 870M, POP 415) 🍽 🛒 🏠 € ⊚ (725.6KM)
For Saint-Privat's first few centuries, the lord lived peacefully with commoners and neighbors. When Jacques Bouchard took over in the 17th century he imperiled that by picking fights with neighboring lords, Church officials, and local inhabitants alike, outraging so many that he was denounced before parliament in Paris and sentenced to death. The town declined after this and then the castle was severely pillaged during the Revolution. The castle today is owned by a family from Lyon and houses an art collection, after many years spent as a nuns' school for girls. The Romanesque church, built out of volcanic stone, dates to the 12th–13th centuries, although most of its chapels were built later, including a sepulchral chamber and mausoleum crypt on the north side.

place description

🏠 Accueil Randonneurs ⊚ 🛒 🍽 🛏 R 🍴 S, 5/15, €15.50/-/31/-, DP20.5, accueil.randonneurs@gmail.com, 0471572912

🏠 Gîte La Cabourne 🛒 🍽 🛏 🍴 R 🍳 W S Z, 2/14, €40/76/110/-, incl DP, jereserve@sfr.fr, 0471572550, open mid Mar–Nov

🏠 L'Abri du Jacquet ⊚ 🛒 🛏 K R S Z, 4/15, €12/-/-/-, DP18, labridujacquet@gmail.com, 0471077553, reservation obligatory Dec–Mar

facilities

🏠 Le Clos de Pierres Rouges 🍽 🛏 🍴 R 🍳 W S, €-/-/95/-, DP32, leclosdespierresrouges43@gmail.com, 0471006478, open Apr–Oct, sauna

▲ Camping Le Marchat R Z, info@mairie-saintprivatdallier.fr, 0471572213, €4.70/tent, open May–Sept, no wifi

The GR65 does not enter the historic core of Saint-Privat, instead skirting the edge before forking right past the service station and bakery. Ascend past the *mairie* (WC, fountain). As the road completes a hairpin turn, fork left onto a footpath ⎣0.5km⎦. Cross **D301** twice in quick succession, following narrow, rocky footpaths before arriving in **Combriaux** ⎣1.1km⎦, 🏠 Gîte L'Estaou ⊚ 🛒 🛏 🍳 R, 4/13, €15/-/-/-, DP18, estaou7@gmail.com, 0471095891 or 0648126380, camping €5/person⎦. A combination of footpaths, dirt roads and a minor paved road lead downhill into

distance between intermediate points

facilities

total distance from previous municipality

distance remaining

3.3KM ROCHEGUDE (ELEV 940M) 🏠 (722.3KM)
WC before village, fountain in center. This short tower and tiny chapel dedicated to Santiago are all that remain of the 13th-century castle ('Rocha Aguda' or 'sharp rock'), positioned on the border between the historic Velay and Gévaudan regions.

🏠 Gîte De Rochegude ⊚ 🛒 🛏 K R W S, 4/14, €16/-/-/-, DP18, contact@gitederochegude.fr, 0471027879 or 0633704810, donkey parking, no wifi

facilities

Infrastructure symbols

catering: restaurants, bars or cafés supermarket/groceries accommodation ATM bus train hospital clinic pharmacy tourist info

MUNICIPALITY INFORMATION HEADINGS

Key towns and villages have their own headings with 10 codes that list available services, such as accommodation, groceries, tourist info, public transport and medical services. The headings also show the distance from the previous municipality and the distance remaining to Saint-Jean-Pied-de-Port. Figure 1 gives an example and identifies the various symbols and codes. Sites worth visiting are highlighted, including admission fees where relevant. Opening hours are generally not listed, as these tend to change monthly, peaking in summer and sometimes shutting down entirely in the winter. Most can be found with a quick look on Google Maps. Churches tend to be accessible during daylight hours, at least. Most municipalities have a public WC, often near the *mairie* (town hall), with an accompanying water fountain or tap, and these are noted as well.

For roads, A or E followed by a number (eg A75 or E11) denotes a major French expressway, while highways are prefaced by an N. You will have limited exposure to those. Instead, you will encounter many country roads that begin with a D (eg D589).

ACCOMMODATION LISTINGS

This guide includes a range of selected gîtes, chambres d'hôtes, hotels, and campsites. Accommodations have a set of 11 possible codes that convey key information related to available facilities. These are followed by the distribution of beds in shared rooms (where available), the price of beds and private

Figure 2: Example of accommodation listing

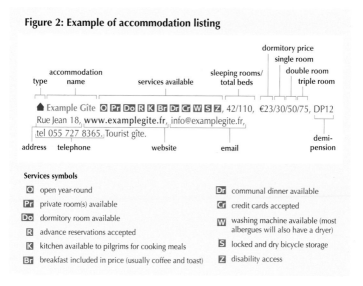

Services symbols

O open year-round

Pr private room(s) available

Do dormitory room available

R advance reservations accepted

K kitchen available to pilgrims for cooking meals

Br breakfast included in price (usually coffee and toast)

Dr communal dinner available

Cr credit cards accepted

W washing machine available (most albergues will also have a dryer)

S locked and dry bicycle storage

Z disability access

rooms, contact information, and other relevant details. Wifi is available, unless otherwise indicated, although connection speeds can vary.

Note that prices are increasingly volatile. Some places charge more during peak months. Some gîtes actually charge more in the winter, when heating is required. Often, chambres d'hôtes charge different amounts for each room. In addition, prices may be higher when using a service like booking.com instead of reserving directly.

ELEVATION PROFILES

These profiles offer a graphical representation of each stage's distance and topography following the main route as described. Optional routes are not included.

MAPS

The stage maps in this guidebook are at a scale of 1:100,000. Six larger towns – Le-Puy-en-Velay, Figeac, Cahors, Moissac, Condom, and Saint-Jean-Pied-de-Port – are shown at around 1:40,000. The recommended route is depicted by a solid red line, with optional route lines in dashed red. See the map key at the start of the book for more details about map symbols.

GPX TRACKS

GPX tracks for the route in this guidebook are available to download free at www.cicerone.co.uk/1102/GPX. If you have not bought the book through the Cicerone website, or have bought the book without opening an account,

please register your purchase in your Cicerone library to access GPX and update information.

A GPS device is an excellent aid to navigation, but you should also carry a map and compass and know how to use them. GPX files are provided in good faith, but in view of the profusion of formats and devices, neither the author nor the publisher accepts responsibility for their use. We provide files in a single standard GPX format that works on most devices and systems, but you may need to convert files to your preferred format using a GPX converter such as GPS Visualizer or one of the many other apps and online converters available.

PLANNING TOOLS

Stage planning tables for the main route and two major variants are provided in Appendix A. These tables include distances between notable villages and towns, all featuring accommodation options, making it easier to break the walk into stages that align with your own preferences. Sources of useful information on transport and other practicalities are listed in Appendix B. There is also a glossary of key terms in French (Appendix C), some recommended further reading (Appendix D), and a non-exhaustive list of major festivals along the *chemin* (Appendix E).

Finally, please keep in mind that despite the author's best efforts, some information in this guide will go out of date almost as quickly as it's printed. Check www.cicerone.co.uk/1102 and https://davewhitson.com for route updates and book corrections. We are grateful to all readers for updates.

THE VIA PODIENSIS

The clock tower in Auvillar (Stage 17)

STAGE 1
Le Puy-en-Velay to Montbonnet

Start	Cathédrale Notre-Dame-du-Puy, Le Puy-en-Velay
Finish	Bar Saint Jacques, Montbonnet
Distance	16.7km (19.9km via Bains)
Total ascent	520m (530m via Bains)
Total descent	100m (110m via Bains)
Difficulty	Easy-to-moderate
Time	4hr 15min (5hr via Bains)
Percentage paved	45% (30% via Bains)
Gîtes	Le Puy-en-Velay, Tallode 9.7km, Ramourouscle 14.2km, Montbonnet 16.7km, Fay 17.8km (via Bains)

The *chemin* begins with a short stage, allowing new pilgrims to ease into their walk while also enjoying a leisurely morning in Le Puy. The morning pilgrim mass and blessing is a must, providing an opportunity to meet many new companions, and most gîtes serve breakfast afterward. If you haven't previously visited the St Michel d'Aigulhe chapel, consider squeezing that in as well. As for the walk, it's fairly mellow, with a consistently moderate ascent early, along mostly agreeable surfaces. Saint-Christophe offers a good spot for lunch, while an alternative route via Bains is worth considering for additional facilities. There's not much in Montbonnet, and for that reason some will push on to Saint-Privat, but it does offer several accommodations with excellent hospitality.

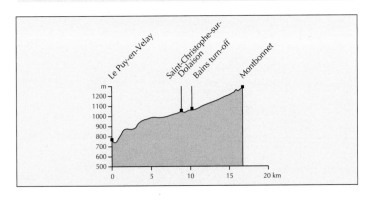

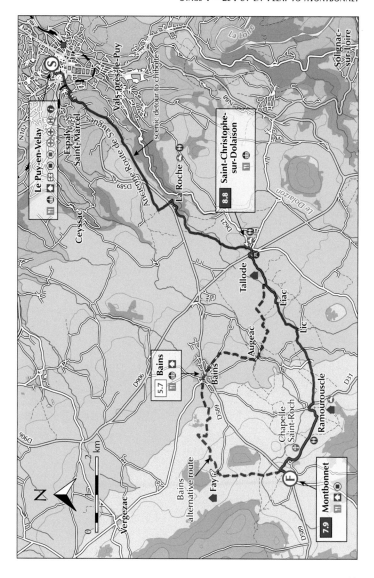

41

LE PUY-EN-VELAY (ELEV 690M, POP 19,000)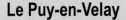
(748.9KM)

Markets on Wednesday and Sunday mornings in **Place du Plot**.

Set in a volcanic landscape and the capital of the Haute-Loire department, Le Puy has been a center of pilgrimage for well over a millennium; indeed, as many as 300,000 pilgrims are claimed to have visited the site in 1622. Originally a Roman temple, the cathedral site was turned over to Christianity in 430 when a sanctuary was built to the Virgin Mary. Legend holds that a feverish woman was

Le Puy-en-Velay

- Cathédrale Notre-Dame-du-Puy
- Rocher St Michel d'Aiguilhe
- ❶ Statue of Notre-Dame de France
- ❷ Le Camino Museum and Pilgrim Welcome
- ❸ Pilgrim mural
- ❹ Pilgrim sculpture

- ❶ Relais du Pèlerin St-Jacques
- ❷ Accueil St-François
- ❸ Accueil St-Georges
- ❹ Les Capucins
- ❺ Auberge de Jeunesse Pierre Cardinal
- ❻ La Maison au Loup
- ❼ La Demeure du Lac de Fugères

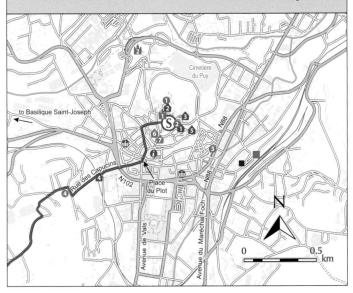

called to a dolmen; after a brief rest, her fever had broken and the Virgin Mary was with her. Mary called for a church to be built in that location; a helpful stag had even marked out the floor plan in the snow. Lacking funds, the bishop settled for planting a hedge to mark the perimeter, only to see it fully bloomed the next morning. Following a miraculous healing, Rome provided Le Puy with funds and permission to build the cathedral. That dolmen remains inside the cathedral today, known as the 'Throne of Mary.'

Cathedral construction spanned a millennium, although the bulk of it occurred in the 11th–12th centuries. It is heavily fortified, reflecting its bishops' quarrels with local lords over sovereignty. It is perhaps most famous for its statue of the Black Virgin. The original suffered an ignominious fate in the French Revolution; when the cathedral was seized, the statue was confiscated, transported to trial in a manure cart, and then burned. A local artist crafted a replacement soon after. Much historical speculation has circled around the phenomenon of the Black Virgins (another can be seen in Rocamadour); are they relics from Coptic Christians, or attempts at more authentic historic representation, or an accidental byproduct of oxidized silver? There is no consensus. In the cathedral's front entrance, the Golden Doorway stands atop the staircase and features scenes from the Nativity on the left and Christ's Passion on the right. Meanwhile, the Romanesque cloister features polychrome mosaics, an allegorical Romanesque frieze, and a celebrated Renaissance fresco in the Reliquary Chapel. Pilgrim mass takes place in the cathedral at 7am daily, with pilgrim credentials (€5) available in the gift shop afterward. The building is open from 6.30am to 7.30pm daily with free access, although there's a fee (€5) to visit the cloisters. Just above the cathedral is a **statue of Notre-Dame de France**, made from metal salvaged from 213 Russian cannons in the Crimean War. It's possible to enter the statue and climb to the top (€4). The nearby chapel on **Rocher St Michel d'Aigulhe** (the Needle) is Le Puy's most iconic site (€5). Built by Godescalc, Bishop of Le Puy, after his pilgrimage to Santiago in 951, it's worth the short trip. Prior to its construction, some accounts attest to agile men scaling the peak; think about that as you wearily climb its 268 steps! A legend holds that a maid, accused of misconduct, was compelled to leap from the peak to prove her purity. She survived. Challenged to confirm the verdict, she leapt safely again. Growing conceited, she made the leap a third time and died. Take those stairs down.

Between April and mid October, the Association des Amis de Saint-Jacques du Velay welcomes pilgrims each evening (5.30–7.30pm) for drinks and conversation in its salon behind the cathedral (2 Rue de la Manecanterie). It also issues credentials and stamps. Le Puy's evening light show, Puy de Lumières, runs from late April through September. Short, dramatic programs are projected across eight different structures, including the cathedral and the Needle. Combine those events with a dinner featuring the local specialty, green *lentilles du Puy*, and you'll have a very memorable first evening! Note that your next supermarket won't come until Saugues (end of Stage 2), unless you take the Bains variant.

🔺 Relais du Pèlerin St-Jacques **Do Br K R W**, 2/27, €Donation, 28 Rue Cardinal de Polignac, 0471094392, open Apr–mid Oct

🔺 Accueil St-François **O Pr Dr Br K R Cf S**, €-/25/50/-, 6 Rue St Mayol, gîte. stfrancois@wanadoo.fr, 0471059886, English spoken

🔺 Accueil St-Georges **O Pr Dr Br K R Cf W Z**, 100/200, €-/28/49/58, DP12, 4 Rue Saint-Georges, grandseminaire43@live.fr, 0471099310, camping €4/person, English spoken

🔺🔺 Les Capucins **O Do Pr Dr K R Cf W Z**, 4/19, €18.5/62/88/129, DP27, contact@lescapucins.net, 0471042874, English spoken

🔺 Auberge de Jeunesse Pierre Cardinal **O Do K R Cf W Z**, 10/50, €15/-/-/-, 9 Rue Jules Vallès, auberge.jeunesse@lepuyenvelay.fr, 0471055240, closed weekends in offseason, breakfast €4.50, English spoken

🔺 La Maison au Loup **Pr Br R Cf**, €-/62/78/-, 10 Rue du Prat du Loup, maisonauloup@gmail.com, 0619533359, open mid Apr–mid Oct

🔺 La Demeure du Lac de Fugères **O Pr Br R Cf S**, €-/95/100/120, 2 Rue Cardinal de Polignac, fugeres@hotmail.com, 0785894907

Throughout Le Puy, watch for the characteristic red-and-white stripes (blazes) marking the way, along with occasional scallop-shell wall plates on buildings. A red-and-white X marks a wrong turn! The Via Podiensis commences from the cathedral's front steps. Descend, continue ahead on Rue des Tables, then turn left onto Rue Raphael/des Farges. Fork right onto Rue Chènebouterie and proceed into **Place du Plot**, a lively little square. Turn right out of the plaza's back corner on Rue Saint-Jacques (distance marker to Santiago on the corner building) and then leave the old town, crossing Boulevard Saint-Louis (**0.6km**).

A steady ascent begins, leading away from town. Continue straight ahead, passing **Gîte Des Capucins**. Turn right on Rue de Compostelle, passing a **pilgrim sculpture** and noting the views back towards Le Puy (**0.7km**). After a short, sharp climb up a footpath, join the **Ancienne Route de Saugues**.

You are now in the **Devés**, France's largest basalt plateau, a consequence of long-ago lava flows. The fertile hills left behind have for two millennia yielded the Puy green lentils, known locally as 'the poor man's caviar.' Some 30 chibottes – round, stone shepherd huts from the 17th–18th centuries – survive in this section and two are accessible via waymarked detours.

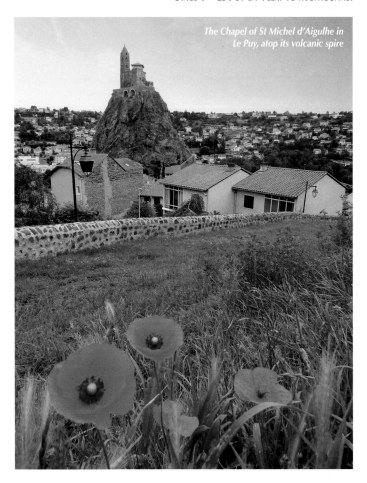

The Chapel of St Michel d'Aigulhe in Le Puy, atop its volcanic spire

Cross **D589** and continue straight on a dirt road through the Dolaison hills (**4.1km**). Turn left onto the La Roche village road and then cross D589 again into **La Roche**. After winding through the village, passing a pilgrim shelter in the middle and a fountain/WC at the end, join a footpath into the countryside, eventually turning left onto a dirt track (**0.8km**). This leads through a wooded area, featuring ash trees. Transition back onto pavement at the entrance to

45

8.8KM SAINT-CHRISTOPHE-SUR-DOLAISON (ELEV 915M, POP 950)
🍴 ⊕ (740.1KM)

Fountain and WC across from the church, outside the *mairie*. The 12th-century church, built of pink basalt (volcanic rock), features a statue of St Roch. While its façade has been rebuilt, two gargoyles survive from the original structure. The town's castle was destroyed in the Wars of Religion; now restored, it is privately owned.

Pass around the church, then fork right on **D31**. Take the next right, pass under **D906**, then bear left, leading to **Tallode** (0.5km, ▲ Gîte La Maison Vieille Do Dr K R, 4/14, €22.5/-/-/-, DP18, michel.allegre38@sfr.fr, 0471031778, open Mar–Oct, English spoken). Soon after, arrive at the **Bains turn-off** (0.5km), where you have the option of detouring to make use of Bains' facilities.

Official track through Chapelle Saint-Roch (6.4km)
Pass through **Liac** (0.6km), not to be confused with **Lic**, which comes next (1km). A longer stretch of dirt track follows, before the *chemin* turns right onto **D621**, leading into **Ramourouscle** (2.4km, fountain at junction, ▲ Gîte Lenti-You O Do Dr K R W, 2/11, €23/-/-/-, DP14, tchap.limis@gmail.com, 0644906470, camping €9.20/person). Note the 17th-century wayside cross and the *travail à ferrer* – a device for securing livestock while they get shod. Turn left in the village and follow this minor paved road as it winds through quiet fields, past the **Chapelle Saint-Roch** (1.4km, WC). This 13th-century chapel, now dedicated to St Roch, was formerly devoted to St James. Watch the waymarks carefully through the scattered village of **Montbonnet**, finally turning left onto **D589**.

Alternative route through Bains (9.6km)
Turning right off the official route, follow a dirt road as it winds through fields (2.1km). Soon after pavement resumes, turn right into **Augeac**, navigating a series of quick turns (0.7km). Leaving the village, fork right onto a dirt track (0.9km). Turn left on Route de Jales and proceed directly into

5.7KM BAINS (ELEV 985M, POP 1350) 🍴 ⊕ 🏕 (737.6KM)
WC on right, before the church; fountain outside its entrance. The 12th-century Église Sainte-Foy, built of volcanic rock, features a Romanesque portal that is dominated by a Moorish-inspired multifoil arch.

▲ La Ferme de Saint-Jacques O Pr Dr Br K R, €-/34/52/-, DP21, 808 Route de Gévaudan, patricia.r43@hotmail.fr, 0471575179, English spoken

Fork right and then left around the church. Soon after, fork left and then right to leave town (**0.3km**). Join a dirt road past a grove of trees; turn right at a T and then make a sharp left (**2.2km**). Bear right through woods, skirting **Fay** (**0.8km**, ⌂ Gîte du Velay 🄾 🄳🄾 🄿🅁 🄳🅁 🅁 🄲🅁 🅆 🅂 🅉, 1/12, €14/31/42/52, DP18.5, sylvetteetlaurent@grand-gite. fr, 0471027160 or 0647759642, dorm open Apr–Oct, donkey parking, English spoken). Just before Montbonnet, transition back onto pavement (**1.8km**). Turn right on D589 to rejoin the GR65 (**0.1km**).

Saint James as he appears in the Église Sainte-Foy in Bains

The routes converge at most of the services, including Bar Saint-Jacques, in

7.9KM MONTBONNET (ELEV 1110M) 🍴 ⌂ ◉ (732.2KM)

A small castle once stood atop the now barren hilltop, established in the early 1200s. Following the Hundred Years' War, the region suffered significant decline, as bandits seized control and ravaged the countryside. The Cardinal Richelieu, famously memorialized as the villain in *The Three Musketeers*, oversaw the further dismantling of many fortifications in the Velay region, including Montbonnet, in 1632.

⌂ Gîte La Grange 🄳🄾 🄳🅁 🅁 🅂 🅉, 4/15, €15/-/-/-, DP18, christiangentes@orange. fr, 0620744743, open Apr–Oct

⌂ Gîte l'Escole 🄳🄾 🄿🅁 🄳🅁 🄺 🅁 🅆 🅉, 4/15, €15.5/-/-/-, DP17.4, 39 Escole Impasse, gite@lescole.com, 0471575103, open 10 Mar–5 Oct, camping €7.20/person

⌂ Gîte La 1ère Étape 🄾 🄳🄾 🄿🅁 🄳🅁 🄺 🅁 🅆 🅂, 4/14, €18/-/57/-, DP21, gr65etape1@gmail.com, 0621471896, camping €6/person, English spoken

⌂ Auberge La Barbelotte 🄿🅁 🄳🅁 🄱🅁 🅁 🄲🅁 🅆 🅂 🅉, €-/54/88/-, DP15, labarbelotte@gmail.com, 0603940219, open Mar–Oct

STAGE 2

Montbonnet to Saugues

Start	Bar Saint Jacques, Montbonnet
Finish	Office de Tourisme, Saugues
Distance	26.1km
Total ascent	805m
Total descent	950m
Difficulty	Strenuous
Time	8hr
Percentage paved	32%
Gîtes	Saint-Privat-d'Allier 6.6km, Combriaux 8.2km, Rochegude 9.9km, Pratclaux 11km, Monistrol-d'Allier 13.9km, Saugues 26.1km

Equal parts challenging and spectacular, this is a wonderfully memorable walk – the first of many to come. A peaceful stroll through wooded countryside delivers you into Saint-Privat by mid morning; hit the bakery for still-warm pastries and make the short detour into the old town to enjoy the view. You then climb gradually to Rochegude, which features another striking vantage point, before enduring a tiring descent to Monistrol-d'Allier. This riverside town marks your arrival in the Margeride region and is a good place to snag a lunch and prepare for an equally demanding ascent, leading past an evocative chapel, built into the cliff face. A seasonal food truck and snack bar offer sustenance along the final stretch (try the blueberry tart in Rognac), before arrival in Saugues, a market town with a beastly past.

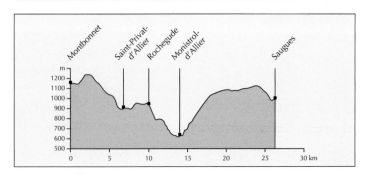

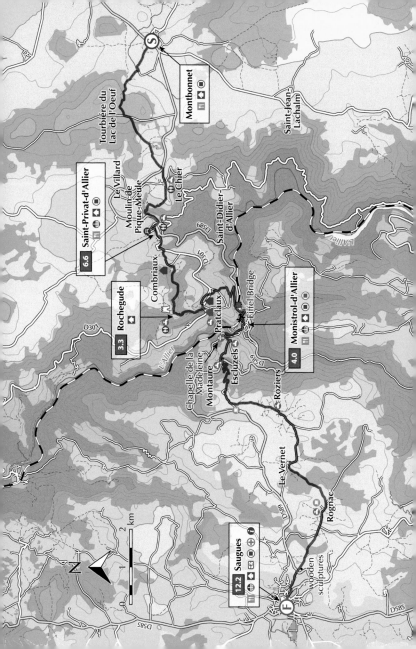

Montbonnet 🏠 ← ⬛

Saint-Jean-Lachalm

Tourbière du
Lac de l'Oeuf

Le Villard

Le Chier

Moulin de
Pique-Meule

Saint-Privat-d'Allier 🏛 🍴 ← ⬛
6.6

Saint-Didier-
d'Allier

L'Allier

Combriaux

Eiffel Bridge

Rochegude 🏠 ←
3.3

L'Allier

Pratclaux

Monistrol-d'Allier 🍴 ← ⬛
4.0

Chapelle de la
Madeleine

Montaure

Roziers

Escluzels

Le Vernet

Rognac

Saugues 🍴 ⊕ ← ✚
12.2

wooden
sculptures

N

↑ 2 km

Leave **Montbonnet** by turning right off D589, just before Bar Saint-Jacques. Turbines span the tree-lined ridge in the distance, as you follow dirt tracks through increasingly wooded terrain. Turn left at **Tourbiére du Lac de l'Oeuf** (**2.5km**). Cross **D589** (**1.9km**) and proceed into the unfortunately named village of **Le Chier** (**0.4km**, WC, fountain), which describes an act one would typically accomplish while seated. Return into woods, ultimately descending along a footpath through a particularly dense grove, then pass an old mill, the **Moulin de Pique-Meule** (**1.8km**). Rejoin **D589** just before the center (WC, fountain), curving right into

6.6KM SAINT-PRIVAT-D'ALLIER (ELEV 870M, POP 415) 🏠 ⊕ 🛏 ◉ (725.6KM)

For Saint-Privat's first few centuries, the lord lived peacefully with commoners and neighbors. When Jacques Bouchard took over in the 17th century he imperiled that by picking fights with neighboring lords, Church officials, and local inhabitants alike, outraging so many that he was denounced before parliament in Paris and sentenced to death. The town declined after this and then the castle was severely pillaged during the Revolution. The castle today is owned by a family from Lyon and houses an art collection, after many years spent as a nuns' school for girls. The Romanesque church, built out of volcanic stone, dates to the 12th–13th centuries, although most of its chapels were built later, including a sepulchral chamber and mausoleum crypt on the north side.

🏠 Accueil Randonneurs ◎ 🗄 🄿 🄳 🅁 🄲 🅂, 5/15, €15.50/-/31/-, DP20.5, accueil.randonneurs@gmail.com, 0471572912

🏠 Gîte La Cabourne 🗄 🄿 🄳 🄱 🅁 🄲 🅆 🅂 🅉, 2/14, €40/76/110/-, incl DP, jereserve@sfr.fr, 0471572550, open mid Mar–Nov

🏠 L'Abri du Jacquet ◎ 🗄 🄳 🄺 🅁 🅂 🅉, 4/15, €12/-/-/-, DP18, labridujacquet@gmail.com, 0471077553, reservation obligatory Dec–Mar

🏠 Le Clos de Pierres Rouges 🄿 🄳 🄱 🅁 🄲 🅆 🅂, €-/-/95/-, DP32, leclosdespierresrouges43@gmail.com, 0471006478, open Apr–Oct, sauna

▲ Camping Le Marchat 🅁 🅉, info@mairie-saintprivatdallier.fr, 0471572213, €4.70/tent, open May–Sept, no wifi

The GR65 does not enter the historic core of Saint-Privat, instead skirting the edge before forking right past the service station and bakery. Ascend past the *mairie* (WC, fountain). As the road completes a hairpin turn, fork left onto a footpath (**0.5km**). Cross **D301** twice in quick succession, following narrow, rocky footpaths before arriving in **Combriaux** (**1.1km**, 🏠 Gîte L'Estaou ◎ 🗄 🄳 🅁, 4/13, €15/-/-/-, DP18, estaou7@gmail.com, 0471095891 or 0648126380, camping €5/person). A combination of footpaths, dirt roads and a minor paved road lead downhill into

Rochegude's tower and chapel

3.3KM ROCHEGUDE (ELEV 940M) 🛏 (722.3KM)
WC before village, fountain in center. This short tower and tiny chapel dedicated to Santiago are all that remain of the 13th-century castle ('Rocha Aguda' or 'sharp rock'), positioned on the border between the historic Velay and Gévaudan regions.

🛖 Gîte De Rochegude **O Do Dr K R W S**, 4/14, €16/-/-/-, DP18, contact@gitederochegude.fr, 0471027879 or 0633704810, donkey parking, no wifi

The GR65 turns left just before the tower. Carefully descend a steep footpath through beech and pine trees (**1km**), then turn left on **D301**. Cut through **Pratclaux** (fountain, 🛖 Gîte de la Ribeyre **O Do Dr Br R W**, 3/12, €36/-/-/-, incl DP, contact@gitedelaribeyre.com, 0663463709, reservation required in offseason, 🛖 La Je Pi **Pr Dr Br K R Cf W S**, €-/30/48/-, DP15, ciboulot1939@hotmail.fr, 0635190407, open mid Mar–mid Oct, reservation required), then continue to descend along dirt tracks and footpaths (**1.5km**). Turn left onto a paved road, then merge with a larger road, with

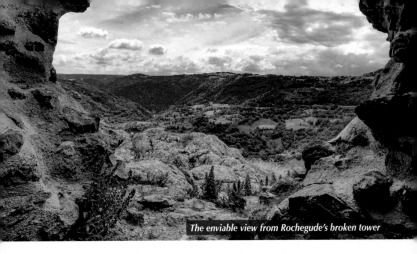

The enviable view from Rochegude's broken tower

many services back to the left (Hotel/Restaurant Le Pain de Sucre, Gîte Au Ricochet, Camping Le Vivier, and the train station). Pass Les Terrasses de l'Allier and cross the Allier River (home to salmon, otters, and the Jean-le-Blanc falcon) on a **bridge** built by Gustave Eiffel into

4KM MONISTROL-D'ALLIER (ELEV 600M, POP 200) 🍴 🏧 🛅 ◉ ◉ (718.3KM)

Fountain near church, WC down by river. The town's Romanesque church was originally linked with the Abbey of Chaise-Dieu, and it preserves statues from the abbey today, including that of Notre-Dame-Estours, a subject of many prayers for help with the Beast of Gévaudan (see Saugues info, below). In the middle of town you may encounter a friendly scallop-shell seller.

🏠 Gîte La Tsabone **Do Dr Br K R**, 2/12, €19/-/-/-, DP33, latsabone@yahoo.fr, 0471061723 or 0615153839, open Mar–Oct, donkey parking

🏠 Gîte Le Repos du Pèlerin **Do Pr Dr Br R Cf S**, 2/15, €33.5/50/82/123, incl DP, reposdupelerin@gmail.com, 0471572357, open Mar–Nov, donkey parking

🏠 Gîte du Pont Eiffel **O Do Pr Dr Br R S**, 3/10, €30/-/60/-, incl DP, 0644728195 or 0471061774

🏠 Gîte Au Ricochet **Do Pr Dr K R W S Z**, 5/20, €15/-/30/-, DP20, auricochet@gmail.com, 0659077066, open Apr–Oct

🏠 Les Terrasses de l'Allier **O Do Pr Dr Br R Cf W S**, 5/15, €32.5/50.5/85/-, incl DP, 2 Rue des Jacquets, lesterrassesdelallier@gmail.com, 0603940473

🛏 **Hôtel Le Pain de Sucre** `Pr` `Dr` `Br` `R` `Cf` `W` `S`, €-/85/120/168, incl DP, peter. paindesucre@orange.fr, 0788212953, open Feb–Nov, donkey parking

⛺ **Camping Le Vivier** `Do` `Pr` `Br` `K` `R` `Cf` `W` `Z`, 1/5, €14/-/29/-, Rue du Pain de Sucre, contact@camping-le-vivier.fr, 0650086570, open Apr–Oct, €6/tent, breakfast €7, washing machine included

Turn right near the end of town and then, at a hairpin turn to the left, continue straight on a footpath that offers excellent views back towards Monistrol (**0.4km**). Follow dirt roads uphill, leading past the evocative **Chapelle de la Madeleine** (**0.7km**). This was built around a grotto in the 17th century. Continue climbing to **Escluzels** (**0.2km**, fountain). Follow dirt tracks out of town, ascending steadily through wooded hillside dominated by conifers to **D589** (**0.8km**). Climb through another series of switchbacks, skirt **Montaure** (**1.9km**, fountain), and fork left past a seasonal food truck (**0.3km**). Cross through **Roziers** (**1.4km**, fountain). Fork right out of the village and follow a paved road onward to **Le Vernet** (**1.8km**). Then, flipping things around, turn left out of Le Vernet and follow a dirt road to **Rognac** (**1.9km**, fountain, snack bar).

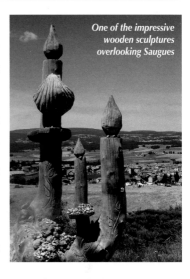

One of the impressive wooden sculptures overlooking Saugues

Enjoy some impressive **wooden sculptures** before descending into **Saugues**, joining D589 for the last approach. The Office de Tourisme is on your right in the town center.

12.2KM SAUGUES (ELEV 965M, POP 1735) 🏨 ⊕ 🛒 🅒 ⊚ ⊕ 🛈 (706.1KM)
WC and fountain near church. Market on Friday mornings.

This is the heart of the Margeride region – a massif (highland zone) lined by a pair of volcanic peaks and 'only' 10 million years old, although the granite itself is 320 million years old. It was originally the realm of the Gabales people, whom legend holds were conquered by Julius Caesar. Control passed from Romans in 476 to Visigoths and then to Franks. During the Umayyad invasions between 725 and 730, the 'Saracens' burned everything. A millennium later, in 1788, Saugues was aflame again, when the communal oven erupted, destroying 104 houses.

The Église Saint-Médard has Romanesque origins (best preserved in its southern portal) but was consistently expanded over the years. Statues of St Roch and St Médard are featured on the western facade. Inside, the stained-glass windows are a particular highlight, although the 12th-century Virgin in Majesty is notable as well. Medardus was an exceptionally highly regarded bishop in sixth-century France; he is invoked against toothache, bad weather, sterility, and imprisonment!

Only the 'Tour de Seigneur' remains of the 13th-century Tour des Anglais, as many stones from the building were salvaged to rebuild homes after the fire. The tower can be visited, and the views are excellent (€2.50). The Diorama de Sainte-Bénilde documents the life of St Bénilde, who lived in Saugues for 20 years and was canonized in 1967. She was one of the White Penitents, a religious order founded in 1652, in part to ward off the plague.

The region was terrorized by the so-called Beast of Gévaudan between 1764 and 1768. The mysterious beast (a super-wolf? A lynx? Something more diabolical?) was blamed for the disappearance of around 60 people. A peasant, Jean Chastel, is said to have slayed the beast, before dragging it to the king's court as proof. The Musée de la Bete du Gévaudan (€5.50) tells the story, in a particularly kitschy manner. English-only speakers will have to employ creative interpretation.

Supplies are very limited between Saugues and Saint-Alban (in Stage 4), so prepare accordingly.

🔺▲ **Gîte Communal** Do K R Cr W, 5/15, €15/-/-/-, 8 Rue de la Margeride, camping@saugues.fr, 0665150432, open Easter–Oct, €5.50/tent

🔺 **Au Lion d'Or** O Do Dr R W S Z, 3/7, €17/-/-/-, DP20, 41 Rue de la Margeride, auliondor43@gmail.com, 0656807562, camping €7/person

🔺 **La Margeride** Do Pr Dr K R Cr W S Z, 15/40, €16.5/19/33/49.5, DP19.5, 8 Rue des Tours Neuves, info.lamargeride@wanadoo.fr, 0471776097, open Mar–Oct

🔺 **Gîte Le Chalet du Pèlerin** O Do Pr Dr Br K R W S, 3/6, €20/-/40/-, DP12, 70 Rue des Cimes, lechaletdupelerin@yahoo.fr, 0609600965, camping €10/person

🔺 **Gîte à la Ferme Itier-Martins** O Do Dr Br R W S, 6/15, €40/-/-/-, incl DP, 65 Rue des Noisetiers, jesusvidal163@gmail.com, 0672754648

🔺🔺 **Gîte La Dentelle du Camino** O Do Pr Dr Br K R S, 1/10, €30/75/100/-, incl DP, 46-48 Rue de la Margeride, ladentelleducamino@gmail.com, 0768751944 or 0687303525

🔺 **La Flore** Pr Dr Br R Cr W S, €-/-/65/-, DP18, 230 Ave Lucien Gires, contact@laflore-saugues.com, 0650284311, open Mar–Nov

STAGE 3
Saugues to Domaine du Sauvage

Start	Office de Tourisme, Saugues
Finish	Auberge du Sauvage en Gévaudan, Domaine du Sauvage
Distance	19.3km
Total ascent	635m
Total descent	305m
Difficulty	Moderate
Time	5hr 15min
Percentage paved	38%
Gîtes	Le Clauze 7.5km, Le Villeret d'Apchier 11.2km, Chanaleilles 13.9+0.5km, Chazeaux 14.6km, Domaine du Sauvage 19.3km

Historically, this was the Gévaudan: a remote and rugged part of France. While the bandits and wolves are gone, it remains sparsely settled; indeed, you will need to detour off the official route should you wish to visit a village that exceeds (only barely) a two-digit population. Not coincidentally, this is the lone stage in the guide that concludes outside of a town or village, finishing instead at an isolated gîte/restaurant in a historic structure, deep in the heart of the Gévaudan. Be sure to reserve ahead – it books up in advance.

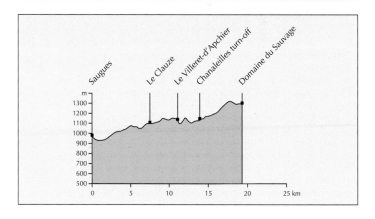

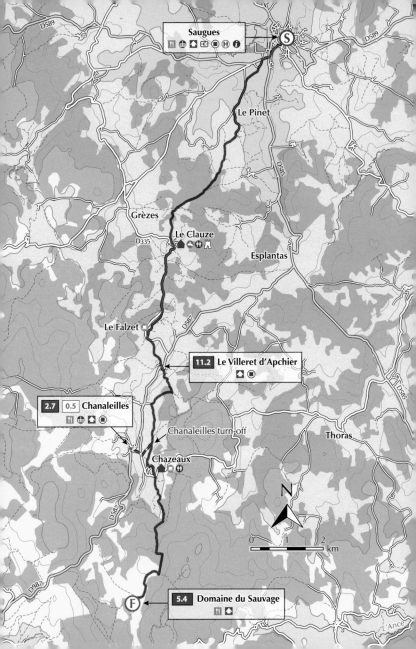

Saugues

Le Pinet

Grèzes

Le Clauze

D335

Esplantas

Le Falzet

11.2 **Le Villeret d'Apchier**

2.7 **0.5** **Chanaleilles**

Chanaleilles turn off

Chazeaux

Thoras

N

0   1   2
km

5.4 **Domaine du Sauvage**

L'Ance

Follow Cours Dr Gervais/D589 westward. Pass through a roundabout at the end of Saugues, then turn left onto Chemin de Saint-Jacques (**0.9km**). Minor paved roads lead through **Le Pinet** (**2.3km**), before transitioning to dirt tracks, winding through increasingly wooded terrain. Merge with D335 and proceed into **Le Clauze** and its tall, singular tower, balanced atop a boulder (**4.3km**, WC, fountain, Refuge Municipal (shelter with stove, tables, but no mattresses), ♠ ♠ Gîte Au Repos d'Antan Do Pr Dr Br R, 4/9, €39/79/118/147, incl DP, sonia.vidal@orange.fr, 0666476718, open Apr–Oct).

Approaching the looming tower in Le Clauze

Continue on D335 (**1.8km**), then fork left onto a minor road into **Le Falzet** (**0.7km**, snack bar). Return briefly to D335 before turning right onto a dirt track. Turn right on **D587** for the final approach into

---

11.2KM LE VILLERET D'APCHIER (ELEV 1125M) 🏠 ◉ (694.9KM)
Fountain and *travail à ferrer*.

🏠 L'Auberge des 2 Pèlerins **Do Pr Dr R W Z**, 7/20, €16/-/96/-, DP20, contact@
aubergedes2pelerins.com, 0607280644 or 0630668845, open Apr–Sept, DP
included with private room

Turn left and descend from the village, soon transitioning onto a series of tracks that wind through green and yellow fields (**2.5km**). After briefly rejoining a paved road through a farm complex, arrive at

---

2.7KM CHANALEILLES TURN-OFF (ELEV 1150M, POP 100) 🍴 ⊕ 🏠 ◉
(692.2KM)
This village café is 0.8km off-route, following a signposted out-and-back detour.

The founding family of Chanaleilles claims regal heritage. Codrus, the likely mythical last king of ancient Athens, had a son named Nélée, who fled following the monarchy's fall. Nélée settled in Germania, although local legend asserts that he came here. On more solid historical ground, a lord of Chanaleilles accompanied Lothaire, first son of Louis I, to battle in Naples in 841, reflecting the town's lengthy past. In the Romanesque Église Notre-Dame de l'Assomption, look for a small commemorative plaque honoring Father Auguste Mayrand, who saved the lives of many young Jewish residents in World War II and was posthumously honored as one of the Righteous among the Nations.

🏠 Gîte Café du Pont **Do Dr K R W**, 4/20, €12/-/-/-, DP19, nic.richard@
wanadoo.fr, 0471744163, open Apr–mid Nov, camping €6/person

Continuing left from the split, proceed into **Chazeaux** (**0.7km**, WC, snack bar,
🏠 Gîte de la Virlange **O Do Dr K R Gr W S**, 3/8, €16/-/-/-, DP22, virlange@outlook.fr, 0632676354, camping €6/person, no wifi, 🏠 Accueil Chrétien Chez Marie-Aimée **Do Dr Br R**, 2/8, €Donation, incl DP, 0670486849, open May–Sept). After winding uphill through the village, transition onto a dirt track, leading into the woods (**0.4km**). It's all unpaved, easy walking from there, onward to the idyllic

Auberge du Sauvage

5.4KM DOMAINE DU SAUVAGE (ELEV 1295M) ▯▯ (686.8KM)

A wild place, long an unpopulated forest frequented by hunters and brigands. Romans and Merovingians passed through but failed to establish a permanent settlement. In around 1000, local lords invested significant manpower in clearing part of the forest to establish a stronghold and public road. Ownership passed to Hôtel-Dieu in Le Puy, the town's historic hospital, for 599 years; they established a pilgrim hospital nearby and operated it quite efficiently. Only after the Wars of Religion did the Hôtel-Dieu abandon the area, leasing the land to farmers. Following a century of steep decline, the Hôtel-Dieu reasserted its control, refurbishing buildings – including the complex that contains today's gîte. The Revolution saw another changing of the guards, with the Saint-Léger family taking over ownership for the next 154 years, until the property passed into the hands of its current operator, the General Council of Haute-Loire. The Knights Templar are often associated with the site; the complex is frequently characterized as a former, Dômerie des Templiers or Templar headquarters, with the knights providing protection in the region.

⬥ L'Auberge du Sauvage en Gévaudan ▯▯▯▯▯▯▯▯▯▯, 10/41, €17.5/-/-/-, DP18.5, domainedusauvage@orange.fr, 0471744030, closed over Dec–Jan holidays, no meals Nov–Mar, reservation required, donkey parking, café/restaurant

59

STAGE 4
Domaine du Sauvage to Aumont-Aubrac

Start	Auberge du Sauvage en Gévaudan, Domaine du Sauvage
Finish	Office de Tourisme, Aumont-Aubrac
Distance	28.2km
Total ascent	480m
Total descent	725m
Difficulty	Moderate
Time	7hr 30min
Percentage paved	24%
Gîtes	La Roche-sur-Lajo 5.5+0.6km, Les Faux 6.7+1.3km, Le Rouget 9.7km, Saint-Alban-sur-Limagnole 13.2km, Les Estrets 20.6km, Bigose 22.2km, Aumont-Aubrac 28.2km

While today's stage leads out of the Gévaudan, it remains on the high-elevation Massif Central throughout, rarely dropping far below 1000m in its persistent undulations. Don't anticipate finding any food between Domaine du Sauvage and Saint-Alban – although the latter provides an excellent spot for a lunch break. And, looking ahead to dinner, the day's destination offers your first excellent opportunity to try aligot, the defining dish of the Aubrac region.

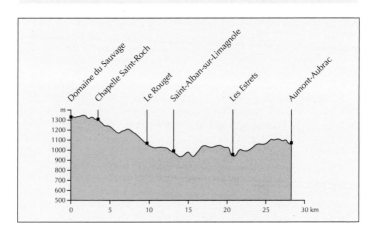

A fountain at the Chapelle Saint-Roch

The GR65 turns right just south of **Domaine du Sauvage**, following a dirt track through thick woods. Turn left onto **D587 (2.9km)**, then pass the ruins of **L'Hospitalet du Sauvage (0.3km)**. Founded in 1198, this once provided shelter to pilgrims and other travelers through the rugged Sauvage, although little remains. Soon after, fork right to visit

3.5KM CHAPELLE SAINT-ROCH (ELEV 1305M) 🔟 ◉ (683.3KM)

Fountain, WC, and pilgrim shelter. First dedicated to St James, this small chapel was rededicated to Roch following the Wars of Religion; note the statue of Roch with his loyal dog above the altar. The current chapel was destroyed by a cyclone in 1897, then rebuilt in 1901. At this point, you cross from the Auvergne-Rhône-Alpes region to the Lozère department in the Occitanie region.

Soon after rejoining **D587**, fork left onto a footpath (**0.2km**). Cross **D987** and then descend a dirt track (**1.6km**). (Alternately, turn left soon after crossing D987 to detour to 🛏 La Bergerie de Compostelle in **La Roche-sur-Lajo** 🆅 🆅 🆅 🆅 🆅 🆅, 4/16, €20/-/-/-, DP19, francoiseastruc@yahoo.fr, 0679698511, open Apr–Oct, closed early July, no wifi.) After an extended off-road stretch, the track transitions into a series of broad switchbacks. Pass the **turn-off for Les Faux** (**1.6km**, 🛏 🛏 L'Oustal de Parent 🆅 🆅 🆅 🆅 🆅 🆅 🆅 🆅 🆅 🆅, 1/10, €16/55/76/90, DP20, oustaldeparent@gmail.com, 0466315009, open Mar–Oct, campers welcome, café/restaurant) before finally descending back to **D987 (2.8km)**. Cross that and join a minor paved road into

6.2KM LE ROUGET (ELEV 1035M) 🅿 (677.1KM)

Picnic area. Named for the region's distinct red stone, the village marks an architectural shift from predominantly red-tile roofs to gray slate.

🛏 🛏 La Croix du Plô 🆅 🆅 🆅 🆅 🆅 🆅 🆅 🆅 🆅, 3/12, €32/60/98/-, incl DP, lacroixduplo@orange.fr, 0633556103, no wifi, English spoken

Turn left at a T, then fork right after a bend in the road, transitioning back onto a dirt track at the village's end (**0.4km**). When approaching the outskirts of Saint-Alban, merge back onto **D987 (1.2km)**. Turn left soon after onto Chemin de Saint-Jacques-de-Compostelle, beginning a circuitous entrance to town. **Resist the temptation to follow**

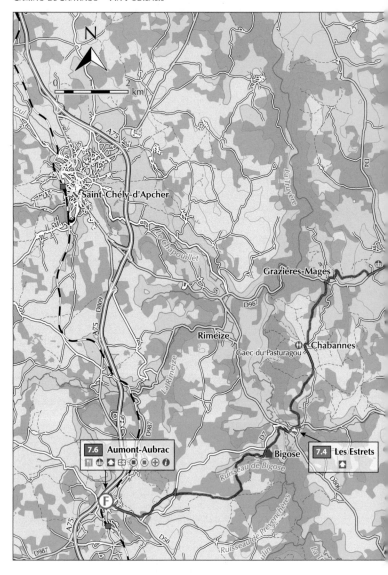

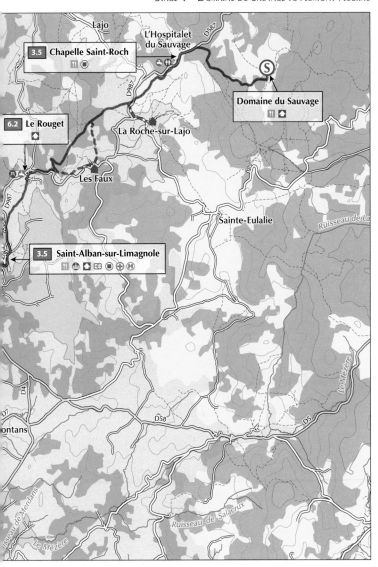

the highway – while shorter, cars speed along the road and there is little shoulder space. Fork left to remain on that street, then turn right, descending through the hospital complex (**0.8km**). After another right turn, follow Rue de l'Hôpital before turning left onto the main road through

---

3.5KM SAINT-ALBAN-SUR-LIMAGNOLE (ELEV 965M, POP 1350)
🏨 ⊕ 🛒 🄲 ◉ Ⓗ ⊕ (673.6KM)

WC next to church. Named after St Alban, England's first Christian martyr – a Briton in the Roman army who sheltered a fugitive priest, Amphibalus, when he was on the run. When soldiers arrived at Alban's home, alerted to Amphibalus's presence, Alban exchanged clothes with him and was taken in his place. When the Roman governor discovered the trick, he interrogated Alban, who rejected his old beliefs and embraced Christianity, declaring, 'I would rather believe in the God of Amphibalus, who teaches people to love one another.' Outraged, the governor ordered his execution.

The town is the former stronghold of the Barony of Apcher. After the Revolution, the castle was converted to an asylum for the department's mentally ill; in 1945, Francois Tosquelles created the concept of institutional psychotherapy here, ushering in the era of the psychiatric hospital. Under German occupation, several surrealists took refuge here, and the hospital played a key role in supporting the underground resistance movement. The Romanesque Église Saint-Alban, built from the local red sandstone and polychrome brick, features a well-preserved choir with impressive capitals.

⌂ Gîte du Centre 🄾 Do Pr Dr R Cr, 1/10, €13/23/42/-, DP19, 32 Grand Rue, hotel.maury@orange.fr, 0466315004, bar/restaurant

⌂ Gîte Le Lit Magnole Do Pr Dr R W S, 8/15, €18/18/36/54, DP21, 27 Grand Rue, lelitmagnole@orange.fr, 0767513851, open Apr–Oct

⌂ Gîte Le Refuge du Pèlerin Do Dr K R W S, 3/12, €18/-/-/-, DP21, 37 Grand Rue, ileane@orange.fr, 0607471261, open Apr–Oct, camping €3/person

⌂ Gîte Antre Nous 🄾 Do Dr K R W S, 4/12, €20/-/-/-, DP15, 9 Rue de la Commette, eric.rondolat@sfr.fr, 0661238511, camping €10/person, donkey parking

⌂ ⌂ Auberge Saint-Jacques Do Pr Dr Br R Cr W S, 2/4, €34/59/92/139, incl DP, 3 Place du Breuil, contact@auberge-saint-jacques.fr, 0466315176, open Feb–Nov, English spoken

⌂ Les Drailles de la Margeride Pr Dr Br R W S Z, €-/55/70/105, DP15, 1 Grand Rue, drailles.margeride@gmail.com, 0670112054, open mid Apr–Oct, English spoken

Proceeding towards Les Estrets

Turn right at Saint-Alban's church, looping around behind it. Descend Rue de la Tournelle, fork left in Place du Breuil, then turn left on Rue de la Baysse. Finally, departing Saint-Alban, turn right on **D987** (**0.4km**). Just before a grove of trees, turn right onto a dirt road (**0.5km**), gradually climbing to **Graziéres-Mages** (**1.4km**). Turn left then right in the hamlet, then left again, crossing **D987** and joining a dirt track (**0.4km**). Another ascent follows, through gradually receding tree cover. Finally, turn right onto a paved road near **Chabannes** (**1.9km**, fountain, WC, cheese vending machine at Gaec du Pasturagou). Curve left around the village, following the paved road, until forking right onto a dirt track (**0.9km**). After emerging from a wooded stretch, navigate a steep descent on dicey footing into

7.4KM LES ESTRETS (ELEV 940M) 🏠 (666.2KM)

Fountain by church. A former command center for the Order of St John, controlling passage over the Truyére River. Its Église Saint-Jean-Baptiste de Fontans features a statue of St Roch, with a scallop shell on its lectern.

🛏 Gîte Le Gévaudan ☒☒ ☒☒ ☒☒ ☒☒ ☒ ☒ ☒, 4/20, €38/48/96/144, incl DP, pas. rousset@orange.fr, 0466456190 or 0688909789, open Apr–Sept, English spoken

Follow D7 through the village, then turn right at a T (**0.4km**). Turn left onto a dirt track, climbing the hill towards **Bigose** (**1.2km**, ♠ ♠ Les Granges de Bigose [O] [Do] [Pr] [Dr] [Br] [R] [Cf] [W] [Z], 2/10, €40/-/120/-, incl DP, contact@grangesbigose.com, 0466471265, donkey parking). Proceed through mostly flat countryside. Turn briefly onto **D7** (**2.9km**), then make a sharp left off it. Just before merging with D7 again, veer right (**1.1km**). Finally, rejoin the highway near town (**0.4km**). Fork right at La Ferme du Barry, descending into Aumont-Aubrac's village center. The Office de Tourisme is on your right.

7.6KM AUMONT-AUBRAC (ELEV 1050M, POP 1035) 🍴 ⊕ 🏠 🄫 ⊙ ⊙ ⊕ 𝟎 (658.6KM)

WC and fountain. Market on Friday mornings.

A town with Roman origins, it preserves some buildings from the 16th–17th centuries. A Benedictine Priory once operated here and the Romanesque Église Saint-Etienne, which dates to 1061, survives from that. It was restored in 1994 with modern stained-glass windows; its choir and Gothic side-chapels are worth a look. A large statue of Jesus stands above town, a monument of the Sacred Heart, established in 1946 after the town survived WWII without casualties. Note the statue of the Beast of Gévaudan before town.

The quintessential culinary experience in the Aubrac region is aligot, a cheesy, mashed potato dish (often served with sausages) that achieves a surprising measure of elasticity. Some local chefs revel in the showmanship of serving it, stretching it wildly out of the pot.

♠ La Ferme du Barry [O] [Do] [Pr] [Dr] [Br] [R] [Cf] [W] [S], 9/32, €40/60/90/120, incl DP, 9 Rue du Barry, fermedubarry@yahoo.fr, 0466429025

♠ Gîte Chemin-Faisant [O] [Do] [Br] [K] [R] [W] [S], 6/14, €25/-/-/-, 15 Ave de Peyre, annie.lautard@live.fr, 0624831936, camping €5/person, English spoken

♠ Gîte Route d'Aubrac [O] [Do] [Pr] [K] [R] [W], 1/8, €12/30/60/-, 4 Route d'Aubrac, 0676684390

♠ Gîte Les Sentiers Fleuris [Do] [Pr] [Dr] [R] [Cf] [S] [Z], 4/13, €20/55/70/105, DP23, 7 Place du Portail, sentiersfleuris48@yahoo.fr, 0466429470, open Apr–Oct

♠ ♠ La Ferme de l'Aubrac [O] [Do] [Pr] [Dr] [R] [Cf] [Z], 1/14, €12/-/65/-, DP23, 2 Place du Foirail, contact@lafermedelaubrac.fr, 0466313897

♠ Le 24 [Pr] [Br] [R] [S] [Z], €-/50/80/-, 24 Route d'Aubrac, francoisechristian. mathieu@gmail.com, 0675917130, open May–Sept

♠ Hôtel Prunières [Pr] [Dr] [R] [Cf] [W], €-/64/66/78, DP23, hotelprunieres@gmail. com, 0466428552, open May–Nov

STAGE 5

Aumont-Aubrac to Nasbinals

Start	Office de Tourisme, Aumont-Aubrac
Finish	Église Sainte-Marie, Nasbinals
Distance	27.3km (25.9km via Montgros)
Total ascent	550m
Total descent	430m
Difficulty	Easy-to-moderate
Time	6hr 45min
Percentage paved	42%
Gîtes	La Chaze-du-Peyre 4.9km, Lasbros 6.8km, Les Quatre Chemins 10.7km, Malbouzon 15.6+1.9km, Finieyrols 16.1km, Montgros 23.4km, Nasbinals 27.3km

This is one of the finest stages on the *chemin*, featuring the Aubrac plateau in all its glory. The rugged and exposed terrain has a majestic openness to it, with rolling hills flecked with yellow and purple wildflowers and some of the most regal cattle you'll ever see. The recommended approach deviates from the GR65 for a short stretch, following an unmarked track past the Cascade du Déroc, a stunning waterfall that is reinvigorating on a warm day. The two routes rejoin just before Nasbinals, a charming small town wrapped around a striking Romanesque church. Regardless of your route choice, food options are limited once again, so plan accordingly.

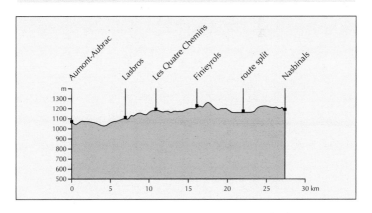

From the Office de Tourisme on Rue du Prieuré in **Aumont-Aubrac**, fork left on Rue de l'Église, then turn right on Avenue de Peyre. Fork right on Route d'Aubrac. After crossing the railroad at the town's end, turn left (**0.5km**). An alternating sequence of paved and dirt roads leads through a small cluster of houses, under the **A75**, and – following a sharp ascent – past a **cemetery** (**4km**). A paved road delivers you into **La Chaze-du-Peyre** (**0.4km**, WC, fountain, ▲ Gîte Aux Chants des Oiseaux **O Do Dr K R S**, 2/5, €22/-/-/-, DP17, colettegr@yahoo.fr, 0632844362). Merge onto D69 briefly, then fork left. Turn left onto **D987**, passing the 16th-century **Chapelle de Bastide** (**1.1km**). Proceed directly into

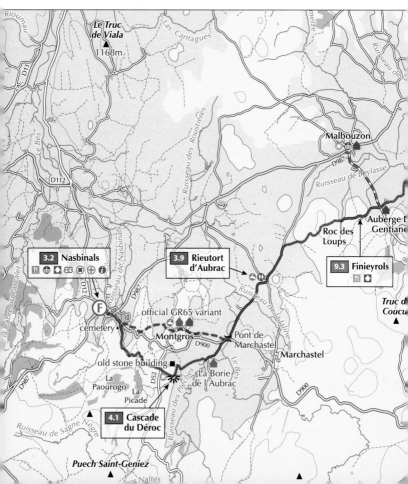

6.8KM LASBROS (ELEV 1090M) 🍴 ⌂ (651.8KM)

⌂ Gîte Chez Marie en Aubrac **Do Pr Dr Br R W S**, 4/12, €36/-/120/-, incl DP, myriamdarz@gmail.com, 0466470894, open Mar–Oct

Soon after Lasbros, turn left onto a minor paved road, which quickly transitions into a dirt track (**0.3km**). An extended off-road stretch (**3.6km**) leads to a small cluster of houses in **Les Quatre Chemins** (café, ⌂ Gîte Aux Quatre Vents **Do Pr Dr R W S**,

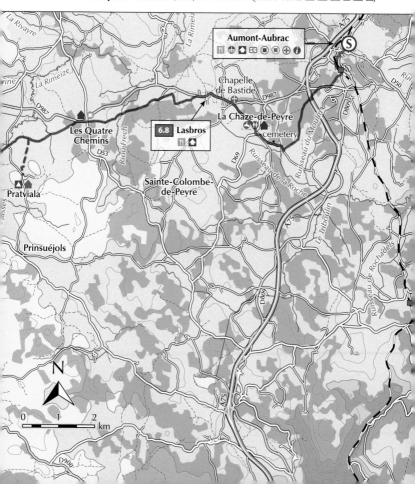

5/13, €20/-/40/60, DP18, granier-jean.marc@orange.fr, 0664193403 or 0652775180, open Apr–Sept, washing machine included, no wifi). Cross **D53** and continue straight on **D987**. Turn left onto a footpath (**0.3km**), passing the turn-off for a 1.2km detour to **Pratviala** (**1.5km**, 🏠 ▲ La Borieta del Prat Do Pr Dr K R W, 1/6, €18/-/52/-, DP21, contact@laborietadelprat.fr, 0430434345, private rooms Mar–Oct, yurt beds May–Aug, €10/tent, donkey parking), and then continue through lovely Aubrac country-side (**2.9km**). Emerge onto a paved road, cross D73, and pass **Auberge Les Gentianes** (**0.2km**). (Alternately, turn right on D73 to detour 1.9km into **Malbouzon** with restaurants, bakery,🏠 Gîte Chez Annie O Do Dr K R Gf W, 4/12, €18/-/-/-, DP21.5, a.fontaine53@laposte.net, 0466325540.)

Keep straight on into

9.3KM FINIEYROLS (ELEV 1190M) 🏔 🏕 (642.5KM)

A memorial near the village's entrance honors native son Louis Dalle, who was deported to and imprisoned at Langenstein-Zwieberge, an annex of the Buchenwald concentration camp, for 10 months during World War II. A Catholic priest, he later characterized his internment as a transformative experience: 'I have suffered so much that I cannot bear to see others suffer.'

🏠 Auberge Les Gentianes O Do Pr Dr R W, 5/21, €18/-/-/-, DP20, auberge. gentianes@orange.fr, 0466325277 or 0673027015, donkey parking

🏠 La Rose de l'Aubrac Do Pr Dr R W S, 1/6, €20/50/70/105, DP20, larosedelaubrac@orange.fr, 0466457855 or 0608315561, open Apr–mid Oct, snack bar

Approaching the Roc des Loups after Finieyrols

Fork right at the village's end (WC and fountain to left), transitioning back onto a dirt track lined with rocks, dandelions, and gentians. Pass a small boulder field, the **Roc des Loups**, with a small labyrinth beneath it (**1.3km**). Turn left on a minor paved road (**1.4km**), curving right into

3.9KM RIEUTORT D'AUBRAC (ELEV 1190M)(638.6KM)
WC and fountain. Note the medieval infrastructure: two granite drinking troughs, a communal oven (which also serves as a pilgrim shelter), and a *travail à ferrer*.

Follow the paved road out of Rieutort. Turn right on **D900** (**2km**) and cross the **Pont de Marchastel** over the Le Bés River. Soon after, you have a choice of routes.

Recommended option via Cascade du Déroc (4.7km)
The GR65 turns right here. However, this guide recommends turning left after the bridge (**0.1km**). The first half of this variant is unmarked, so note these instructions. Follow a paved road through flat terrain, passing ▲ La Borie de l'Aubrac 🄾 🄿🄵 🄳🄵 🄱🄵 🅁 🅆 🅉, €-/-/100/130, DP30, contact@borie-aubrac.com, 0466457697 (**0.5km**). Turn right, towards Gambaise (**0.3km**). Look straight ahead to the hilltop – you'll see a rocky outcropping and an old stone building. That building is your target, so use it to keep your bearings. The road you're on curves to the right at the base of the hill. At the apex of that curve, fork left onto a footpath (**0.9km**). Take the next left (**0.1km**). Soon after, arrive at that **stone farmhouse** (**0.3km**). Look for a break in the stone wall to your left. This provides access to a viewpoint overlooking the **waterfall**. Footpaths to the left allow you to descend, if you wish, to the base of the falls.

4.1KM CASCADE DU DÉROC (ELEV 1210M) 🄷 (634.5KM)
A 30m waterfall, with the Gambaïse River plunging into a small glacial valley. It's easy to admire from above, but even more invigorating to stroll beneath and behind it.

Backtrack to the footpath and continue onward. Upon intersecting **D52** (bar), turn right towards Le Baules, then fork left on a stone-lined footpath (**0.5km**). Red-and-white blazes resume here, although you are not on the GR65. In quick succession, fork right, turn left, turn left again, and then fork left onto a dirt road (**1.2km**). As you approach Nasbinals, pavement resumes (**0.7km**). Briefly rejoin D900 at a **cemetery**, before forking left onto a footpath. The GR65 rejoins here (**0.4km**).

Official GR65 track through Montgros (3.3km)
After crossing the Le Bés, take the first right on a dirt track. Merge onto a paved road and proceed directly into **Montgros** (**1.4km**, fountain, ▲ ▲ La Maison de Rosalie 🄳🄾

Pr Dr Br R Gr W S, 4/14, €45.6/70.6/111.2/-, incl DP, maisonderosalie@orange.fr, 0637106454, open mid Apr–mid Oct, ▲ Aurelle **Pr Br R S**, €-/-/69/-, aurelle.aubrac@gmail.com, 0632824496, open Apr–Sept). At the village's end, fork left onto a dirt track (**0.2km**). Near Nasbinals, transition back onto pavement (**1.5km**). Turn left, then right, onto D900, rejoining the recommended route.

Reunited for the final approach, the *chemin* crosses **D987** and follows a minor paved road uphill to the church in

---

3.2KM NASBINALS (ELEV 1170M, POP 525) ⊞ ⊕ ⌂ Ⓔ ◉ ⊕ ❶ (631.3KM)

Like Saugues, Nasbinals claims a visit from Julius Caesar. Its Christian era dates to the seventh century, when Gregory of Tours evangelized the region. Its impressive 11th-century, Romanesque Église Sainte-Marie has pride of place in the center and features a statue of St Roch and a lovely octagonal bell tower. A monument commemorates Pierre Brioude, or Pierrounet, a 19th-century local hero. Born a shepherd, local legend holds that he stopped one day to repair a damaged roadside cross. Following a short prayer, he received a response: 'Pierre, you will repair everything you touch.' And indeed, he did. At his peak, he treated over 10,000 patients annually, setting and repairing the bone fractures of humans and animals alike.

- ▲ Gîte Communal **Do K R Gr W Z**, 4/19, €15/-/-/-, 5147A Rue de las Janas, mairiedenasbinals@orange.fr, 0466325947, open Apr–Oct

- ▲ Gîte La Grappiere **O Do Br K R**, 1/15, €21/-/-/-, marjori.lagrappiere@laposte.net, 0466321560, reservation required in offseason

- ▲ ▲ Gîte Le Sorbier / Hotel de France **O Do Pr K R Gr S**, 4/20, €16/-/55/-, Rue Principale, chaletderoc.rey@free.fr, 0466325019, breakfast €7

- ▲ Gîte de l'Association NADA **O Do Pr K R**, 2/14, €12/14/28/42, contact@nada-aubrac.com, 0466325042

- ▲ Gîte Lo Fenador **Do K R**, 2/10, €12.5/-/-/-, Chemin de la Grange du Four, accueil@lofenador.fr, 0695083668, open Apr–Oct, English spoken

- ▲ Hôtel La Route d'Argent **O Do Pr Dr R Gr**, €16/44/62/65, DP30, contact@bastide-nasbinals.com, 0466325003

- ▲ Camping Municipal de Nasbinals **R Gr W Z**, follow D12 1km from center, camping.nasbinals@orange.fr, 0466325187, €5.70/person, open Apr–Sept

STAGE 6
Nasbinals to Saint-Côme-d'Olt

Start	Église Sainte-Marie, Nasbinals
Finish	Église Saint-Côme-et-Saint-Damien, Saint-Côme-d'Olt
Distance	32.7km (35.6km via GR6)
Total ascent	640m (740m via GR6)
Total descent	1440m (1560m via GR6)
Difficulty	Strenuous
Time	10hr (11hr via GR6)
Percentage paved	22% (15% via GR6)
Gîtes	Aubrac 9km, Sarbonnel 4.6+0.7km, Saint-Chély-d'Aubrac 16.4km, L'Estrade 23.2km, Saint-Côme-d'Olt 32.7km

This lengthy walk bridges two of the most evocative regions on the *chemin*: the Aubrac plateau and the Lot Valley. The opening ascent from Nasbinals brings you high into the Aubrac's green hills and then to its eponymous village. The first of the day's two significant descents follows, dropping 500m into the town of Saint-Chély-d'Aubrac, perfectly positioned for a lunch break. Indeed, many will opt to split this stage in two, spending the night here. The walk's second half mirrors the first, with an initial ascent giving way to another substantial drop, yielding another 500m. Sore knees will be amply rewarded for their labors, though, with an evening spent in lovely Saint-Côme-d'Olt. An alternative stretch between Aubrac and Saint-Chély on the GR6 offers solitude and a bit less pavement, but adds several kilometers.

Follow Rue Principale uphill around the church and then out of **Nasbinals**. Fork right into Le Coustat (**0.7km**), then continue on a dirt track. After winding through a series of unpaved roads, cross the **Pont de Pascalet** and fork right onto a footpath (**2.7km**). **Bikes and dogs are not allowed along the chemin between the Pont de Pascalet and Aubrac; stick with the road if riding or walking with your four-legged friend.** This leads steadily higher into the hills, first skirting a thicket and then curving right uphill. Pass the **Buron de Ginestouse** – a summer base for shepherds with seasonal flocks – and continue onward (**2.9km**). The hill to the right is Trois Eveques, the historic border between three regions. Today, it marks the line between the Lozère and Aveyron departments. Cross **D987** (**2.1km**), passing modern sculptures, and follow a footpath into Aubrac, looping beneath the church and tower (**0.5km**). Turn right on **D533** (WC on left) then left on **D987** in

Nasbinals

Aubrac

9

Saint-Chély-d'Aubrac

7.4

Le Coustat

D12

Pont de Pascalet

Ruisseau de la Cabro ou Pascalet

Ruisseau de Na

La Paourogo
La Picade

Places Hautes

1276m

Puech Saint-Geniez

1271m

Ruisseau de Places Hautes

Alte Teste

1448m

Ruisseau de Sagne Nègre

D987

1375m

Roc de Campiels

1354m

Buron de Ginestouse

D987

Puech du Pommier

1302m

La Roque

1303m

CR6 variant

Trois Eveques

Pic de Gudette

1427m

D15

D987

D533

Sarbonnel

Les Enfrux

D19

Aubrac

Wooden cross

Belvézet

Bonneval variant

cemetery

Ruisseau du Vaysolie

N

2 km

Map continues on page 81

Map continues on page 76

D900

Condom-d'Aubrac

D987

5

D15

The village of Aubrac

9KM AUBRAC (ELEV 1310M) ⏸ 🏠 ◉ (622.3KM)

Adelard de Flandres, a Flemish knight who was attacked by bandits en route to Santiago, founded Aubrac in 1120 as a place of refuge for pilgrims. The Église Notre Dame has a large, modern painting depicting the town's history. Watch for gentian: a yellow-flowered plant, 1m high and common to the area. Its root is used for Suze, a liqueur.

The region is famous for its annual Transhumance Festival, which celebrates the long tradition of 'herding the herds' to the high plateau each summer. It occurs on the weekend closest to May 25 and draws thousands to the region to witness the parade of flower-covered cattle. Events are often centered here and in nearby Saint-Chély-d'Aubrac, but its impact is felt throughout the Aubrac region. While exciting to witness, if walking at that time, plan carefully! Accommodations, including gîte beds, are booked far in advance.

🛏 La Tour des Anglais ᴅᴏ 🅺 🆁, 2/16, €12/-/-/-, DP22 at Hôtel de la Dômerie, mairie-st-chely-daubrac@wanadoo.fr, 0565442842, open May–Sept

🛏 Gîtes du Royal Aubrac ᴅᴏ ʙʳ 🅺 🆁 ᴄʳ 🆂 🆉, 14/57, €30/-/-/-, contact@royal-aubrac.fr, 0565442841, open spring–summer, €10/tent

🛏 La Colonie ᴏ ᴘʳ ʙʳ 🆁 ᴄʳ 🆂, €-/80/110/-, contact@la-colonie.com, 0565516479 or 0632140571

🛏 Hôtel de la Dômerie ᴘʳ ᴅʳ ʙʳ 🆁 ᴄʳ 🆉, €-/66/104/-, incl DP, david.mc@wanadoo.fr, 0565442842, closed Dec–Jan

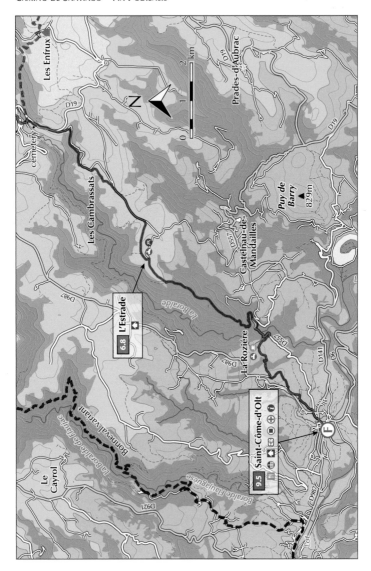

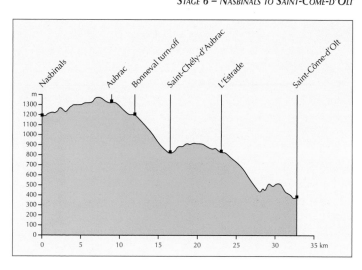

Leaving Aubrac, you have two waymarked options en route to Saint-Chély-d'Aubrac.

GR65 through Belvezet (7.8km)
Fork left off D987 onto a footpath (**0.7km**) and descend through wooded terrain. Beech, chestnut, oak, and walnut all proliferate here. Pass a **wooden cross** and the turn-off for the Bonneval variant (**2.3km**, described below), before emerging onto a paved road in **Belvezet** (**1.2km**, fountain). Follow a dirt track out of the village, passing the **turn-off for Sarbonnel** (**0.4km**, ⬧ ⬧ Ecologîte Sarbonnel Dd Pr Dr K R W S, 2/6, €14/51/52/72, DP23, gitesarbonnel@gmail.com, 0565448189, open Apr–Oct), and then eventually merging onto a minor paved road (**1.7km**). Turn right on D19 and proceed into

7.4KM SAINT-CHÉLY-D'AUBRAC (ELEV 810M, POP 530) 🏨 ⊕ 🛖 ⓒ ◉ ⊕ (614.9KM)
Market on Wednesday mornings. The 15th-century Église Saint-Éloy, rebuilt after being destroyed by English raiders, pays homage to St Roch, with both a gold statue and stained-glass window. Its gallery, added later to accommodate more people, is an unusual design element in this region. Near the bridge over the Boralde River, look closely at the 16th-century cross to spot a tiny pilgrim at its base.

🏠 ▲ Chez Fanny et Jérémy **Do** **K** **R** **W**, 7/26, €16/-/-/-, Route d'Espalion, fannyligniercocq@gmail.com, 0629835882, open Apr–Oct, camping €6.50/ tent, breakfast €6, no wifi

🏠 Gîte Saint-André **Do** **Dr** **R** **W** **Z**, 5/20, €19/-/-/-, DP21, randogitestandre@free. fr, 0565442687, open mid Mar–mid Oct

🏠 🏠 Le Relais Saint-Jacques **Do** **Pr** **Dr** **Br** **R** **S**, 1/6, €40/70/95/-, incl DP, 0647320408, open mid Mar–mid Nov

🏠 Côté Boralde **Pr** **Dr** **Br** **K** **R** **W** **S**, €-/49/65/97, DP17, romiazam@orange.fr, 0678134647, open mid Apr–Oct, swimming pool

🏠 La Carderie **Pr** **Dr** **Br** **R** **W** **S**, €-/57/95/141, incl DP, lacarderie. chambresdhotes@gmail.com, 0565441296, open Apr–Oct, vegetarian

🏠 Hôtel Les Coudercous **O** **Pr** **Dr** **R** **Gr** **W** **S**, €-/51/61/73, DP34, lescoudercous@orange.fr, 0565442740, closed Dec–Jan holidays

Turn left at the post office (WC on right). Turn right through Place de la Mairie, then left on Rue du Pont Vieu (turn right for Église Saint-Éloy). Cross the Pont des Pèlerins and then climb switchbacks to the **cemetery**. Turn right onto a dirt track (**0.4km**), where the GR6 intersects from the left.

GR6 through Les Enfrux (10.7km to GR65, 11.1km to Saint-Chély services)
Backtrack on **D533** from Aubrac center and pick up the GR6 waymarks soon after, forking left off the highway. The first third of this walk involves a gentle descent along a grassy trail, followed by an equally measured rise through woods. The second third flattens out, eventually emerging from the woods to wide-open skies, with impressive views of the surrounding valley. This transitions to an extended descent in the last third, dropping some 450m, but it's consistently gradual on good footing. Pass through the lone village on this alternative, **Les Enfrux** (**7.9km**, 🏠 Galtier **O** **Pr** **Br** **R**, €-/-/90/-, gerard.galtier12@orange.fr, 0672913443, English spoken), then continue on a stone-lined footpath back into thick woods. The trees only yield as you rejoin the **GR65** at the exit from Saint-Chély (**2.8km**). To reach the town's services, backtrack **0.4km**, following the GR65's waymarks.

Routes reunited, turn left on **D19**, then right onto a footpath, rejoining D19 soon after (**0.9km**). Fork right on a minor paved road, then fork right again onto a dirt track through woods. A series of tracks leads to **Les Cambrassats** (**2.1km**). Follow a footpath from the village, later turning right onto a paved road (**1km**). Fork right onto a dirt track (**1.1km**), then proceed into

6.8KM L'ESTRADE (ELEV 825M) ▱ (608.1KM)
Covered rest stop with fountain.

🛏 Gîte de L'Estrade `Do` `Dr` `Br` `R` `W` `Z`, 5/15, €39/-/-/-, incl DP, gitelestrade@orange.fr, 0675590091, open Apr–Sept

Turn right in the village and then follow a long, winding track through an extended descent (**4.3km**). Transition onto pavement, cross **D557**, and join another footpath. Turn left onto D557 (**0.5km**). Turn right onto a dirt track and proceed into **La Roziére** (**1.2km**, fountain, snack bar). Alternate between dirt tracks, footpaths, and paved roads in quick succession, ultimately rejoining **D557** (**2.8km**). Cross **D987**, turn right at a T, and then fork left back under **D987** (**0.4km**). Continue straight along Rue Mathat and then through an arched passageway into **Saint-Côme**'s pedestrian-only center. Curve left past Gîte del Roumiou and proceed to the church in

9.5KM SAINT-CÔME-D'OLT (ELEV 370M, POP 1350) ▯ ⊕ ▱ Ⓒ ◉ ⊕ ❶ (598.6KM)
WC and fountain across from church. Market on Sunday mornings in July/August.

One of the 'most beautiful villages in France,' Saint-Côme features a well-preserved medieval core, with three fortified entryways and many curving alleys. The 16th-century Église Saint-Côme et Saint-Damien is built in flamboyant Gothic style and known for its unusual, twisted spire (*clocher*). Its carved oak doors include 360 hand-forged nails that date to 1532. The saints, Côme/Cosmas and Damien, were twins and Arab doctors in third-century Roman Syria; they accepted no payment for their medical services and, in the process, won over many to Christianity. Captured by the prefect under the period of Emperor Diocletian's persecution, they were extensively tortured – crucified, stoned, pierced by arrows – but stayed true to their faith. Ultimately, they were beheaded, along with their three younger brothers.

The 10th-century Chapelle des Pénitents formerly had a pilgrim hospital and was the church for peasants in the Middle Ages; it now hosts exhibits. Meanwhile, the 14th-century château is now the Hotel de Ville. Note that street names come in both French and Occitan; 'Olt' is the old Celtic name for the Lot River.

🛏 Gîte del Roumiou `Do` `Dr` `K` `R` `W` `S`, 3/18, €16/-/-/-, DP22, 12 Rue Crémade, gitesaintcome@gmail.com, 0635591605, open Apr–Oct, English spoken

🛏 Gîte l'Antidote `O` `Do` `Dr` `R` `S`, 1/8, €15/-/-/-, 22 Chemin des Plantiers, laurent.auz@gmail.com, 0641906289, breakfast €5, donation-based dinner

Approaching the steep descent towards Saint-Côme-d'Olt

🏠🏠 Couvent de Malet Ⓞ Do Pr Dr R Cf W Z, €16/41/62/73, DP18.5, contact@hotel-malet-aveyron.fr, 0565510320, donkey parking

🏠 Gîte Halte d'Olt Ⓞ Do Pr Dr K R W S, 2/7, €16/26/-/-, DP21, 15 Route de Boraldette, lahaltedolt@gmail.com, 0679083872 or 0676266989

🏠 Gîte Le Chat en Boule Ⓞ Pr K R W S, €-/-/45/60, 19 Ave de Saint-Geniez, danielebarre@orange.fr, 0687044951, reservation required in offseason, English spoken

🏠 Au Pont d'Olt Pr Dr Br R W S, €-/65/72/79, DP18, 25 Ave de Saint-Geniez, aupontdolt@gmail.com, 0652462420, open Mar–Oct, English spoken

▲ Camping Belle Rive R Cf, 40 Rue du Terral, contact@camping-bellerive-aveyron.com, 0698229159, open Apr–Sept, camping €10/person

Alternative route from Aubrac to Espalion (36.7km) via Abbaye de Bonneval (28.6km)

It's possible to detour to the Bonneval Abbey, leaving the GR65 3km after Aubrac. Founded by Cistercians in the 12th century, the abbey thrived in the Middle Ages but was hammered in the 14th century by the double-whammy of the Black Death and Hundred Years' War. A group of Trappist nuns moved into the abbey in 1875, launching a chocolate factory and river turbine for electricity. Accommodation (and chocolate) is offered to pilgrims.

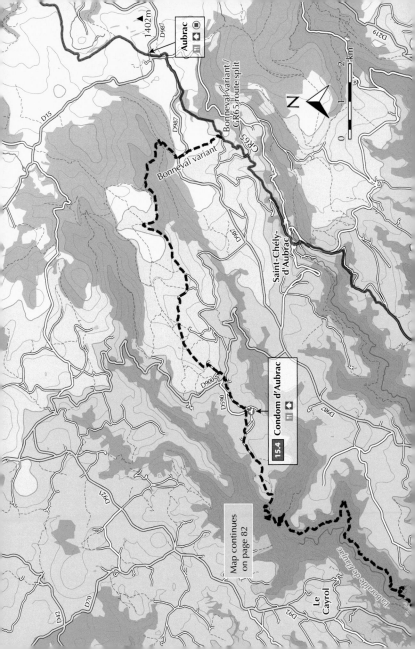

1402m

D987

Aubrac

D987

Bonneval Variant/
GR65 route split

Bonneval variant

GR65

D987

Saint-Chély-
d'Aubrac

D900

D590

15.4 Condom d'Aubrac

D987

Map continues
on page 82

La boralde flaujergue

Le
Cayrol

D97

D70

D42

D219

D15

N

0   1   2 km

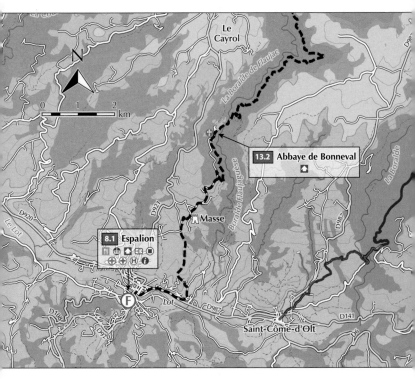

The route is not frequently walked. Consequently, pilgrims should be prepared for faded waymarks (light blue is not an ideal color!) and overgrown trails. The terrain is strenuous (1165m ascent, 2025m descent), descending – often steeply – from the Aubrac to the Lot Valley with a pair of river crossings en route that also necessitate sharply rebounding ascents.

From Aubrac, the walk divides as follows: **15.4km Condom d'Aubrac** (fountain, basic accommodation in *mairie* – 0565442711, meals by reservation only at Café Aux Portes d'Aubrac – carlasur12@gmail.com, 0682341502), **13.2km Abbaye de Bonneval** (gîte, hotellerie.bonneval@gmail.com, 0565442449), and **8.1km Espalion**, where it rejoins the GR65 (see Stage 7 for further info). Services, including water points, are very limited, so prepare accordingly.

STAGE 7
Saint-Côme-d'Ôlt to Estaing

Start	Église Saint-Côme-et-Saint-Damien, Saint-Côme-d'Olt
Finish	Église Saint-Fleuret, Estaing
Distance	21.3km (19.7km via low-level alternative)
Total ascent	570m (445m via low-level alternative)
Total descent	615m (490m via low-level alternative)
Difficulty	Moderate-to-strenuous
Time	6hr (5hr 30min via low-level alternative)
Percentage paved	57% (64% via low-level alternative)
Gîtes	Espalion 7.8km, Bessuéjouls 11.3km, Estaing 21.3km

The three towns visited on today's itinerary – Saint-Côme, Espalion, and Estaing – could easily keep this region's postcard industry in good health. Leaving Saint-Côme, the *chemin* joins the Lot River for its opening kilometers, before climbing high to a dramatic viewpoint overlooking the valley. An equivalent descent loops past a lovely Romanesque church before arriving in Espalion, famous for its graceful bridges spanning the Lot. The route then veers inland, passing another impressive church, before returning to the river just before Estaing. For a second consecutive night, the stage concludes in one of France's most beautiful villages – a castle-topped, medieval settlement perched on a promontory overlooking the confluence of the Lot and Coussane Rivers. Those preferring a less demanding walk have the option to bypass the initial climb, instead following a quiet, paved road to the Perse chapel.

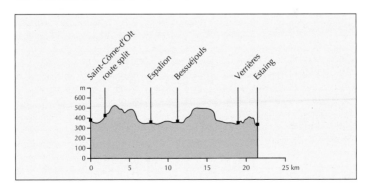

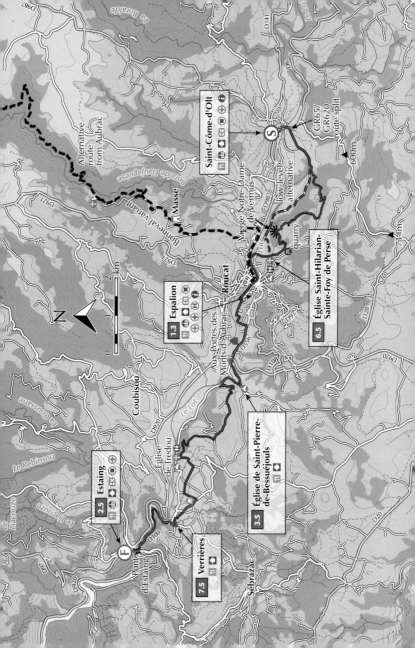

Saint-Côme-d'Olt

S ← GR65/GR620 route split

600m

low-level alternative

Alternative route from Aubrac

la Boralde

Boralde Flaujaguese

la Masse

Bonneval variant

Vierge Notre-Dame de Vernus

quarry

Espalion 1.3

Roucat

Aux-Portes des Monts d'Aubrac

Église Saint-Hilarian-Sainte-Foy de Perse 6.5

Le Lot

Coubisou

Église de Tredou

Église de Saint-Pierre-de-Bessuéjouls 3.5

Estaing 2.5

Le Rebinsou

Le Goussane

la Lacourte

Verrières 7.5

Sebrazac

F

Pont d'Estaing

N

0 1 2 km

Loop around **Saint-Côme**'s church, then turn right, passing through the medieval gate. Continue straight on Rue du Terral, fork right, then merge onto D6. Cross the **Lot River** and turn right towards Gîte de Combes (**0.4km**). The GR620 continues straight; don't be tricked! After a flat, easy walk along the Lot (**1.4km**), you have two options.

GR65 via the Vierge Notre-Dame de Vermus (4.7km)

Turn left onto a footpath, climbing steadily through woods. Emerge onto a minor paved road (**2km**). After a string of scattered houses, fork right onto another footpath, leading past an old quarry, and then to the **Vierge Notre-Dame de Vermus** (**1.4km**). The Virgin has an envious vantage point, with sweeping views of the valley, Espalion, and its castle. A sharp descent follows (**1km**), made slightly gentler by recent route changes. After transitioning back onto a dirt track, arrive at the **Perse chapel**.

Low-level alternative via the Lot (3.1km)

This unmarked alternative allows pilgrims to opt out of a significant up-and-down. Follow the flat, paved road until turning left on a dirt track towards 'Chapelle de Perse' (**2.5km**). Rejoin the GR65 at the **Perse chapel**.

6.5KM ÉGLISE SAINT-HILARIAN-SAINTE-FOY DE PERSE (ELEV 345M) (592.1KM)

Fountain and WC. This 11th-century Romanesque chapel is dedicated to Saint-Hilarian d'Espalion. Hilarian was born in nearby Lévinhac, around 760. Legend – but not the historical record – holds that Hilarian was raised to the priesthood by Charlemagne and later served as his confessor. Hilarian was decapitated by 'Saracens' while he officiated mass in an earlier church here. However, holding true to a promise, he calmly lifted his head and washed it, before bringing it to his mother. Note his representation in the church, similarly with head in hands. He is celebrated in Espalion annually on the third Sunday in June. The church was placed under the Conques Abbey's authority in 1060, hence the link to Sainte-Foy.

The capitals and tympanum are notable. The tympanum portrays the Last Supper, and features dueling tetramorphs (symbolic arrangements of four differing elements) – Jesus is surrounded by the four evangelists on the right (Matthew's angel, Mark's lion, Luke's winged ox, and John's eagle), while a *tétramorphe diabolioque* looms to the left, with an evil foursome gathered around a seated devil. The latter is believed to be unique in European religious architecture.

Routes reunited, with the chapel at your back, proceed through a sports complex and its parking lot, then join a riverside walkway (**0.4km**). Entering Espalion, follow Rue Saint-Joseph. Turn right past Gîte Au Fil de l'Eau in Place du Plô onto Rue Canel in

1.3KM ESPALION (ELEV 345M, POP 4515) 🍴 ⊕ 🛏 🅒 ⊛ Ⓗ ⊕ ⊕ **ℹ** (590.8KM)
Market on Friday mornings. A Roman town formed here around a bridge; in the Middle Ages, it became a Templar command post. At its peak, medieval Espalion featured three towers, 20+ shops, and a drawbridge, all organized around the Place du Griffoul. The pilgrim bridge over the Lot, the Pont Vieux, was built in the reign of St Louis out of pink sandstone. In the Middle Ages, the Lord of Calmont imposed a toll for passage over it, to cover maintenance expenses. Today, it's closed to motorized traffic but open to cattle, particularly as part of the transhumance in late May. On the Lot's right bank, between the bridges, flat stones can be seen jutting out from some buildings; those buildings were once tanneries, the stones used to wash hides.

The Église Paroissiale Saint-Jean-Baptiste is newer construction – dating to the late 19th century – but its dramatic spires and striking red sandstone façade are attention-getters. Meanwhile, its predecessor, the 15th-century Ancienne Église Saint-Jean-Baptiste, was converted into the town hall in the 19th century, and then more recently transformed into the Musée du Scaphandre. That museum tells the story of residents, Rouquayrol and Denayrouze, who invented the autonomous diving machine in 1864; they're also commemorated with a riverside statue.

🏠🏠 Gîte Au Fil de l'Eau 🅳🅾 🅿🆁 🅳🆁 🅱🆁 🆁 🆆 🆉, 5/15, €21.40/49.50/59/-, DP15, 5 Rue Saint-Joseph, aufildeleaumireille@gmail.com, 0677585308, open Apr–Oct, private rooms at adjacent Au Jardin des Sens

🏠 Gîte La Halte Saint-Jacques 🅾 🅳🅾 🅿🆁 🆁 🆆, 4/18, €16/-/52/-, DP21, 8 Rue du Trémolières, lahaltesaintjacques@hotmail.fr, 0628303830 or 0565663561, reservation required in offseason, English spoken

🏠 Gîte du Pont Vieux 🅾 🅳🅾 🅿🆁 🅺 🆁 🅶🆁 🆆 🆂 🆉, 3/12, €17/-/50/68, 7 Rue Canel, espasport12@orange.fr, 0647758119 or 0565449081, reservation required in offseason, breakfast €5

🏠 La Fontaine 🅾 🅿🆁 🅱🆁 🆁 🅶🆁, €-/-/54/-, 15 Chemin De Calmont, christian.regis3@wanadoo.fr, 0565484591, swimming pool

🏠 La Maison du Pèlerin 🅾 🅿🆁 🆁, €-/45/60/-, 3 Rue de Bouquiès, nicolemonnaye@orange.fr, 0565442677

🏠 Aux Portes des Monts d'Aubrac 🅾 🅿🆁 🅳🆁 🅺 🆁 🅶🆁 🆆, €-/17/30/45, DP19, 66 Ave de Saint-Pierre, apdma@orange.fr, 0565488505, located 1km after Espalion, swimming pool

Turn right on Rue Droite, left on Quai Affre, and then cross Boulevard Poulenc (Office de Tourisme to left). Continue straight ahead, alongside the Lot, and then fork right onto a riverside footpath (**0.4km**). Turn left onto a paved road (**0.4km**), passing

Espalion and the Pont Vieux over the Lot River

through a residential neighborhood. Turn right onto **D556** (**1.1km**), with a pedestrian walkway, then turn left onto a minor road (**1.1km**). Continue to

3.5KM ÉGLISE DE SAINT-PIERRE-DE-BESSUÉJOULS (ELEV 340M) 🍴 ⌂ (587.3KM)

A UNESCO site, Bessuéjouls is a Celtic term meaning 'clearing in the woods.' Most of the present church dates to the 14th century, although it was over-restored in the 19th. The interior features a simple barrel vault and a baroque retablo. However, the bell tower preserves a rare high chapel, which dates to the 11th-century Chapelle Saint-Michel, and it includes a ninth-century altar and interesting historiated capitals. To the altar's left is a carving of St Michael, stabbing a spear into a dragon's throat. The archangel Gabriel stands to the right.

🏠 🏠 **Domaine d'Armagnac** Ⓞ Ⓓⓞ Ⓟⓡ Ⓓⓡ Ⓚ Ⓡ Ⓒⓡ Ⓦ Ⓢ Ⓩ, 1/8, €20/95/105/150, DP19, domainedarmagnac@gmail.com, 0603256347, breakfast included with private rooms

Turn right across the Hom River, then pass behind the *mairie* (fountain). Continue straight onto D556e, then turn left at a T (**0.6km**). After passing through a cluster of houses, join a footpath through woods (**0.5km**). Transition onto a minor paved road for a stretch (**1.9km**), before returning to another footpath, descending this time. After emerging from the woods, arrive at the **Église de Tredou** (**1.9km**, fountain, WC). A series of mostly quiet, paved roads lead past a snack bar and into

A sign before Bessuéjouls alerts drivers to pilgrim traffic

87

7.5KM VERRIÈRES (ELEV 330M, POP 455) 🍴 ⬜ (579.8KM)

The Chapelle Saint-Michel sits near the village's end, overlooking an elegant medieval bridge.

⬥ Picard Pr Dr Br K R, €-/-/60/80, DP20, alpicard13@gmail.com, 0687018240, open May–Sept

Following D556 from the village, merge soon after with **D100** (0.3km). Fork left onto a footpath for one last up-and-down before returning to D100 (1.3km). While the GR65 bypasses Estaing's center, that would be a crime. Turn right instead onto the **Pont d'Estaing** and cross the Lot. Turn right and then left immediately after on Rue François d'Estaing. The Église Saint-Fleuret is on your right.

2.5KM ESTAING (ELEV 325M, POP 475) 🍴 ⊕ ⬜ 🄲 ⊙ ⊕ (577.3KM)

Market on Friday mornings in July/August. WC next to bridge. The municipal swimming pool, located on the way into town, is open July/August (€3).

Dieudonné d'Estaing saved King Philippe Auguste at the Battle of the Bouvines in 1214, and from that point the town boomed – at least, until the Revolution, when Admiral Charles Henri Hector d'Estaing testified on behalf of Marie Antoinette in her trial. He was labeled a Reactionary and sent to the guillotine. The 15th-century Château d'Estaing sits proudly in the center, owned by the family of Valéry Giscard d'Estaing, the former President of France. The extensively restored castle is open for visits (€6).

Directly across from the castle, the 15th-century, Gothic Église Saint-Fleuret has a stone cross outside with a tiny pilgrim. The chapel in the back-left corner is dedicated to St Fleuret and includes his relics; he is believed to have originally converted Estaing to Christianity in 621. The Feast of St Fleuret takes place on the first weekend in July, which corresponds to the feast day for Francois d'Estaing, former Bishop of Rodez, who was beatified but never canonized. On that Sunday, a procession features townsfolk dressed as the Heavenly Host and pilgrims to Compostela.

⬥ Hospitalité Saint-Jacques O Do Dr Br R, 2/12, €Donation, incl DP, 8 Rue du Collège, 0565441900, no wifi, reservations 24hrs before, closed Sundays, English spoken

⬥ Gîte Communal Do Pr K R Cf W Z, 5/20, €15/-/-/45, Place du Foirail, gitecommunalestaing@gmail.com, 0644955214, open Mar–Oct

⬥ Au Paradis sur Terre Do K R, 4/14, €15.40/-/-/-, 3 Rue d'Estaing, marietthereserampony@gmail.com, 0641858667, open Mar–Oct, breakfast €5.60

The village of Estaing, topped by its magnificent château

🔺 Gîte Saint-Christophe **Do** **Pr** **K** **R** **W** **S**, 5/15, €16.40/-/32.80/-, 5 Rue St Fleuret, gite.etape.st.christophe@gmail.com, 0608254170, open Apr–Oct, breakfast €6

🔺 Gîte Chez Aurélie **O** **Do** **Dr** **K** **R**, 3/8, €16.40/-/-/-, DP22, 3 Rue du Collège, ChezAurelie12@outlook.fr, 0695821595, breakfast €6

🔺 Gîte Haut-Doubs d'Estaing **O** **Do** **Dr** **K** **R** **Gr** **W** **S** **Z**, 1/6, €16.40/-/-/-, DP22, 31 Rue d'Estaing, gite-hd-estaing@outlook.fr, 0644187295, restaurant

🔺 Gîte Les Pieds dans l'Olt **Do** **Pr** **Dr** **R** **Gr** **W** **S**, 3/10, €16.60/-/64/-, DP21, 1 Ave d'Espalion, lespiedsdanslolt@gmail.com, 0663338822, open mid Mar–mid Dec

🔺 Chez Tifille **O** **Pr** **Dr** **Br** **R** **Gr** **W** **S**, €-/45/55/-, DP21, 4 Rue du Château, contact@cheztifille.fr, 0651124146

🔺 Chez Jeannot **Pr** **Br** **R** **W** **S**, €-/37/42/52, Le Pont d'Estaing, jean.dijols12@orange.fr, 0565447151 or 0670384281, open Mar–Nov, donkey parking

🔺 Camping Municipal La Chantellerie **R** **Gr** **W** **Z**, commune-estaing@orange.fr, 0686772720, €6.50/tent, open May–Sept, 2km outside of the center

STAGE 8
Estaing to Conques

Start	Église Saint-Fleuret, Estaing
Finish	Abbaye Sainte-Foy, Conques
Distance	35.3km (35.1km via Golinhac)
Total ascent	980m (955m via Golinhac)
Total descent	1010m (985m via Golinhac)
Difficulty	Moderate-to-strenuous
Time	10hr
Percentage paved	48% (58% via Golinhac)
Gîtes	On GR6: Campuac 11.5km, Le Barthas 12.7+0.7km. On GR65: Fonteilles 7.7+0.3km, Massip 12.5km, Golinhac 14.1km. After routes merge: Le Soulié 20.5km, Espeyrac 23km, Sénergues 25.9km, Conques 35.3km

While many will prefer to break this lengthy stage in half, it's presented here as a single stage because there are two routes to choose between, and that choice may influence where you overnight. Both have their virtues. This guide favors the GR6, which climbs steadily out of Estaing and passes through Campuac, as it offers a bit less pavement and better views. The GR65, meanwhile, hews closer to the Lot early on, although a significant ascent follows; those taking that approach might opt for a night in Golinhac. Whether it takes one day or two, though, the reward is significant. Beautiful Conques is rivaled only by Le Puy as the town most deeply associated with this pilgrimage to Compostela. Be ready for a later bedtime – the pilgrim blessing, organ concert, and light show are all must-dos.

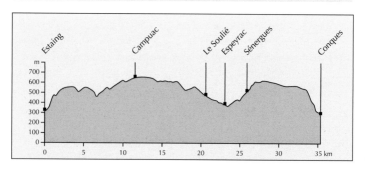

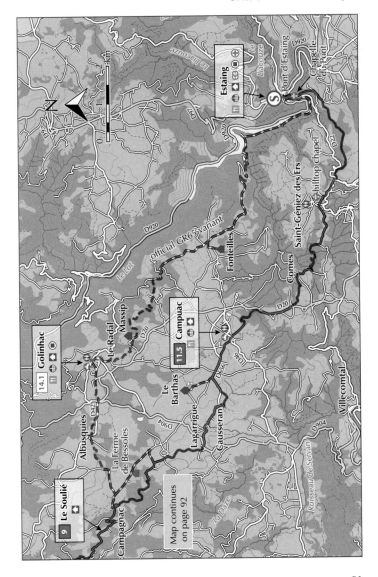

Map continues on page 92

91

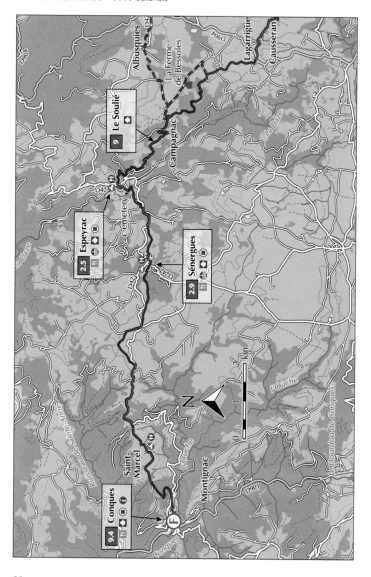

Backtrack across the **Lot River**, to the first intersection after the **Pont d'Estaing** (0.2km). At this point, you have two waymarked options.

Recommended GR6 track through Campuac (19km)

To follow the GR6, turn left and then immediately fork right onto a minor road, passing to the **Chapelle du Pont**'s left. Proceed steadily uphill, transitioning onto a footpath through the woods, before emerging back onto pavement just before a hairpin turn (**0.9km**). Soon after forking right, the pavement recedes once again (**0.6km**), giving way to an extended stretch on a dirt track (**2.5km**). Merge with **D22**, fork onto a minor paved road, and wind through hills. Loop past a small, **hilltop chapel** (**0.7km**); the village of **Saint-Géniez des Ers** (WC) is just off-route to the right. The paved road concludes at a cluster of farmhouses (**1.3km**). Continue straight, joining a footpath into dense woods, descending through a gully, and then climbing into **Comes** (**1.8km**). Merge with **D20** (**1.1km**), then fork left onto a dirt track (**0.8km**). Merge with another paved road and then cross **D46** to arrive at the church in

---

11.5KM CAMPUAC (ELEV 660M, POP 450) 🏠 ⊕ 🎒 (565.8KM)

WC and fountain in front of church. The first commune here was established during the Revolution. The Église Saint-Pierre-ès-Liens dates to the 19th century.

🔺 🔺 Gîte L'Arche d'Yvann 🄳🄾 🄿🄵 🄳🄵 🄺 🅁 🄶🄵 🅆 🅂 🅉, 6/15, €15/45/55/-, DP20, 28 Place de la Fontaine, larchedyvann@gmail.com, 0637753880, open Apr–Oct, breakfast included with private rooms, English spoken

---

Proceed along the church's right side; fork right and then left (**0.3km**). Merge onto **D656** (**0.4km**). A series of minor roads, paved and unpaved, lead past the turn-off for **Le Barthas** (**0.5km**, 🔺 Gîte du Barthas 🄾 🄳🄾 🄳🄵 🄺 🅁 🅆 🅂, 7/14, €17.50/-/-/-, DP17, gitedubarthas@gmail.com, 0565515938) and through the villages of **Causseran** (**1km**) and **Lagarrigue** (**0.8km**). Continue through a longer stretch in the quiet hills, dotted with cattle and little else, before reaching a third village, **Campagnac** (**4.7km**). The GR65 rejoins you here, on a minor paved road.

Official GR65 track through Golinhac (18.8km)

Continue straight from the intersection after the Pont d'Estaing, then take the first right onto a minor paved road. This parallels the Lot River as it surges south and then doubles back north (**3.1km**). Turn left onto a dirt road (**0.9km**), initiating a stretch of pinging back and forth between paved and unpaved tracks as you switchback uphill (**0.9km**). Another long section of pavement follows, passing the turn-off for 🔺 🔺 Gîte de Fonteilles Lo Soulenquo 🄳🄾 🄿🄵 🄳🄵 🄺 🅁 🄶🄵 🅆, 9/18, €17/40/60/-, DP20, losoulenquo@gmail.com, 0610970871, camping €5/person, open mid Mar–Nov, vegetarian, English spoken (**2.4km**). Finally leave the pavement behind (**2km**), following a roughly equivalent series of dirt tracks through **Massip** (**2.8km**, 🔺 Gîte L'Orée du Chemin 🄳🄾

Pr Dr R W S Z, 6/22, €16/-/32/-, DP21, stephan.dissac@wanadoo.fr, 0671380757, open Apr–Oct, English spoken) and **Le Radal** (**1.2km**). Continue straight onto D519, leading into

---

14.1KM GOLINHAC (ELEV 635M, POP 335) ⊞ ⊕ ◪ ◉ (562.8KM)
WC and fountain across from church. A 15th-century pilgrim cross, the Croix dels Roumious, featuring three scallop shells and a pilgrim with staff, marked the town's entrance for centuries. For the sake of preservation, it has today been replaced with a reproduction.

⬥ Gîte Bellevue Do Pr Dr K R W Z, 6/31, €15/-/35/-, DP19, pole-bellevue12@orange.fr, 0689554632, open Apr–Sept, camping €12/tent, chalets available, swimming pool

⬥ Les Rochers O Pr Br R W S, €-/60/68/88, lesrochersgolinhac12@gmail.com, 0681864405, includes picnic lunch

⬥ Hôtel La Bastide d'Olt Pr Dr Br R Cf Z, €-/77/89/103, labastide.golinhac@orange.fr, 0689549685, open mid May–Oct, English spoken

---

Fork left on a paved road and move through another quick series of paved and dirt tracks through a rich prairie (**1.2km**). Cross **D904** and continue straight ahead on **D42**. Fork right onto a dirt track and then turn right back onto D42, leading into **Albusquies** (**1.1km**). Leave the hamlet on a dirt track. Turn right at a T on a paved road (**1.8km**). (Alternately, turn left at the T to detour to ⬥ La Ferme de Bessoles Pr Dr Br R W, €-/40/52/75, DP16, soulie.xavier@wanadoo.fr, 0665501031 or 0565661886, open Apr–Oct, also accessible from the GR6.) Shortly after, the GR65 reunites with the GR6. Le Soulié is **6km** from Golinhac.

Routes reunited, follow minor roads, winding downhill through switchbacks, to

---

9KM LE SOULIÉ (ELEV 480M) ◪ (556.8KM)
⬥ Accueil du Soulié de Saint-Jacques O Do Pr Dr Br R W S Z, 6/19, €Donation, incl DP, mroudil@yahoo.fr, 0642356901 or 0649074661, tents welcome, rest area with snacks for passing pilgrims

---

Continue following a series of minor paved and dirt tracks, descending into the valley. Join **D42** (**2.4km**), then fork left at the church in

Pilgrims approach the village of Espeyrac

2.5KM ESPEYRAC (ELEV 390M, POP 245) 🍴 ⊕ ⛰ ◉ (554.3KM)
Fountain outside church, WC in village center. The Église Saint-Pierre features an almost life-size statue of St Roch. The church is mentioned in the *Book of Sainte-Foy*. A pilgrim, Guibert, was passing through here on his return home from a pilgrimage to Conques when he was assaulted by brigands. They ripped his eyes from his head; those were later carried by bird to Conques. Sainte Foy subsequently appeared to Guibert in a vision, encouraging him to return to Conques for mass. He followed her advice and, following a night spent in prayer, miraculously recovered his vision.

🛏 Gîte de l'Ancienne École 🅾 Do Dr Ⓚ Ⓡ, 5/14, €18/-/-/-, gite.ecole@gmail.com, 0611396463, no wifi

🛏 Gîte Chez Benjamine Do Ⓚ Ⓡ Ⓦ, 2/4, €20/-/-/-, benjamine.bruni@gmail.fr, 0609161240 or 0565461664, open Apr–Oct, breakfast €5

🛏 Hôtel de la Vallée Pr Dr Br Ⓡ Cr Ⓢ Ⓩ, €-/50/100/-, incl DP, sarl.lavallee@orange.fr, 0565698761, open mid Apr–mid Oct, English spoken

Make a sharp right off the main road through Espeyrac, cross D42, and proceed past a **cemetery** and onto a dirt track (**0.4km**). Turn right on D42 (**0.9km**), then left onto a dirt track (**0.7km**) for the ascent to town. On the final approach, pass a small park (fountain), then the church (WC), before turning left back onto D42 in

2.9KM SÉNERGUES (ELEV 515M, POP 420) 🍴 ⊕ 🏠 ◉ (551.4KM)

The Église Saint-Martin is built upon ninth-century foundations that date to Louis, son of Charlemagne. The current structure, though, is the work of Conques' abbot in the 16th century, and the stained-glass windows are even more recent, credited to a Benedictine monk, Ephrem Socard, in 1965. The château dates to 1385, when it was built to protect the town from the English in the Hundred Years' War.

🛏 **Domaine de Sénos** Do Pr Dr K R W S Z, 4/15, €20/-/40/60, DP24.5, bienvenue@gites-aveyron.com, 0565729156, open Apr–Oct

🛏 **Gîte Ginette et Maurice** O Do Br K R W S, 3/6, €25/-/-/-, ginette.panissie@orange.fr, 0565728447

Fork left onto **D242** leaving town, then turn right onto a footpath with steps, climbing briefly uphill (**0.2km**). The next section loosely parallels D42, holding to its left side before briefly joining it (**1.9km**), and then swinging to the right. After returning to D42 once more (**1.8km**), stick with it for a longer stretch (**1.1km**). Fork right onto a footpath (**0.9km**), then continue straight on a minor paved road into **Saint-Marcel** (**0.8km**, WC, fountain). The Église Saint-Marcel dates to 1561, although the chapel survives from an earlier Romanesque church. A leprosarium was here in the 17th and 18th centuries. Continue along the road downhill, perhaps saying hello to a most loquacious donkey on the right, then fork left onto what soon becomes a footpath (**1.3km**). This is the original pilgrim road, making for a lovely final approach to Conques, although the footing can be quite unforgiving in wet weather. As the village begins, transition back onto a minor paved road (**0.9km**). Join the main road through Conques, curving left around the abbey, and then turn left into the plaza in front of the stunning church.

9.4KM CONQUES (ELEV 295M, POP 250) 🍴 🏠 ◉ ❶ (542KM)

The abbey offers a full slate of evening programming: pilgrim blessing at 8.30pm, tympanum presentation (in French) at 9pm, organ concert and tour of the upper gallery (€6 ticket for the latter) at 9.30pm, and a tympanum light show at 10.15pm.

The abbey was founded in 819 – the same year that Santiago's remains were discovered in Compostela – by Spanish monks. It is dedicated to St Foy (Faith) of Agen, who was martyred as a young woman when she refused under torture to engage in pagan worship. Her relics attracted attention in Agen, with a basilica built upon her place of martyrdom in the fifth century. Many miracles were linked to Foy, often involving cures for blindness or liberated captives. Others were more colorful. For example, when a local official took his deceased first wife's ring, which was promised to Foy, and used it instead in a second marriage, trouble followed. The new wife's finger became horribly and painfully swollen; seeking relief, the couple attended Foy's shrine for three consecutive nights. Finally, on that third night, the poor woman blew her nose, and the ring miraculously flew – with tremendous force – off her aggrieved finger.

To elevate Conques to a major pilgrimage site, monks conspired in 866 to steal relics of St Foy from Agen. A Conques monk, Aronisdus, was sent by Abbot Bégon to live at Agen for 10 years, gradually earning their trust and confidence, until he had the opportunity to steal the remains. As hoped, this shifted the pilgrim's road away from Agen and through Conques.

The boom in visitors necessitated a larger church. The Église Sainte-Foy, one of the Camino's oldest Romanesque pilgrimage churches, was built 1045–1120. Its tympanum, featuring the Last Judgment, is a masterpiece, with Christ enthroned weighing souls while flanked by Archangel Michael on one side and a demon on the other. Below, heaven and hell are depicted as roofed buildings, each with an entrance door. To the right, the damned are pushed into the jaws of hell. An unpopular local bishop is ensnared, while poachers on abbey property are roasted by a rabbit. To the left are the righteous, welcomed by angels. Abraham stands in the center, embracing two saved souls. The light show hints at how it might have once looked, fully painted.

Part of Conques Abbey's tympanum

The austere church interior features little decoration. Unusually tall for a Romanesque church (nearly 30m), it has an arch-lined, barrel-vaulted nave. The cloister's 212 columns, topped with Romanesque capitals, are an exception to the dearth of embellishment. Unfortunately, much of the cloister was destroyed in 1837; miraculously, the rest of the church survived, thanks to the French Romanticist Prosper Mérimée's intervention. Indeed, this is the only medieval shrine on the French pilgrimage routes to Compostela that survived the Wars of Religion and the French Revolution unscathed. The lone modern addition is a stained-glass window devoted to the only saint to live at the monastery, St George of Conques. Traditionally, pilgrims circled the shrine of St Foy three times and then stopped in front of the reliquary to ask for a safe journey to Santiago.

The church's small-but-mighty treasury (€4.50) also survived revolutionary turbulence. A clever mayor and loyal villagers saved the day, distributing the treasures to each home. When Republicans arrived, they were informed that justice had already been served, with villagers claiming their share. Satisfied, the rabble departed, and the treasures were restored to the church. The treasury's highlight is the reliquary of St Foy, the only surviving example of a statue-reliquary shrine. Remnants of the saint's skull are stored in the statue's back. It also contains a fragment of the True Cross (gifted by Charlemagne), a golden 'A' from Charlemagne (legend holds he had 24 golden letters made, giving Conques the A; history dates this to 1100), and the reliquary of Pope Pascal.

Most of Conques' houses date from the late-medieval era and match the style of the abbey. There was almost no construction between the French Revolution and World War II. Imagine: in the 13th century, Conques had 3000 inhabitants!

▲▲ Accueil Abbaye de Sainte-Foy ◯ Do Pr Dr R Cf S Z, 4/49, €12/25/38/51, DP19, Rue Charlemagne, saintefoy@abbaye-conques.org, 0565698944, no wifi

▲ Chez François ◯ Do Dr R Cf S, 8/21, €30/-/-/-, DP24, francois@gite-francois-conques.fr, 0688702766

▲ Chez Alice et Charles Pr Dr Br R S, €-/-/78/-, DP12.5, Rue du Chanoine Benazech, lecomptoirdegermain@gmail.com, 0683183487, open Easter–Oct, no wifi

▲ La Bonne Étoile Pr Dr Br R, €-/40/80/120, incl DP, jgissero@yahoo.com, 0663731075, open mid May–mid Oct,

▲ L'Alcôve Pr Br R, €-/71/80/-, conques.lalcove@gmail.com, 0608643288, open Apr–Oct, English spoken

▲ Au Castellou Pr Dr Br R W S, €-/76/87/111, DP30, castellou.conques@gmail.com, 0648156691, open Apr–Oct, English spoken

▲ Auberge Saint-Jacques Pr Dr R Cf S, €-/-/73/77, DP, info@aubergestjacques.fr, 0565728636, closed Jan, English spoken, breakfast €9

▲ Camping Beau Rivage Pr Dr R Cf W S Z, €-/51/55/66, camping.conques@wanadoo.fr, 0661174773 or 0565698223, open May–Sept, no single-night mobile home rentals in high season, camping €7/person or €35DP

98

STAGE 9
Conques to Livinhac-le-Haut

Start	Abbaye Sainte-Foy, Conques
Finish	Église Saint-Adrien, Livinhac-le-Haut
Distance	24.3km (26km via GR6)
Total ascent	780m (930m via GR6)
Total descent	865m (1015m via GR6)
Difficulty	Strenuous
Time	7hr 30min (8hr via GR6)
Percentage paved	72% (48% via GR6)
Gîtes	Noailhac 6.7km, Les Brefinies 7.3km (GR6), Decazeville 18.9km, Chapelle Saint-Roch 21.5km, Livinhac-le-Haut 24.3km

Tired legs might protest today's start: after a brief descent from Conques, a sharp climb follows, leading past a small chapel in the woods. Once that ascent has been vanquished, though, the terrain smooths out – certainly not flat, but much more manageable. Once again, there are two options. This time, the guide prefers the GR65 over the GR6 alternative, as it includes an additional stop in the village of Noailhac, although the GR6 does offer a break from pavement and a donkey farm. A short detour is required to visit Decazeville's center – it's a gritty and workaday town, but it offers the best resupply options on this stretch. A final up-and-down brings you to Livinhac, a small, gîte-filled town occupying a veritable peninsula in the Lot.

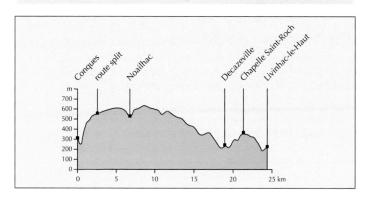

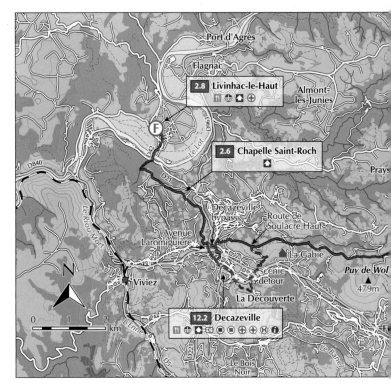

In **Conques**, with the abbey behind you, leave the plaza, then take the first left, downhill, following Rue Charlemagne. Fork left downhill, cross **D901**, the Pont Romain, and the Dourdou de Conques river, and then continue ahead on D232. Fork left onto a footpath at a hairpin turn (**0.6km**). Get ready! This is a tiring climb, but the **Chapelle Sainte-Foy** (**0.5km**), a perfect little chapel and the site of a local pilgrimage, offers a nice rest stop back with lovely views back towards Conques. Its spring water is reputed to cure eye problems. Following the ascent's second half, continue forward on a dirt track (**0.8km**, WC).

Just ahead (**0.5km**), you have two waymarked options.

GR65 through Noailhac (9.3km)

For the recommended route, continue straight on. Soon after, turn left onto a minor paved road. Then, turn left on **D606** (**1.6km**). At a T, turn left onto **D580**, following it to

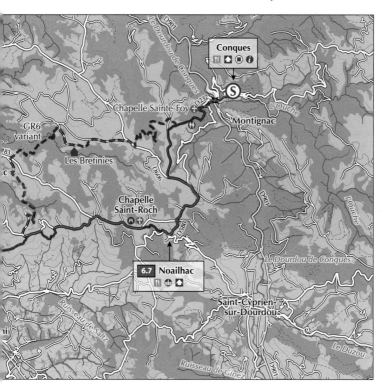

6.7KM NOAILHAC (ELEV 520M, POP 175) 🍴 ⊕ 🏠 **(535.3KM)**
The Église Saint-Jean-Baptiste was restored in the 17th century.

🏠 Gîte Communal **O Do Dr K R**, 3/18, €12/-/-/-, DP19, gaillacaurelien@aol.
   com, 0565729125, check-in at Restaurant du Chemin de St Jacques, no wifi

🏠 Montbigoux **O Pr Br K R**, €-/44/54/72, falip.michel@wanadoo.fr,
   0565698501, swimming pool

Near the town's end, fork right towards La Merlaterie. After a short climb, following the fourteen Stations of the Cross, arrive at **Chapelle Saint-Roch (0.9km)**.

This is the **site of a local pilgrimage** on August 16 (St Roch's Day). The tradition originated in 1847 when, during a typhoid epidemic, a procession of townspeople came here to pray, resulting in a dramatic improvement. The chapel was built in 1884.

Follow D580 onward (**2.8km**). Fork left to descend a dirt track, then rejoin D580 (**0.8km**). Soon after, fork left again, with the GR6 rejoining immediately after.

GR6 alternative through Les Brefinies (11km)

Turn right to join the GR6. A dirt track leads onto a deeply wooded trail winding through heavily undulating terrain. After a sharp ascent, emerge on a paved road, where the route straightens and smooths out for a bit (**3km**). That comes to an end **1.2km** later. Fork left to descend back into a gorge, passing the **Les Brefinies** donkey farm (**0.7km**, ♠ Accueil Les Ânes des Monédiès ⭕ 🅳🅾 🅿🆁 🅳🆁 🅱🆁 🆁, lesanes@monedies.fr, 0633304478, accommodation in yurt, donkey rentals available!), crossing the Ruisseau de la Brousse, and climbing back the other side. Cross **D183** (**2.9km**) and arrive in **Prayssac** village soon after (**0.4km**). After a short descent, one last notable ascent remains before rejoining the GR65 (**2.8km**).

The routes reunite for an off-road descent, leading eventually past an odoriferous agricultural complex (**2.4km**). Join a minor paved road (**0.9km**); it's almost exclusively pavement for the rest of this stage. Pass the turn-off for ♠ La Gabie (🅿🆁 🅱🆁 🆁 🆂 🆉, €-/-/80/-, 165 Chemin de La Gabie, lagabie12@gmail.com, 0686713716, open Apr–Oct, transport provided to restaurants) (**2km**). Fork right off Route de Soulacre Haut (**0.2km**) to continue on the GR65, although a scenic alternative is available for those interested in Decazeville's history:

Optional scenic detour around Decazeville (4km)

A newly waymarked route offers an extended and scenic approach into Decazeville. A large informational sign is available at the intersection with Soulacre Haut; note the special waymark in the bottom-left corner. Fork left to take this detour. After looping through **La Découverte** (**2km**), a park that highlights the town's mining history, double back through the town center, following Rue Cayrade to the church (**1.5km**), where you rejoin the main route below.

Those who stick with the GR65 will descend towards Decazeville's northern outskirts (**1.3km**). After merging with Avenue Maruéjouls, the GR65 takes the next right off the D580 for a short-cut, but an approach through Decazeville center is recommended instead. This approach is unmarked. Continue forward on D580. Proceed through an underpass, curve left, and then curve right with the main road towards church steeples. Fork right, passing to the church's right (reuniting with the scenic approach), and then turn right at a T in

12.2KM DECAZEVILLE (ELEV 220M, POP 5360) ⊞ ⊕ ⬆ Ⓒ ◉ ◉ Ⓗ ⊕ ⊕ ❶
(523.1KM)
Markets on Tuesday and Friday mornings. Named after Napoleon's Minister of Industry, Duc de Decazes, who promoted large-scale mining in the area, Decazeville had the largest open-pit coal mine in Europe and produced over 10 million tons of coal. In conjunction with this, a set of related industries flourished here, most notably steel production, capitalizing on the region's significant iron ore deposits.

A miner strike in 1886 became a symbol of working-class resistance, part of a series of increasingly violent strikes flaring up across France. Jules Watrin, a tremendously unpopular manager of the mine, was literally defenestrated, while the strike persisted for 106 days, winning notable concessions for the miners. Labor disputes erupted into major strikes in 1948 and 1961 as well. However, the mines are now shuttered, with the last one closed in 2001. The Musée du Patrimoine Industriel et Minier aims to preserve this history.

Decazeville gets a bad rap among pilgrims, many of whom opt to bypass it. In this, they are consistent with 19th-century travel writers. Davies and Christopher, who stayed nearby, wrote that, 'Decazeville is dirty, outrageously dirty, but it is not picturesque.' Meanwhile, Freda White lumped it together with another area town in her harsh condemnation: 'Capdenac-Gare... is the typical graceless product of the Industrial Revolution, without form or soul, made on the orders of the employers to whom men are hands, not human beings. Decazeville, further east... has the same inhuman sluttishness.' Nonetheless, Decazeville's history is distinct on the Via Podiensis and quite compelling in its own way.

🛏 Gîte Les Volets Bleus ⓓ ⓟ ⓓ Ⓚ Ⓡ Ⓖ Ⓦ Ⓢ, 2/12, €13/15/34/-, DP19, 3 Rue Camille Douls, voletsbleus12@gmail.com, 0649899716, open Apr–Oct, donkey parking, English spoken

🛏 Eco-Gîte Le Mineur Paysan ⓓ ⓟ Ⓚ Ⓡ Ⓦ Ⓢ, 4/14, €14/-/40/-, 760 Route de Viviole, lemineurpaysan@laposte.net, 0623202997, open Apr–Oct, breakfast €6, camping €10/person

🛏 Libellules et Papillons ⓓ ⓓ Ⓔ Ⓡ Ⓦ, 2/4, €10/-/-/-, DPdonation, 241 Côte des Estaques, jeanmarierival58@gmail.com, 0641089101 or 0668140114, open Feb–Nov

🛏 Bernard Pourcel Ⓞ ⓟ ⓓ Ⓔ Ⓡ, €-/40/50/75, DP13, 17 Rue Lassalle, bernard. pourcel@sfr.fr, 0603670860 or 0581469233

🛏 Hotel Malpel Ⓞ ⓟ ⓓ Ⓡ Ⓖ Ⓢ, €-/55/68/-, 16 Ave Bos, hotelmalpel@gmail. com, 0565430433, breakfast €8

Continue straight through a roundabout onto Avenue Laromiguière. The GR65 rejoins soon after. Routes reunited, turn left on Route de Nantuech (fountain, WC), and begin a sharp ascent (**0.6km**). Turn left again soon after, onto Chemin du Boutigou, following it to

2.6KM CHAPELLE SAINT-ROCH (ELEV. 350M) 🏔 (520.5KM)
The second Roch chapel today, this is a larger structure with a stamp and three different statues of the saint.

🏠 Gîte Le Chemin ⬛ ⬛ ⬛ ⬛ ⬛ ⬛, 3/10, €15/-/-/-, DP20, 465 Route de Saint-Roch, gitelechemin@gmail.com, 0695306513, open Apr–Oct, campers welcome

Gîte Le Chemin in Chapelle Saint-Roch

Continue along the paved road (**1km**). Turn right onto a footpath, descending through woods towards the Lot River (**1km**). Turn left on **D21**, then merge with **D42**. Cross the **Lot** and then turn left, entering Livinhac's outskirts (**0.3km**). Cross D627 and fork left on Rue de la République, then fork left again into the central plaza and the Église Saint-Adrien in

2.8KM LIVINHAC-LE-HAUT (ELEV 210M, POP 1120) 🏨 ⊕ 🛒 ⊕ (517.7KM)
Named after Livinius, the Roman general who had a camp in the area, Livinhac suffered from the so-called 'Revolt of the Lepers' in 1321, when a marauding band of lepers looted and burned the region. The town has also been hit hard by the plague on many occasions – 1348, 1439, 1610, 1710, and 1891. A church has been documented here as early as 924, but the current structure has gone through many different permutations, and weaves together Romanesque, Gothic, and much more recent elements.

🏠 Le Chant des Étoiles **Do** **Pr** **Dr** **K** **R** **Gr** **Z**, 8/29, €15.50/-/52/-, DP19, gitelivinhac@orange.fr, 0676869477, open Apr–Oct, English spoken

🏠 La Fontaine du Chemin **O** **Do** **Pr** **Dr** **K** **R** **Gr** **W** **S**, 4/14, €17/-/52/-, DP20, 215 Ave Ramadier, lafontaineduchemin@gmail.com, 0687074170 or 0675807677, reservation required in offseason, donkey parking, English spoken

🏠 A Chacun Son Chemin **O** **Do** **Pr** **Dr** **K** **R** **W** **S**, 2/10, €15/-/40/-, DP19, 30 Impasse Panassié, jm.bonnici@laposte.net, 0646893641 or 0632496885, reservation required in offseason, camping €9/person

🏠 Gîte La Coquille Bleue **O** **Do** **Pr** **R** **W**, 3/14, €16/-/44/60, 25 Rue Couderc, lacoquillebleue@gmail.com, 0651010288, English spoken, reservation required in offseason, breakfast €5.50

🏠 Gîte La Magnanerie **Do** **Pr** **Dr** **K** **R** **W** **S** **Z**, 2/9, €19/-/58/-, DP19, 170 Rue du Faubourg, magnanerie.gite@gmail.com, 0637004785, open 15 Apr–15 Oct, camping €8/tent

🏠 Sur le Chemin **O** **Pr** **Dr** **Br** **K** **R** **W** **S** **Z**, €-/35/55/70, DP12, 5 Place du 14 Juin, surlechemin@orange.fr, 0616985477

🏠 Le Potager du Peyssi **O** **Do** **Pr** **Dr** **Br** **K** **R** **W**, 4/9, €30/-/60/-, DP20, 530 Route du Peyssi, solange.cayrade@orange.fr, 0565633592 or 0637980135, English spoken

▲ Camping Beau Rivage **Pr** **R** **Gr** **W**, campingbeaurivage.livinhac@gmail.com, 0565435693, open Apr–Oct, camping €10/person, mobile homes, swimming pool, restaurant/*épicerie*, English spoken

STAGE 10
Livinhac-le-Haut to Figeac

Start	Église Saint-Adrien, Livinhac-le-Haut
Finish	Pont d'Or, Figeac
Distance	23.2km
Total ascent	495m
Total descent	510m
Difficulty	Moderate
Time	6hr 15min
Percentage paved	43%
Gîtes	Montredon 5.4km, Lacoste 7.8km, Le Terly 10.8km, Felzins 13.6+1.8km, Saint-Félix 14.6km, Seyrignac 16.4+3.5km, Figeac 23.2km

And on the tenth day, the *chemin* rested. After nine days of compelling walks with consistently significant sights, today's stage is much mellower. There's nothing unpleasant about it; it merely suffers in comparison to the preceding and succeeding highlight reels. The villages of Montredon and Saint-Félix offer chances to rest and refill water bottles, while the Romanesque Église Sainte Madeleine is a good spot for a picnic. Ultimately, though, today's journey is all about the destination. Figeac, the largest town encountered since Le Puy, has a vibrant historic core, filled with medieval houses, delicious bakeries, and even hieroglyphics.

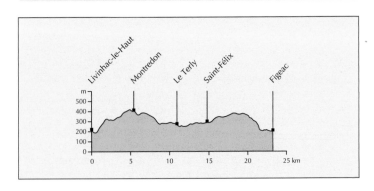

With the church's entrance behind you, leave **Livinhac** on Rue du Couderc. Cross D21 and join **D627**, curving to the right, and then fork right onto a dirt track (**0.6km**). Cross a paved road and proceed into **Peroc** (**0.7km**). Continue mostly on dirt tracks from there, through another small cluster of houses and an agricultural complex, and then past **La Croix des Trois Eveques** (**3.1km**). The cross historically marked the border between Quercy, Rouergue, and Auvergne, and today represents the junction of the Lot, Aveyron, and Cantal departments. Merge onto D2 (**0.7km**). Fork right and then turn left into

---

5.4KM MONTREDON (ELEV 400M, POP 295) 🛏 **(512.3KM)**
Fountain in plaza. The Chapelle Notre-Dame has a 16th-century *vierge de pitié*, or *pieta* – a statue of the Virgin Mary cradling Jesus's body. Local friends of the *chemin* offer cold drinks to pilgrims from an adjacent building. This marks the entrance into the Lot department in the Occitanie region.

⌂ Accueil Pèlerin La Mariotte Do Dr Br R W S, 3/9, €42/-/-/-, incl DP, lamariotte46@free.fr, 0565343820, open mid Apr–mid Oct, English spoken

⌂ Halte Pèlerin Le Saint-Michel Do K R S, 3/12, €14.50/-/-/-, Place de l'Église, haltepelerinmontredon46@gmail.com, 0783384959, open 15 Apr–15 Oct, donation-based breakfast

---

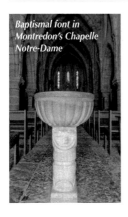

Baptismal font in Montredon's Chapelle Notre-Dame

Turn right at a T. Cross a paved road, then fork left immediately after (**0.9km**). Turn left onto a dirt road, leading first past a farm and later by ⌂ Gîte Lacoste Do Pr Dr K R Cf S, 1/3, €30/30/50/60, DP23, gitelacoste@gmail.com, 0783777399, open Apr–Oct, English spoken (**1.5km**). Turn left at a T onto a paved road, then fork right onto a footpath that leads to the Romanesque **Église Sainte-Madeleine** (**0.9km**, snack bar). The church features 14th-century murals of the four evangelists over its altar and 16th-century frescoes in its choir. Turn right on **D2**, right again soon after towards Guirande, and then fork right a third time onto a tree-lined dirt track (**0.4km**). After winding along shady tracks through fields, cross **D41** into **Le Terly** (**1.7km**, ⌂ Le Fournil du Terly Do Pr Dr K R W Z, 2/12, €16/-/44/-, DP21, fournilduterly@mailo.com, 0607748896, open Apr–Oct, on-site bakery, camping €3/person, no wifi, English spoken). Descend past **Lac de Guirande** (**0.5km**) and then continue along dirt tracks into the village of **Les Cordiers** (**1.4km**). Cross D2 (**0.9km**) and continue towards Saint-Félix. (Alternately, turn left on D2 and continue to **Felzins** and ⌂ ⌂ Gîte Le Pentadou Do Pr Dr Br K R W S, 2/10, €25/52/75/99, DP20, info@lepentadou.com, 0565404812, open Jan–Oct, swimming pool, English spoken.)

Turn right onto a paved road leading into

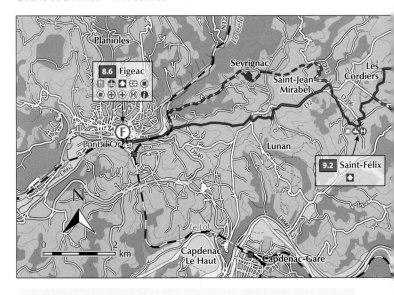

9.2KM SAINT-FÉLIX (ELEV 280M, POP 520) (503.1KM)

WC and fountain next to *mairie*. The Romanesque Église Sainte-Radegonde features Adam and Eve, complete with Tree of Life and tempting serpent, in its 11th-century tympanum. Look as well for the bearded man adorned with a cockle shell, linking this to Santiago. Radegonde was a sixth-century Frankish queen and one of six wives and concubines of Clotaire I, a Merovingian king. When Clotaire I killed her brother, she fled and took shelter in the Church, becoming a nun, and eventually founding the Poitiers Abbey around 560.

⛺ Chez Thierry ▢ ▢ ▢ ▢ ▢, 2/4, €Donation, incl DP, 0665919252, pick-up from church

⛺ Marathon'elle ▢ ▢ ▢ ▢ ▢ ▢, €-/-/80/90, didier.bonnefoy@sfr.fr, 0565341288 or 0609302446

Turn left shortly after the church. A series of minor paved roads and dirt tracks lead through a residential neighborhood. Merge onto **D206** (**1.4km**), then fork right on a tree-lined footpath. Continue straight on D31, then turn left through **Saint-Jean-Mirabel** (**0.4km**). (Alternatively, stick with D31 to detour into Seyrignac – although both gîtes will pick you up here – with ⛺ Gîte Le Relais de la Bourrache ▢ ▢ ▢ ▢ ▢ ▢ ▢ ▢ ▢, 2/10, €17/-/60/-, DP17, delabourrache.lerelais2@orange.fr, 0676741607,

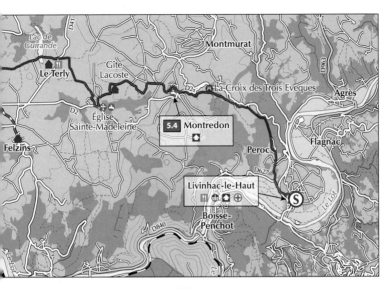

camping €5/person, washing machine included, bar/épicerie; and ⌂ Gîte de Seyrignac Ⓞ Ⓓⓞ Ⓟⓡ Ⓓⓡ Ⓡ Ⓦ, 1/4, €17/-/50/75, DP20, jean.malbouires@gmx.com, 0606459382, swimming pool.)

Join D2 and follow it until forking left onto a dirt track (**1.7km**). Later, briefly rejoin D2, turning right onto it and then making a sharp left off it (**1.2km**). A long dirt track (**2km**) ultimately yields to pavement, just in time for a sharp descent to the **Célé River** (**0.6km**). Follow a riverside road through Figeac's outskirts, then merge onto **D840**. Fork right onto Rue du Griffoul, then cross the **Pont d'Or** into

Saint James is portrayed in the stained glass of Saint-Félix's Église Sainte-Radegonde

8.6KM FIGEAC (ELEV 195M, POP 9790) ⓐ ⊕ ⓐ ⓒ ⓞ ⓜ ⓗ ⊕ ⊕ ⓘ (494.5KM)

Market on Saturday mornings, WC near tourism office. Pilgrim welcome in Église Saint-Sauveur (Jun–Sept, 4.30–6pm) and pilgrim blessing (Tue–Fri, 6.30pm).

In 753, Pepin the Short (Charlemagne's father), having just won a battle against the Duke of Aquitaine, saw a flock of doves rise from the ground here and thus decided to build a town. By 838 there was an abbey; two centuries later, it was linked to Cluny. In 1302, the town moved into the hands of King Philip IV, who bequeathed great wealth upon it. Figeac was taken by the English briefly in the Hundred Years' War and then hit hard by plague in 1348. It was hit harder by Protestants, with Catholicism banned by the late 16th century. Indeed, the Protestant conquest in 1576 was accomplished only through treachery; the first consul's wife was successfully bribed by Protestant leaders to smuggle a gate key to them. Disguised as peasants, Protestant soldiers quietly filled the town before unmasking and seizing control. Following the Edict of Nantes, Figeac was established as a Protestant safe zone. Skipping ahead to the modern era, Figeac was occupied by Nazis during World War II and 540 citizens were deported to Dachau and Auschwitz in April/May 1944. Of those citizens, 145 never returned. Nazis abandoned the town a month later.

The main industrial focus today is Ratier, an aeronautical firm. Figeac is also home to the smallest university in France. Its most famous resident was Jean-François Champollion, one of the great Egyptologists, who is honored today with the **Musée Champollion** (€5). Born in Figeac in 1790, by the age of 14 he had command of Greek, Latin, Hebrew, Arabic, Chaldean, and Syrian; five years later, he lectured at the University of Grenoble. His fame, though, derives from him being the first to translate the Rosetta Stone, paving the way for the deciphering of hieroglyphics. He later founded the Egyptology Museum at the Louvre.

Le Vieux Figeac, the historic core, preserves its medieval layout, with today's boulevards replacing the old moats. Many buildings date to the 13th–15th centuries. In these multi-story edifices, the bottom floors were often open and arcaded, while the top floors were typically open as well, used for drying clothes and storage. The **Commanderie des Templiers**, established in the 13th century, was a pilgrim hospital; it is wonderfully preserved and worth a visit (€5).Unfortunately, Figeac's religious architecture is disappointing, worn down by some difficult years. The **Église Saint-Sauveur** was largely destroyed in the Wars of Religion; only parts of the south side survive from the original 11th-century structure. Meanwhile, the **Église Notre-Dame-du-Puy** is just north of the center and has been largely restored. Legend holds that the Virgin called for its construction, signaling this with the sudden growth of a rose bush through the snow at Christmas.

If you're not taking the Rocamadour variant, you might consider an extra day in Figeac to make a daytrip to Rocamadour, one of France's most significant pilgrimage sites. A train links the two towns, although the Rocamadour station is inconveniently positioned 4km from the sanctuary. Several taxi companies, including Bernard Taxi (0565500020), can whisk you there directly.

If you're headed to the Célé Valley from Figeac, note that you will not see another ATM until Saint-Cirq-Lapopie (71km) or Cahors (104km). Stock up on euros before you leave.

🛖 Gîte du Gua **O Do Pr Dr R W S Z**, 4/15, €16/-/40/-, DP19, 14 bis Ave du Maréchal Joffre, gitedugua.figeac@gmail.com, 0674732269, vegetarian, English spoken

🛖 Gîte Le Soleiho **O Do Pr Br K R**, 2/6, €17/65/75/-, 8 Rue Prat, jeanlouisroyer@yahoo.fr, 0565384262 or 0675899653, reservation required in offseason

🛖 Gîte Chez Celia **Do Pr Dr R W**, 4/11, €15/-/40/-, DP20, 29 Rue Emile Zola, gitechezcelia@gmail.com, 0605109659, open Apr–Sept

🛖 Gîte du Carmel **Do Dr Br R**, 2/8, €Donation, incl DP, 9 Ave Jean Jaurès, carmel.figeac@gmail.com, 0614320551, open May–Sept, no wifi

🛖 Le Repos du Célé **Do Pr Dr R Cf W S**, 5/15, €20/-/40/, DP19, 94 Chemin de Roussilhe, lereposducele@gmail.com, 0763595024, open Apr–Oct, tents permitted when the camping is closed (€8/tent)

🛖 Gîte Le Coquelicot **Do Pr Dr K R W**, 4/15, €14.50/-/40/-, DP19, 20 Ave du Faubourg du Pin, lecoquelicot46100figeac@outlook.fr, 0581715593 or 0627586754, open Mar–Dec

🛖 Hôtel des Bains **O Pr R Cf S Z**, €-/58/71/89, 1 Rue du Griffoul, figeac@hoteldesbains.fr, 0565341089, breakfast €8.50

🛖 Hôtel Champollion **O Pr R Cf S**, €-/-/57/-, 3 Place Champollion, hotelchampollion@orange.fr, 0565340437, breakfast €8, English spoken

🔺 Domaine du Surgié **R Cf W**, contact@marc-montmija.com, 0561648854, open May–Sept, camping €13/person, restaurant in Jul–Aug, swimming pool

Figeac

🏛	Église Saint-Sauveur	2	Gîte Le Soleiho
🏛	Église Notre-Dame-du-Puy	3	Gîte Chez Celia
🏛	Église Saint-Thomas	4	Gîte du Carmel
1	Place de la Halle	5	Le Repos du Célé and Domaine du Surgié
2	Musée Champollion	6	Gîte Le Coquelicot
3	Commanderie des Templiers	7	Hôtel des Bains
1	Gîte du Gua	8	Hôtel Champollion

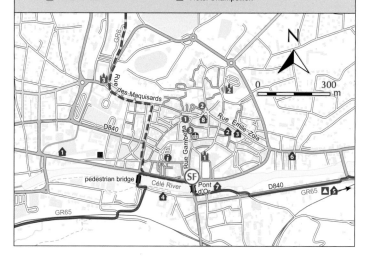

An oversized replica of the Rosetta Stone honors Jean-François Champollion in Figeac

STAGE 11
Figeac to Cajarc

Start	Pont d'Or, Figeac
Finish	Église Saint-Étienne, Cajarc
Distance	30.8km
Total ascent	620m
Total descent	670m
Difficulty	Moderate
Time	8hr 15min
Percentage paved	41%
Gîtes	Lacassagnolle 4km, Le Puy Clavel 18.5km, Gréalou 20.1km, Ussac 21.9+2.5km, Cajarc 30.8km

It's decision time: do you stick with the GR65, or branch off onto the Célé Valley or Rocamadour variants? If the former, today's walk begins with a tiring climb out of Figeac and concludes with a sharp descent into Cajarc – with stunning limestone cliffs towering above the historic village and the Lot River below – the bulk of the walk meanders through rocky, isolated terrain. Only Faycelles and Gréalou offer food stops along the way, and quite limited ones at that, so plan ahead. Watch out for *caselles* – small, circular, stone huts in fields – and your first dolmen in this stretch, an indicator of this region's ancient quality.

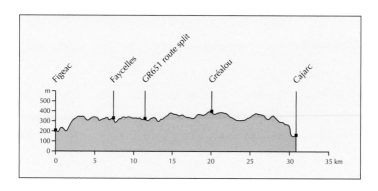

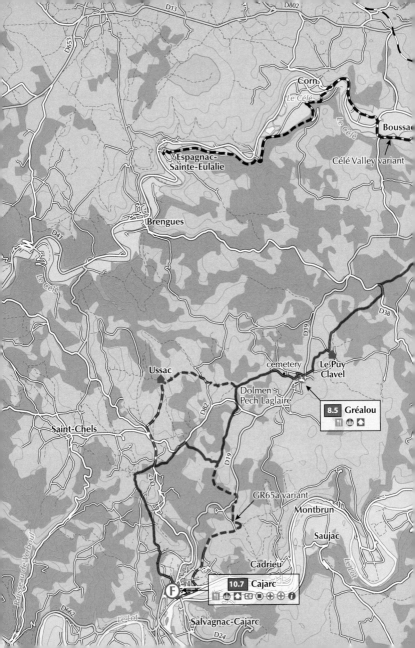

Corn

Le Célé

Boussac

Le Célé

Espagnac-
Sainte-Eulalie

Célé Valley variant

Brengues

Le Célé

D47

D38

D19

Ussac

cemetery

Le Puy
Clavel

Dolmen
Pech Laglaire

8.5 Gréalou

D62

Saint-Chels

D19

GR65a variant

Montbrun

Saujac

Cadrieu

F

10.7 Cajarc

Le Lot

D662

Salvagnac-Cajarc

D24

Le Lot

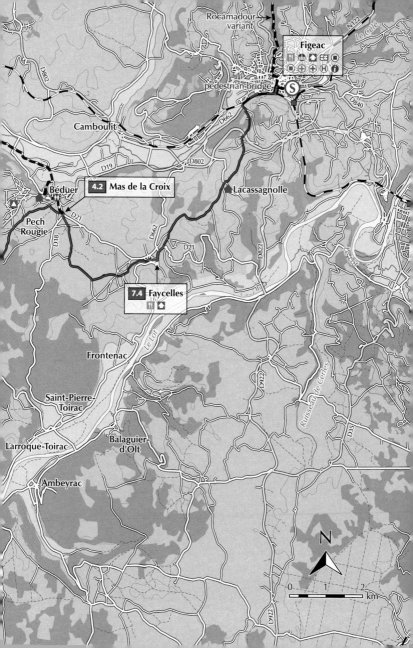

Rocamadour variant

Le Célé

N122

Figeac

pedestrian bridge

D662

Camboulit

D19

D802

4.2 Mas de la Croix

Lacassagnolle

Béduer

D21

Pech Rougie

D18

D662

D21

D822

7.4 Faycelles

Le Lot

Frontenac

D922

Ruisseau de Certes

Saint-Pierre-Toirac

Larroque-Toirac

Balaguier-d'Olt

D35

Ambeyrac

D922

N

0   1   2 km

Those diverting from the GR65 to the Rocamadour variant should follow the Célé River to the pedestrian bridge and then turn right on D840, where the waymarked route begins. See Stage R1. From the Pont-d'Or in Figeac, turn left along the Célé River, then turn left back across it over the next **pedestrian bridge**. Cross to the road skirting the left side of the opposing parking lot, then fork left twice in quick succession, passing under the railroad (**0.5km**). Turn right at the T. Turn left to briefly join **D662** (**1km**), then turn left off it. Fork right towards Bois de Palhasse and then ascend steadily along a series of minor roads through **Lacassagnolle** (**2.5km**, ⌂ Relais Saint-Jacques 🅳🅾 🅿🆁 🅳🆁 🅺 🆁 🆆 🆂, 2/7, €16/20/40/-, DP20, jesus.gomez.46@orange.fr, 0565340308, open Apr–Oct). Continue onward, eventually merging onto **D21** (**2.7km**). Cross **D662**, then turn right into the village center, arriving at the church in

7.4KM FAYCELLES (ELEV 325M, POP 660) 🍴 ⌂ (487.1KM)
Charlemagne's twin sons, Lothaire and Louis, were born in Faycelles in 778; the latter became king. A Merovingian graveyard was discovered here in 1960.

⌂ La Caselle 🅾 🅿🆁 🅳🆁 🅱🅵 🆁 🆆, €-/45/68/78, DP15, lacaselledhotes@gmail.com, 0631832098

⌂ La Petit' Pause 🅿🆁 🅳🆁 🆁 🅲🅵, €-/40/60/-, DP20, thierry.frugnac@wanadoo.fr, 0565346509 or 0642479293, open Apr–Oct

Fork left onto a dirt road away from the village. Weave through a series of minor roads and dirt tracks through quiet terrain (**3.9km**). Turn right on **D18**, then left on **D21** into

Dolmen Pech Laglaire

4.2KM MAS DE LA CROIX (ELEV 300M)(482.9KM)
At this point the GR651 Célé Valley route splits from the GR65; for route directions see 'Célé Valley variant', Stage C1.

Turn left to continue on the GR65. This becomes a dirt track, which leads through **Pech Rouge** (**1.1km**). Continue winding through a series of mostly unpaved tracks until turning left onto **D38** (**3.1km**). Fork right soon after (**0.3km**), beginning another primarily off-road stretch. Pass through **Le Puy Clavel** (**2.4km**, ⏶ Ecoasis 🄳🄾 🄿🅁 🄳🅁 🄱🅁 🅁 🅆 🅂 🅉, 8/26, €16/-/44/66, DP21, 305 Route de Puy Clavel, bonjour@ecoasis.fr, 0671004830 or 0950077466, open Apr–Sept, English spoken). Cross **D19** and continue straight on a paved road (**1.1km**). Make a sharp left, then turn right at a T, leading into

8.5KM GRÉALOU (ELEV 365M, POP 280) 🄸🄸 ⊕ 🄰 (474.4KM)
Fountain in park. Once a stronghold for the Barasc family, the founders of Béduer's château, its rough terrain is reflected in its name. Linguists see plausible links to the Germanic word for 'gravel' and the Occitan word for 'crickets.' The region's rich prehistoric past is reflected in the abundance of megalithic monuments. Note that there is no water between Gréalou and Cajarc.

⏶ Gîte la Fontaine 🄾 🄳🄾 🄿🅁 🄳🅁 🅁 🅆 🅂, 3/9, €18/-/40/-, DP21, Mas de Lafon, nathalie.robic@sfr.fr, 0581716058, donkey parking, English spoken

⏶ Atelier des Volets Bleus 🄳🄾 🄳🅁 🄱🅁 🅂, 1/8, €48/-/-/-, incl DP, Place de l'Église, esther.marcoux@gmail.com, 0684376473

Turn right after the church, fork left at the **cemetery**, and then continue straight onto a dirt track. Pass by the **Dolmen Pech Laglaire** (**1.8km**). (Alternately, fork right from the dolmen to detour to ⏶ ⏶ Gîte La Source d'Ussac 🄾 🄳🄾 🄿🅁 🄳🅁 🄺 🅁 🅆 🅂, 4/12, €16/51/62/78, DP19, dominique.pourcel@orange.fr, 0565407989, camping €5/person, reservation required in offseason.) Cross **D82** (**0.5km**). Continue straight ahead past an agricultural complex, then turn right onto a paved road (**1.7km**). It's possible to continue straight here on the waymarked GR65a. At 5.8km it's 0.8km shorter than the GR65. It's less scenic but a good option for bikers and those wary of the official route's sharper descent. Turn left, briefly joining **D82**, then fork left onto a dirt track (**1.3km**). Descend through thick woods, cross **D17**, then return to a dirt track through forest, now ascending (**0.9km**). Turn left and begin the final, rocky descent (**0.6km**). Briefly merge with a paved road and then fork right onto a footpath plunging along the cliff face (**2.4km**). Finally, emerge onto Rue de Lacaunhe at the town entrance, curving past Gîte Le Pèlerin and the Gîte Communal before proceeding straight into the historic center on Rue Centrale (**1km**). Arrive at the church soon after in

10.7KM CAJARC (ELEV 145M, POP 1125) ⊞ ⊕ ⬛ ⓒ ⓞ ⊕ ⊕ ❶ **(463.7KM)**
Markets on Wednesday and Saturday mornings. Mass and pilgrim blessing Mon–Fri at 6pm.

This bastide town preserves some 12th-century houses. Its 13th-century Église Saint-Etienne was a pilgrimage destination in the Middle Ages, devoted to the blessed sacrament. Until the 18th century, the region was known for its saffron production; this has experienced a resurgence in recent years and the town now celebrates a saffron festival on the penultimate Saturday in October. On 10 April 1944, Jean-Jacques Chapou, the Lot's famed resistance leader, occupied Cajarc. Impersonating the mayor, he called the Gestapo, pleading for their help; when they arrived, he ambushed them.

Cajarc was the home of Françoise Sagan, a prolific writer who authored 50 novels over the course of her lifetime. She was also an effective recruiter, drawing famous friends to Cajarc, including two former French presidents: François Mitterand and Georges Pompidou. The latter founded a contemporary art center in Cajarc, the Maison des Arts Georges & Claude Pompidou.

⬢ Gîte Le Pèlerin **Do Pr K R Z**, 1/10, €13/16.50/33/49.50, 11 Rue Lacauhne, gitelepelerincajarc@orange.fr, 0674324440, open Apr–mid Oct, breakfast €5, English spoken

⬢ Gîte Communal **Do Dr Br K R Cr**, 4/20, €23/-/-/-, DP16, 1 Rue de la Cascade, lecommunal46@orange.fr, 0614665489, check-in at La Peyrade, open mid Mar–mid Nov, no wifi

⬢ ⬢ La Peyrade **Do Pr Dr K R Cr W S Z**, 3/9, €22/64/69/94, DP23, 52 Rue Lapeyrade, lapeyrade@orange.fr, 0565104203, open Apr–mid Oct, donkey parking, Nordic bath, English spoken

⬢ Chez Sylvie **O Pr Dr Br R W S**, €-/40/56/-, DP15, 16 Lotissement Camp de Poux, sylvie.de-boussiers12@orange.fr, 0631850056, located across Lot from Cajarc

⬢ Hôtel Cajarc Blue **Pr Dr R Cr W Z**, €-/-/67/89, DP available, 380 Ave Mitterand, contact@cajarcbluehotel.fr, 0565406535, open Easter–Oct, swimming pool

▲ Camping Le Terriol **Pr R Cr W Z**, 2/4, €-/14.50/29/-, info@campingleterriol.com, 0565407274, open Apr–Sept, camping €8–10/person

STAGE 12
Cajarc to Varaire

Start	Église Saint-Étienne, Cajarc
Finish	Mairie, Varaire
Distance	27.5km
Total ascent	510m
Total descent	340m
Difficulty	Easy-to-moderate
Time	7hr
Percentage paved	36%
Gîtes	Saint-Jean-de-Laur turn-off 10.4km, Mas de Delat 15.4km, Mas de Gascou 15.4+0.7km, Limogne-en-Quercy 19.1km, Varaire 27.5km

After a notable early ascent to Gaillac, this stage settles into a largely unpaved stroll through the softly undulating Causse de Limogne. This limestone-dominated, agriculturally limited terrain originated with the Atlantic Ocean, some 70 million years past, formed by the Jurassic carbonate rocks deposited here at that point. Not much grows in this area, but the *Quercus pubescens*, or downy oak, has found the soil quite inviting; it provides the bulk of the shade you'll enjoy, although blackthorn and juniper make their presence felt as well. Humans have long settled here, and the distinct conditions have helped to preserve evidence of their impact. Once again, an ancient dolmen speaks to that past in this stage. In terms of more recent construction, the architectural highlight, reflected in the place names, is the *mas* or traditional farmhouse, designed for self-sufficiency in this isolated context.

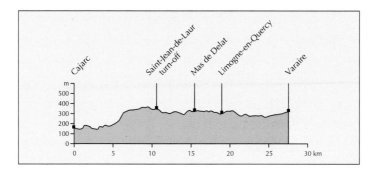

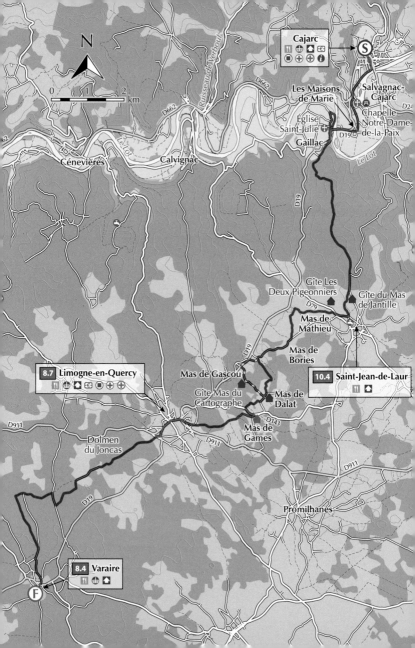

N

0   1   2 km

Cajarc
S

Les Maisons de Marie

Salvagnac-Cajarc

D662

D19

D2

Chapelle Notre-Dame-de-la-Paix

Église Saint-Julie

D19

Gaillac

Le Lot

Cénevières

D662

Calvignac

D19

Gîte Les Deux Pigeonniers

Gîte du Mas de Jantille

D79

Mas de Mathieu

Mas de Bories

D19

10.4 Saint-Jean-de-Laur

8.7 Limogne-en-Quercy

Mas de Gascou

Gîte Mas du Cartographe

Mas de Dalat

D143

Mas de Games

D911

Dolmen du Joncas

D911

D911

Promilhanes

D19

8.4 Varaire

F

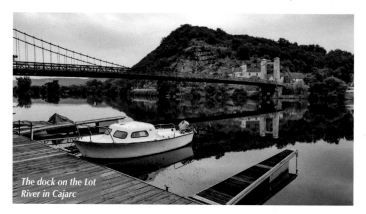

The dock on the Lot River in Cajarc

Proceed south past the church in **Cajarc**, through Place de l'Église, and then continue directly onto Rue du Faubourg. Turn right alongside the **Lot River** (**0.4km**). Fork right uphill, briefly joining **D662** before forking left onto a minor paved road, passing **Chapelle Notre-Dame-de-la-Paix** and a picnic area (**1km**). Fork right soon after. Turn right just after **Les Maisons de Marie** and join **D19** (**1.3km**, ⏶ Chez Babet 🄾 🄿🅕 🄳🅁 🄱🅁 🅁, €-/25/44/66, DP13, Lieu-Dit Andressac, babet@hotmail.fr, 0781361803, camping €10/person). Cross the **Lot River**, then turn right (**0.5km**), beginning a circuitous approach to Gaillac that entails swinging wide, ascending, and then doubling back around. You are now officially in the Causse de Limogne. Pass Église Saint-Julien (**0.9km**) en route to the center of **Gaillac**. Cross **D19** and proceed onto a dirt track (**0.7km**). Wind through a wooded stretch, then continue straight onto a paved road (**2.8km**). Fork right back onto a dirt track, walking past Gîte du Mas de Jantille (**2.1km**) to

10.4KM SAINT-JEAN-DE-LAUR TURN-OFF (ELEV 350M, POP 240) 🍽️ ⌂
(453.3KM)
A beautifully decorated pilgrim rest stop with a fountain and seasonal snack bar. Turn left here to make a 350-meter detour into Saint-Jean-de-Laur. Retrace steps to return to the main route.

⏶ **Gîte du Mas de Jantille** 🄳🄾 🄺 🅁 🅆, 1/10, €17/-/-/-, masdejantille@gmail.com, 0688850718, open Apr–Sept, breakfast €6, mini-*épicerie*

⏶ **Gîte Les Deux Pigeonniers** 🄳🄾 🄳🅁 🅁 🅆, 3/7, €23/-/-/-, DP19, maxime. boisset854@orange.fr, 0609930548 or 0565407013, open Apr–mid Oct

⏶ **Le Couvent** 🄾 🄿🅕 🄳🅁 🄱🅁 🅁 🅂, €-/-/100/-, contact@aucouvent.fr, 0565397705, swimming pool

Turn right onto a paved road to cross **D79** and proceed through **Mas de Mathieu** (**0.7km**). An extended off-road stretch follows through **Mas de Bories** (**2km**). After a short return to pavement (**1km**), turn left back onto a dirt track leading to **Mas de Dalat** (**1.3km**, ÀTÉKÔTÉ offers handcrafted walking sticks, ♠ Gîte Dalat'Etape `Do` `Pr` `Dr` `K` `R` `W` `S`, 2/9, €15/-/30/-, DP20, contact@dalatetape.fr, 0607316961 or 0630035981, open Apr–Oct, campers welcome) or continue straight on the road for a 1.1km detour to reach **Mas de Gascou** and ♠ Gîte Mas du Cartographe `Do` `Pr` `Dr` `K` `R` `W` `S`, 4/13, €16/-/65/-, DP19, lemasducartographe@gmail.com, 0675373549, open Mar–Oct, camping €10/two people. Fork right back onto a dirt track, then turn left on **D143** (**0.8km**). Fork right in **Mas de Games** (**0.2km**, ♠ La Hulotte `Pr` `Dr` `Br` `K` `R` `G` `W` `S`, €-/-/70/-, DP19, chambreslahulotte@orange.fr, 0617388447, open Apr–mid Nov), then make a sharp right. Fork right onto a dirt track, then continue onto a paved road (**2km**). Merge onto **D911** as it curves left, following it into Place de l'Occitanie in

---

8.7KM LIMOGNE-EN-QUERCY (ELEV 295M, POP 760) ⎾⎿ ⊕ ⌂ Ⓒ ⊙ ⊕ ⊕
(**444.6KM**)

Markets on Friday and Sunday mornings. A lively small town, with lots of activity in the summer. In both winter and summer, the Sunday market specializes in truffles. Aside from Varaire's modest *épicerie* (check ahead to confirm hours), Limogne offers your last supermarket until Cahors (41km).

♠ Gîte Communal La Halle `O` `Do` `K` `R` `W`, 4/9, €17.5/-/-/-, Rue de la Halle, gite.limogne@orange.fr, 0612848647

♠ Gîte La Maison en Chemin `O` `Do` `Pr` `Dr` `Br` `R` `W` `S`, 5/11, €29/-/52/-, DP16, 99 Rue de Lugagnac, bonjour@lamaisonenchemingr65.fr, 0619730311, English spoken

♠ Gîte Au Bon Marché `O` `Do` `Dr` `R` `Gr` `W` `S`, 4/12, €16/-/-/-, DP19, 8 Rue du Grainetier, gite.aubonmarche@gmail.com, 0695194018

▲ Camping Municipal Le Bel Air `Pr` `Dr` `K` `R` `Gr` `W`, €-/30/40/50, DP19.50, 311 Rue de la Piscine, camping.lebelair@free.fr, 0565243275, camping €9/person, open Apr–mid Oct, swimming pool

---

Fork left to remain on D911, then fork left again onto **D19** (**0.2km**). Turn right on Chemin du Jouncas, then fork left soon after onto a dirt track (**0.4km**). This leads to a short detour to see the **Dolmen du Joncas** (**1.2km**). It's one of 13 such Neolithic structures in the greater Limogne area. Fork right onto a paved road, then fork left back onto a dirt track (**1km**). After an extended off-road stretch through the rocky *causse*, continue onto a paved road (**4.5km**). Finally, at a T, fork left into Varaire, proceeding to the *épicerie*, church, and *mairie* on D19.

Colorful scallop shells line a rest stop near Saint-Jean-de-Laur

8.4KM VARAIRE (ELEV 315M, POP 310) 🏨 ⊕ 🛏 (436.2KM)
WC across from the restaurant. A town with Roman origins, situated on the historic Rodez-Cahors route. In the Middle Ages it was owned by the Cardaillac family, which built the 13th-century tower.

🛏 Clos des Escoutilles Do Pr Dr K R Gr W S, 5/15, €16/-/46/69, DP18, info@clos-des-escoutilles.eu, 0565245084 or 0673470236, open mid Mar–Oct, swimming pool, English spoken

🛏 Gîte Chez Titi Do Dr R S, 1/3, €15/-/-/-, DP13, jtpayet@gmail.com, 0780021544 or 0565224123, open Apr–Oct, English spoken

🛏 Gîte Les Marronniers Do Pr Dr K R Gr W S Z, 2/7, €17/-/50/-, DP21, lesmarronniers46@sfr.fr, 0611121278 or 0565315385, open Apr–Oct, camping €5/person

STAGE 13
Varaire to Cahors

Start	Mairie, Varaire
Finish	Cathédrale Saint-Étienne, Cahors
Distance	32.5km (33.5km via Vaylats)
Total ascent	365m
Total descent	550m
Difficulty	Easy
Time	7hr 15min
Percentage paved	24%
Gîtes	Bach 5.6km, Vaylats 7.1+1.5km, Mas de Vers 14.3km, Le Pech 19.3+0.5km, Cahors 32.5km

The relatively mild terrain earns this stage an 'easy' rating, but it still requires prudent preparation. The distance, of course, is significant. The route is quite exposed, and the heat is unforgiving in midsummer. On top of that, there are precious few services available to pilgrims along the way; were it not for a pair of purpose-built pilgrim shelters, water would be a rare commodity. There are lots of ways you can customize the route, including a short detour to Vaylats and its convent, a long variant to Saint-Cirq-Lapopie (16.1km, moderately difficult, 38% paved), many gîtes at which to split the stage, and the possibility of bypassing Cahors altogether, via the truffle center of Lalbenque (21.5km, easy walking, 54% paved). If you follow the stage as planned, though, you'll be rewarded with a splendid view of Cahors and the encircling Lot as you approach the town.

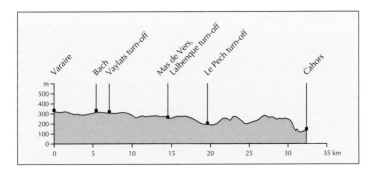

124

From the *mairie*, backtrack along your path of entry, then fork left at the cemetery. Fork left twice more, then turn right on **D52** (**0.8km**). Wind through a series of dirt tracks, passing a nice surprise: a snack bar at La Lune ô 4 Saisons (**1.7km**), where campers are also welcome. Turn left at a T (**1.1km**). Continue straight through a crossroads (**1.1km**). Alternately, turn right if you wish to detour through Saint-Cirq-Lapopie, following the GR36; that route is described at the end of this stage. Fork right and then transition back onto a paved road (**0.6km**). Cross **D19** into

---

5.6KM BACH (ELEV 388M, POP 180) 🏨 ⛺ (430.6KM)
Pilgrim rest area at end of town, with fountain and WC.

The Phosphatière du Cloup d'Aural, located 1.5km east of Bach, was an open-pit phosphate mine. In the mid 19th-century, phosphate became highly desired for agriculture; this mine was discovered soon after and at peak operation by the 1870s. This triggered a figurative explosion of phosphate production throughout the Quercy region, with 161 active mines by 1886. And then, as suddenly as the industry appeared, it shut down, the phosphate deposits exhausted. By 1902, only two of those 161 mines were still in business. On the bright side, this particular mine has been redeveloped as a historic site, and it's possible to follow a guided tour into the old pit, with special attention paid to fossils, flora, and phosphate (€9).

🛏 Gîte La Grange Saint-Jacques 🄳🄿🄳🄱🅁🅂🅉, 3/10, €36/62/96/-, incl DP, lagrangesaintjacques@gmail.com, 0565310875, open Apr–Nov, camping €15DP/person

🛏 Gîte Relais Arc en Ciel 🄾🄳🄿🄳🅁🅆, 4/12, €21/-/80/-, DP19, relaisarcenciel46@gmail.com, 0665090482, reservation required

🛏 Gîte La Rose de Bach 🄾🄳🄳🄺🅁, 10 beds, €13/-/-/-, DP12, Route de Caylus, larosedebach@gmail.com, 0677556294, campers welcome

🛏 Gîte ChanteBach 🄾🄳🄳🄱🄺🅁🅆🅂, 1/4, €20/-/-/-, DP15, fouchet. chantal@gmail.com, 0659009805

Turn right at the church into an alley. Turn right and then left on D19, soon joining a footpath alongside it (**0.2km**). Fork right onto a dirt track, then turn right at a T (**1.3km**). At the next intersection (**0.1km**) you have two waymarked options to choose from.

GR65 direct to Mas de Vers (1.7km)
Continue forward on the GR65. Cross **D42** (**1.4km**) and keep straight on. The Vaylats detour rejoins from the left **0.3km** later.

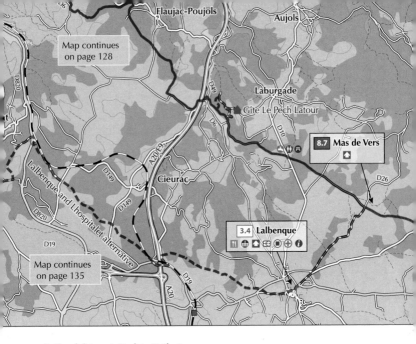

Map continues on page 128

Flaujac-Poujols

Aujols

Laburgade

Gîte Le Pech Latour

8.7 Mas de Vers

Cieurac

D26

3.4 Lalbenque

Lalbenque and L'hospitalet alternative

Map continues on page 135

Optional detour to Vaylats (2.7km)

Turn left off the GR65 onto a dirt track. Fork left, just after a cemetery, onto a foot-path, marked with shell stickers (**1.1km**). Cross **D19** and continue straight, transitioning soon after onto a paved road. Turn right at a T in **Vaylats** (**0.4km**). The 19th-century ⌂ Couvent de Vaylats is on your left (O Do Dr Br R W S Z, 7/14, €31.50/-/-/-, incl DP, accueil@couventdevaylats.fr, 0565316351). The Sisters have been providing hospital-ity to pilgrims since 1983. The last Gallic resistance to Julius Caesar occurred nearby, much earlier than that.

Waymarks are less reliable leaving Vaylats. Turn right again at the next T, then fork left past the front of the church. Turn left on **D19** (**0.2km**). Turn right on a dirt track towards Bascot (**0.3km**). Turn left at a T, rejoining the GR65 (**0.7km**).

With the two routes rejoined, continue straight, crossing first **D55** (**3.7km**) and then **D26** into

8.7KM MAS DE VERS (ELEV 314M) ⌂ (421.9KM)

⌂ Gîte De Poudally Do Pr Dr K R Cf W S Z, 5/22, €17/-/46/69, DP21, manu. elsa@poudally.com, 0565220869, open Apr–mid Oct, camping €6/person

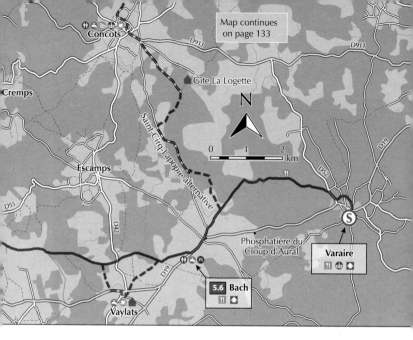

The Lalbenque alternative route diverges here; see the description at the end of this stage. Follow a minor paved road, which later transitions back into a dirt track (**1.6km**). Cross **D10** (**1km**), where a pilgrim rest stop is available (fountain, WC). Pass the turn-off for Gîte Le Gascou, then turn left at a T onto a minor paved road (**1km**). Fork right at the next T, then left onto a dirt track (**1.4km**). (Alternately, fork right, remaining on the paved road, to ascend 0.5km to ⛺ **Gîte Le Pech Latour** Do Pr Dr Br K R S Z, 1/8, €21/-/60/-, haneliese@hotmail.com, 0637436013, open Apr–Sept, camping €5/person.)

Fork left, cross **D49**, and then immediately fork left onto a footpath (**0.9km**). Bear right alongside D6, pass under **A20/E9**, then fork right soon after (**0.2km**). Turn left at a T, then fork right onto a footpath (**0.3km**). Pass alongside **D6**, then fork away from it (**0.8km**). Turn right onto a dirt track, beginning a winding stretch on unpaved roads, until finally turning right onto **D6** (**5.3km**). On clear days you'll enjoy quality views of Cahors in this stretch. Fork right off D6 almost immediately onto Route de la Marchande and then left onto Chemin de la Marchande. Merge onto **D6** again and then fork left onto Chemin de Cabridelle (**0.6km**). Continue straight along a dirt track through a small cluster of houses (**0.3km**). Fork left, then right, then later emerge back onto a paved road (**2.2km**).

The road winds downhill, looping around a basketball court and parking lot (**1.2km**). Turn left on D6 (**0.3km**). Fork right at a roundabout on **D620**. At the next roundabout, fork left to cross **Pont Louis-Philippe** into Cahors (**0.3km**). A **pilgrim**

welcome center is on the left soon after. Ignore GR65 waymarks calling for a left turn along the Lot. Proceed straight to the next roundabout, then take the second right onto Rue des Maures, a very minor street (**0.2km**). Turn left at a T on Rue Nationale and proceed straight to the cathedral in

18.2KM CAHORS (ELEV 130M, POP 19,340) 🍴 ⊕ 🏠 ⓒ ⊚ ⊛ ⊞ ⊕ ⊕ 𝒊
(403.7KM)

Markets on Wednesday and Saturday mornings, in front of cathedral. Pilgrim welcome (Apr–Sept, 4pm–7pm) and pilgrim blessing (Mon–Fri, 6.15pm) in cathedral. CAMINOLOC, located near Cahors' southern entrance, is a pilgrim-focused gear shop (17 Cours Vaxis, 0565221206, mahdiducamino@caminoloc.com).

Set atop a limestone promontory, flanked by the Lot, Cahors was originally a Roman town, with an amphitheater seating 1000 and significant baths. Cahors was known for its linen and wine, and its merchants were so poorly reputed that they were featured in Dante's vision of hell. The arrival of Lombard bankers in the 13th century also drew in the Knights Templar, who set up a hospital and chapel. Most of the town's great sights date from this boom time.

Boulevard Gambetta, now the main thoroughfare, formerly the moat, is named after native son Léon Gambetta (1838–82). He moved to Paris in 1856, playing an active part in both Napoleon III's downfall and the proclamation of a republic in 1870. Imperiled, he escaped Paris in a balloon a month later. Years later, he was elected back to the National Assembly and raised to Premier of France for a short time.

The oldest part of Cahors is Les Badernes, located south of the **Cathédrale Saint-Étienne**. The cathedral was originally built as a fortress; remains of its 14th-century ramparts are still visible. While it features a large nave, there is (unusually) no transept. One of Aquitaine's first domed churches, the cathedral's rare twin domes are 32m high, inspired by the architect's experience on crusade in the Holy Land. One of the domes is decorated with 14th-century frescoes, depicting the stoning of St Stephen and eight prophets, each riding an animal. Its north door (built 1135) depicts the Ascension, capturing the moment when Jesus is about to rise, and angels are calming the disciples' fears. The 16th-century cloister was built in the flamboyant Gothic-style.

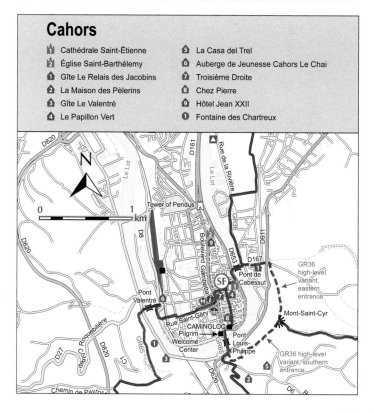

Cahors

- Cathédrale Saint-Étienne
- Église Saint-Barthélemy
- 1 Gîte Le Relais des Jacobins
- 2 La Maison des Pèlerins
- 3 Gîte Le Valentré
- 4 Le Papillon Vert
- 5 La Casa del Trel
- 6 Auberge de Jeunesse Cahors Le Chai
- 7 Troisième Droite
- 8 Chez Pierre
- 9 Hôtel Jean XXII
- 0 Fontaine des Chartreux

Weekly markets in Cahors take place just outside the cathedral

The **Pont Valentré** is a six-arched stone bridge, built 1308–78 and funded by city merchants. It's often regarded as the best-preserved medieval bridge in France. Note the devil on the upper-right side of the second tower. The legend is that the master mason, worried that he wouldn't finish on time, made a deal with the devil to help him finish. However, he tricked the devil, asking the devil to get water for the last batch of mortar – but giving him a sieve instead of a bucket. As such, the job could never be finished. The devil backed out of the deal but cursed the bridge – removing a central stone and swearing that it would always fall loose again. In 1879, a devil statue was placed in that void. Turn left on the west side of the bridge to visit **Fontaine des Chartreux**, a spring once revered by Gauls and Romans alike.Other than Gambetta, Cahors celebrates two other famous residents: Joachim-Napoléon Murat (described in the Rocamadour variant, Stage R4) and Jacques of Cahors. Jacques was born the son of a shoemaker in Cahors, but he's better known as Pope John XXII, the second Avignon pope, elected by a conclave in 1316 and selected by the future King Philip V of France. He challenged the policies of the Holy Roman Emperor, Louis IV of Bavaria, who then invaded Rome and established an Antipope, Nicholas V. Cahors also has a notably infamous resident: Louis Darquier, the Commissioner for Jewish Affairs under Vichy rule, who sent thousands to die in Nazi extermination camps in World War II. He subsequently fled to Spain, where he comfortably escaped justice, dying of old age.

Cahors is loaded with other interesting sights: secret gardens sprinkled around town, the old medieval walls, the Tower of Pendus, and assorted small museums devoted to art, wine and truffles, and resistance efforts in World War II. There are far worse places to take a day off.

⌂ Gîte Le Relais des Jacobins `Do` `Dr` `K` `R` `W`, 4/15, €16/-/-/-, DP20, 12 Rue des Jacobins, lerelaisdesjacobins@gmail.com, 0662658166 or 0565210084, open mid Mar–mid Oct, camping €8/person

⌂ La Maison des Pèlerins `Do` `Pr` `Dr` `Br` `K` `R` `W`, 2/8, €20/-/50/-, DP15, 158 Rue des Cayssinnes, alain.houadec@gmail.com, 0565300306, open Apr–Oct, reservation required, no wifi

⌂ ⌂ Gîte Le Valentré `Do` `Pr` `Dr` `K` `R`, 2/10, €16/-/56/-, DP20, 250 Chemin de la Chartreuse, frederiquegauvrit@gmail.com, 0612267868, open Mar–Nov

⌂ Le Papillon Vert `Do` `Pr` `Dr` `R` `W` `S`, 2/6, €15/30/36/54, DP20, 51 Rue du Tapis Vert, papillonvert.cahors@gmail.com, 0675805842, open Apr–Oct, vegetarian, English spoken

⌂ La Casa del Trel `Do` `Dr` `Br` `R` `W`, 2/5, €35/-/-/-, incl DP, 101 Combe del Trel, lacasadeltrel@bbox.fr, 0687868901, open Apr–mid Oct, walkers only, free shuttle from CAMINOLOC at 3pm

▲ Auberge de Jeunesse Cahors Le Chai 🅾 🔟 🅿️ 🅱️ 🅺 🆁 🅶 🆆 🆂 🆉, 38/94, €26/31/62/-, 52 Ave Breton, cahors@hifrance.org, 0536040080, closed mid Dec–mid Jan

▲ Troisième Droite 🅾 🅿️ 🅱️ 🅺 🆁 🆆 🆂, €-/70/80/-, 85 Blvd Gambetta, 3droite@ gmail.com, 0647081527, washing machine included

▲ Chez Pierre 🅾 🔟 🅿️ 🅱️ 🅺 🆁 🆆 🆂, 5/11, €25/35/55/70, 68 Rue Brives, noderpac@gmail.com, 0609962832

▲ Hôtel Jean XXII 🅿️ 🆁 🅶 🆂, €-/62/85/95, 2 Rue Albe, contact@hotel-jeanxxii. com, 0565350766, open May–Oct, breakfast €7.90

▲ Camping Rivière de Cabessut 🆁 🅶 🆆 🆂 🆉, 1180 Rue de la Rivière, contact@ cabessut.com, 0565300630, open Apr–Sept, camping €9.45/tent, breakfast €7.50

Alternative route to Saint-Cirq-Lapopie (16.1km)

It's possible to deviate from the GR65 to visit Saint-Cirq-Lapopie, considered by some to be the most beautiful village in France. From there, the GR36 leads onward to Cahors (described in the Célé Valley variant, Stage C5). The route is waymarked in both directions, so it's equally possible to walk this southward, connecting from the Célé Valley route to the GR65.

Turning right off the GR65 and onto the GR36, follow a dirt track northward. Turn right at a T, then fork left (**0.8km**). Once again, turn right at a T, this time onto a paved road (**1km**). Turn right onto a dirt track (**1.5km**). Turn left (**1.2km**), then continue straight onto a paved road (**1.8km**). Fork left onto **D911**, then fork right onto a minor road (**0.4km**), just before the church in **Concots** (WC, fountain, bakery/*épicerie*, Sunday market, ▲ Gîte La Logette 🅾 🔟 🔩 🅺 🆁 🆆, 3/13, €15/-/-/-, DP20, 2km outside Concots, jeanmarie.aillet@orange.fr, 0565315504).

The town's highlight is its 13th-century **clock tower**. A local proverb asserts that hard bread underpins a solid house. This is not to be taken literally! Rather, the implication is that people will eat less of the hard bread, thus saving money.

Turn right just before the *mairie*, then left at a T, with even more turns coming in quick succession (**0.9km**). Follow a series of mostly unpaved tracks through the *causse*, emerging back on asphalt (**3.4km**) as you pass ▲ À la Ferme (🅾 🅿️ 🆁, bsorenza@ orange.fr, Les Bories Basses, 0565312602 or 0688041324). Fork right and then turn right onto a dirt track (**0.4km**). Turn left on **D42**, then fork left on **D197** towards Berganty (**0.4km**). Fork right onto a dirt track, then proceed back onto a paved road (**1.5km**). Turn right and then make a sharp left immediately after (**0.2km**). At a five-way

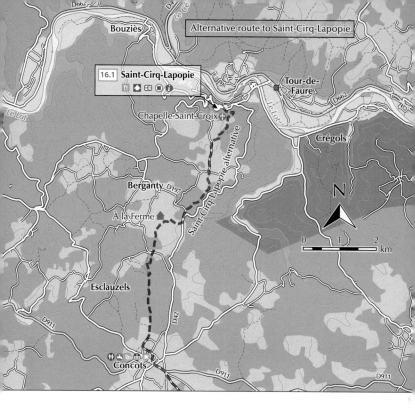

intersection, take the second left (**0.9km**), winding gradually uphill. Continue straight through the middle of three forks (**0.8km**). Follow a dirt track to **Chapelle Saint-Croix**, then enjoy excellent views of Saint-Cirq while descending. Fork left, then cross D8/D40 into the village (**0.4km**). At a T, turn right for the church, or left to reach the Office de Tourisme.

Alternative route to bypass Cahors, via Lalbenque and Lhospitalet (21.5km)
Those disinterested in Cahors have the option of instead passing south of it, along this variant, visiting two towns with historic ties to the pilgrimage. It rejoins the GR65 well into Stage 14, at Gîte La Ferme de Trigodina, 8.5km before Lascabanes.

Leave the GR65 at Mas de Vers, turning left on **D26**. There are no waymarks during this first stretch, but it's straightforward – just stay on D26 for **2.6km**. Turn left on **D55** towards Escamps and then right immediately after on Chemin des Grèzes. Continue straight through a roundabout and then fork right soon after on Rue de l'Étang (**0.7km**). Turn right on Rue du Marché aux Truffes, just before the church in

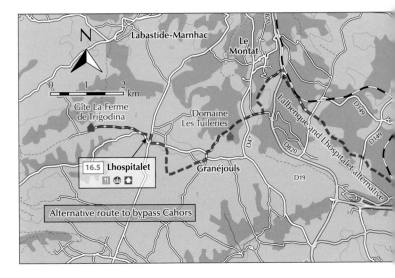

Gîte La Ferme de Trigodina

Domaine Les Tuileries

16.5 **Lhospitalet**

Granéjouls

Alternative route to bypass Cahors

3.4KM LALBENQUE (ELEV 270M, POP 1735) (406.7KM)
Once the world's truffle center, Lalbenque still has a truffle market in the winter and preserves that legacy through 'truffle days' that occur throughout the year.

▲ Gîte Mango **O Pr Dr Br K R W S Z**, 3/6, €-/24/48/-, DP13.50, 51/67 Route de Puylaroque, philpariat@yahoo.fr, 0780029469 or 0962522300, washing machine included, free pick-up from Mas de Vers

▲ La Vayssade **O Pr Br R Cr**, €-/-/110/140, 205 Chemin de la Vayssade, contact@lavayssade.com, 0565243151, swimming pool

Fork left at the post office on Place de la Poste. Before passing tennis courts on the left, watch for a signpost with several waymarks. Here, you'll see your first marker for today's route: an orange stripe. Orange is your color, from here to Lhospitalet.

Follow Chemin de la Vignasse out of town. Fork right onto a dirt track (**0.7km**). Cross **D19**, briefly rejoin a paved road, then continue back onto a dirt track (**0.4km**). After a long off-road stretch (**2.9km**), turn left onto a paved road just before the **A20/ E9**. Cross the railroad then turn right on D19, crossing the expressway as well. Fork right onto a dirt track running first alongside the railroad and then forking away from it (**0.9km**). Cross **D149** (**1.6km**). Later, join D149 (**1.9km**), as it parallels the railroad. Veer left onto a footpath, then turn right just before **D820**. Rejoin D149, crossing through

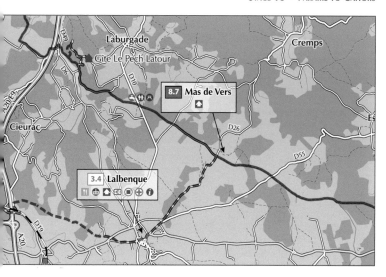

a roundabout towards Le Montat (**1.6km**). Fork left onto a minor paved road that soon becomes a dirt track (**0.5km**). Cross **D47** (**1.6km**) and pass ⛰ Domaine Les Tuileries (**Pr Dr Br R**, €-/66/75/90, DP20, domainelestuileries@orange.fr, 0565210472 or 0607657686, open Mar–Nov). Descend into the woods. Emerge on a paved road and enter the village of **Granéjouls**, looping around its Église Notre Dame de l'Assomption (**1.8km**). Transition onto a dirt track away from the village (**0.2km**). Turn right at a T (**1km**). Turn left onto a paved road (**0.7km**). After passing Gîte Conviviale, turn right (**0.4km**). Arrive at the church in

16.5KM LHOSPITALET (ELEV 240M, POP 500) 🍴 ⊕ 🏠 (390.2KM)
Founded by Pons I of Gourdon's wife, Hélène, who suffered a scare when her horse toppled into a gully here. She vowed to open a hospice for the poor if she survived and followed through on that, later adding a chapel.

⛰ Gîte Conviviale **O Do Dr K R Gr W**, 2/12, €15/-/-/-, DP20, letapeconviviale@outlook.fr, 0650939914, camping €7/person

Turn left at the church and proceed **1.6km** to ⛰ Gîte La Ferme de Trigodina (**Do Pr Dr K R W S**, 5/12, €15/-/30/-, DP19, trigodina@orange.fr, 0671069872, open mid Mar–Oct), rejoining the GR65. The route description continues in Stage 14.

STAGE 14
Cahors to Lascabanes

Start	Cathédrale Saint-Étienne, Cahors
Finish	Église Saint-Georges, Lascabanes
Distance	23.8km
Total ascent	475m
Total descent	415m
Difficulty	Moderate
Time	6hr 30min
Percentage paved	35%
Gîtes	Fontanet 4.1km, Les Mathieux 7.5km, Labastide-Marnhac 12.1km, Trigodina 15.3km, Lascabanes 23.8km

Leaving Cahors, you cross a significant transition point on the Via Podiensis. While you won't believe it at first, as you climb sharply up the hillside opposite the town, the most strenuous terrain on the GR65 is now behind you. As you pause mid-ascent, huffing and puffing, turn around to admire both the Pont Valentré and the Lot. It's your last chance to appreciate this river, as the *chemin* now veers steadily south of it. As the landscape flattens out, the land use patterns shift as well. Fewer cows line the trail. In their place, at least over the next few stages, are sprawling fields of sunflowers – a truly marvelous sight to behold when they are in full bloom in summer.

Through Cahors, the route described here does not strictly follow the GR65. With the cathedral's entrance to your right, proceed straight on Rue du Marechal Joffre. Cross Boulevard Leon Gambetta and turn left. Turn right after the Office de Tourisme and pass through the plaza. Continue straight on Rue Saint-Géry. Turn right at a T, then left immediately after on Rue Gustave Sindou. Turn right onto a riverside walkway, then left across the **Pont Valentré**. Once on the other side, join a footpath to the left, the

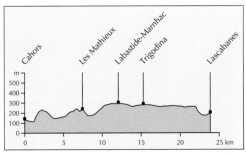

'Passage Sportif,' climbing the hillside (**1.4km**). At the top, fork right onto a dirt track (**0.6km**). Alternately, fork left, remaining on a footpath that leads to an impressive viewpoint at La Croix de Magne. From there, follow a dirt road inland, rejoining the GR65 soon after. This adds 0.2km.

Turn right onto a paved road. Turn left at a T, then take the next left (**0.8km**). Turn right to pass under **D820**, then turn right immediately after the tunnel to climb a small footpath and join Route de Fontanet (**1.2km**). Pass ⌂ Gîte Au 1082 (**O Pr Dr K R W S**, 3/8, €-/20/40/60, DP15, au1082cahors@gmail.com, 0781094204, camping €5/person) soon after. Fork left onto a dirt track (**1.3km**). Rejoin a paved road, then fork right at a T, just after a church (**1km**). Turn right on a dirt track (**0.2km**). Continue straight onto a paved road (**0.8km**), then loop through

7.5KM LES MATHIEUX (ELEV 220M) 🏠 (396.2KM)

⌂ **Domaine des Mathieux** **Do Pr Dr Br R W**, 3/12, €22/-/50/-, DP17, domainedesmathieux@gmail.com, 0667556817, open Apr–Nov, no wifi

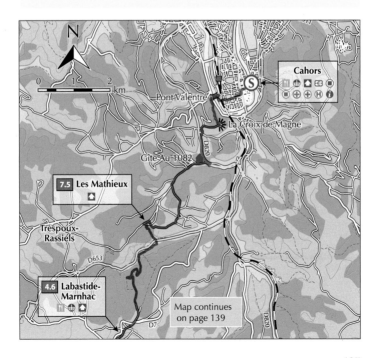

Map continues on page 139

Turn right onto a footpath after Domaine des Mathieux. After a sharp, rocky descent, this smooths out into a good dirt road (**0.4km**). The day's second significant ascent follows. Cross **D653** (**0.4km**) and then stick with the unpaved road through a series of turns, finally emerging back on pavement (**2.9km**). Cross **D7** and continue straight onto a dirt track, veering to the right as it becomes paved once more (**0.5km**). Pass a church and proceed through

---

4.6KM LABASTIDE-MARNHAC (ELEV 270M, POP 1225) ⊞ ⊕ ◪ (391.6KM)
Markets on Monday and Friday mornings. A bastide town established in the 13th century by wealthy Cahors merchants to monitor the road. Nearly destroyed by the English for switching loyalties to France, it was saved by Irlande de la Popie, wife of Guillaumont III. She cleverly called for townsfolk to line the ramparts and impress the English with their numbers. Surprised to see such a large force, the English troops backed off.

⌂ Gîte de l'Église 🅳🅾 🆁 🆂, 1/5, €15/-/-/-, 15 Rue de Viguiérmes, michenaud. patrice@orange.fr, 0565239150, open mid Apr–Sept

⌂ Gîte Chez Bernie 🅳🅾 🅿🆁 🆁 🆂, 3/6, €15/15/30/-, DP20, 547 Chemin du Pech de Capy Saint-Remy, bernadette.dechet@free.fr, 0683643533 or 0565210683, open Apr–Oct, camping €10/person

---

Fork right on a footpath, then merge onto D7 (**0.4km**). Turn left onto a dirt track, sticking with it through many intersecting roads, and finally turning left at a T (**2.6km**). Turn right onto a paved road (**0.2km**), passing ⌂ Gîte La Ferme de Trigodina (🅳🅾 🅿🆁 🅳🆁 🅺 🆁 🆆 🆂, 5/12, €15/-/30/-, DP19, trigodina@orange.fr, 0671069872, open mid Mar–Oct). The Lalbenque-Lhospitalet variant from Stage 13 rejoins here. At a complicated intersection, continue straight onto a dirt track (**0.5km**). Soon after merging with another dirt track (**2.7km**), fork right onto a footpath. Rejoin a dirt road (**0.6km**), then cross **D239** (**1.8km**). Continue forward, winding through a series of paved and dirt tracks to the outskirts of Lascabanes (**2.7km**). Pass a WC and fountain, then turn left at the *mairie* onto the main road through the village. Turn right, then right again, arriving at the church in

---

11.7KM LASCABANES (ELEV 190M, POP 180) ⊞ ◪ (379.9KM)
A pilgrim hospital operated here in the 15th century. Today, a pilgrim blessing is offered in the church every evening at 6pm.

⌂ Le Nid des Anges 🅾 🅳🅾 🅿🆁 🅳🆁 🆁 🆆 🆂, 4/15, €14.50/-/33/-, DP19.50, chihamaupoux@wanadoo.fr, 0565318638, reservation required in offseason, mini-épicerie, donkey parking

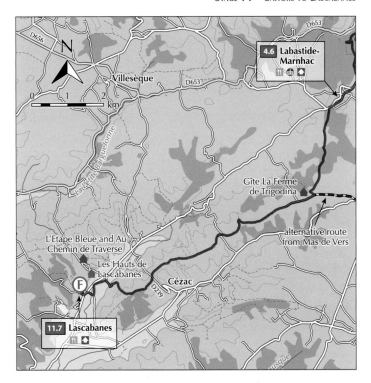

● **L'Etape Bleue** Do Pr Dr K R W S, 1/4, €14/42/56/-, DP20, mc.cayon-glayere@orange.fr, 0565353477, open Apr–Sept, no wifi

● ● **Au Chemin de Traverse** O Do Pr Dr Br R W S, 1/4, €36/60.50/102/-, incl DP, auchemindetraverse@gmail.com, 0614086646, camping €20DP/person

● **Gîte en Yourte Le Sabatier** Do Dr K R W, 3/11, €18/-/-/-, DP19, located after village exit, jslascabanes@gmail.com, 0565239854, open Apr–Oct, English spoken, swimming pool, donkey parking

● **Laniès** Pr Dr Br R W S, €-/35/50/-, DP13, lanies46800@gmail.com, 0622563261 or 0565350647, open Mar–Nov

STAGE 15
Lascabanes to Lauzerte

Start	Église Saint-Georges, Lascabanes
Finish	Place des Cornières, Lauzerte
Distance	23.7km
Total ascent	615m
Total descent	595m
Difficulty	Moderate-to-strenuous
Time	6hr 45min
Percentage paved	30%
Gîtes	Gamel 2.6+1.1km, Escayrac 2.6+1.4km, Janès 7+1.7km, Montcuq 9.4km, Lauzerte 23.7km

It's another beautiful day in sunflower country! Be prepared that the GR65 today actually bypasses the two towns on the itinerary, so small detours are required to make visits. Those extra meters are worth the walking, though, as Montcuq especially is a history-rich town, dominated by its medieval tower. Take the time to climb to the top. By contrast, Montlauzun is a much smaller place, with no food available, but a very agreeable spot for a rest nonetheless. Fortunately, no detour is required to reach Lauzerte, a charming hill town overlooking Tarn-et-Garonne. This is also a day to celebrate: midway between Lascabanes and Montcuq, you pass the halfway mark to Saint-Jean-Pied-de-Port on the GR65.

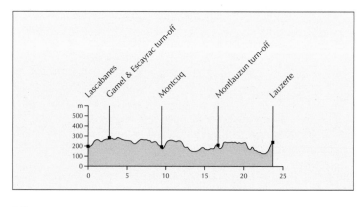

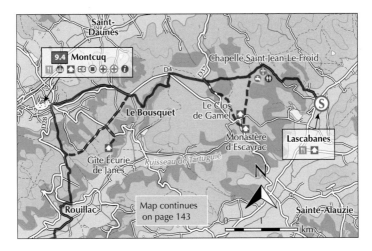

Proceed behind the church in **Lascabanes**, through sunflower fields, transitioning onto a dirt track. Fork left. Turn right at a T onto a paved road (**1.3km**). Turn left, passing **Chapelle Saint-Jean-Le-Froid** (**0.8km**, WC, fountain). This neighbors a miraculous spring that is said to always flow on the night of Saint-Jean. Fork right onto a dirt track (**0.5km**). (Alternately, turn left to detour to 🛏🛏 Le Clos de Gamel Do Pr Dr K R W, 3/6, €20/40/80/-, DP23.50, contact@closdegamel.com, 0581225161, open Apr–Oct, swimming pool; and 🛏 Monastère d'Escayrac Do Dr Br K R, 3/8, €Donation, incl DP, communaute@mariemeredeleglise.fr, 0563322887, open May–Sept, no wifi.)

Make a sharp left, doubling back onto **D37**, then turn right onto a tree-lined dirt track (**1.4km**). Emerge from the trees and turn left, cross **D4**, and fork left in quick succession (**1.2km**). Another wooded section leads to the village of **Le Bousquet** (**1.3km**). Turn left, then fork right, then merge with D4 (**0.5km**). (Or, to reach 🛏 Gîte Écurie de Janès Do Dr Br K R W, 1/10, €22/-/-/-, DP8, ecuriedejanes@gmail.com, 0648435361, open May–Oct, donkey parking, turn left instead of joining D4.)

Fork right and then turn left on a footpath. Continue straight, alternating between paved and dirt roads (**2.2km**). The GR65 bypasses the center of Montcuq, turning left on D28. It's well worth the short detour, though, so instead continue straight on D4 into

9.4KM MONTCUQ (ELEV 190M, POP 1200) 🍴⊕🏠🅲◉⊕⊕ℹ (370.5KM)
Markets on Thursday and Sunday mornings.

The town's name is unfortunately similar to *mon cul*, which has resulted in a proliferation of postcards featuring exposed backsides. Its other significant

141

Dawn breaks over Montcuq

landmark is the 12th-century keep, which stands 24m high, and offers 360-degree views of the surrounding valley of Petite-Barguelonne (€2.50). Montcuq was attacked repeatedly by Simon de Montfort during the Albigensian Crusade; 83 of its residents were ultimately convicted of Catharism. It was later captured by the English during the Hundred Years' War and then ravaged by Calvinists in the Wars of Religion. The Église Saint-Hilaire suffered badly in the latter conflict, but was rebuilt soon after and now enjoys a set of impressive stained-glass windows.

- **Gîte Le Cantourel** Do Pr Dr K R W S, 5/15, €17/-/34/-, DP20, 32 Rue du Faubourg Saint-Privat, gite.cantourel@gmail.com, 0682131865, open Apr–Oct, camping €6/person, English spoken
- **Gîte Le Soleillou** Do Pr Dr K R W S Z, 1/6, €12/-/40/-, DP19.50, 356 Rue du Souleillou, lesouleillou@gmail.com, 0761516941, open Apr–Oct, camping €6/person
- **Gîte l'Evidence** O Do Pr Dr K R Cr W, 4/9, €17/-/34/51, DP18, 8 Rue du Couvent des Cordeliers, levidence.sas@orange.fr, 0630689505, no wifi
- **Gîte Celtic Camino** O Do Dr R W S, 1/5, €20/-/-/-, DP18, 51 Rue Marcel Bourrières, pause@gitecelticcamino.com, 0749374656, reservation required in offseason

Backtrack to the town's entrance and turn onto **D28** (WC on left). Fork left onto a footpath. Merge onto a dirt road and then turn right (**1.6km**). Turn left on D28, then fork left on a minor paved road towards Charry (**0.2km**). Fork right on a footpath, then turn right back onto D28 (**1.2km**). Fork left onto a dirt track, turn left at a T, and then fork left on a paved road past Église Saint-Pierre in **Rouillac** (**0.6km**). Fork right, then turn left onto a dirt track (**0.9km**). Merge onto a paved road, loop through a small cluster of houses, then turn right at a T on **D256** (**1.7km**), leading to

7.2KM MONTLAUZUN TURN-OFF (ELEV 210M, POP 120)(363.3KM)
WC and fountain. A 0.3km detour leads to this hilltop village, with a small church and many benches. After Montlauzun, you'll leave the Lot department and enter Tarn-et-Garonne.

After following D256 away from Montlauzun, turn left on **D45**. Turn right on a dirt track that converges with a paved road soon after (**0.7km**). (Alternately, continue straight on D45 to detour 1.2km to ⌂ Auberge du Canabal 🅾 Pf Dr Br R W, €-/70/85/100, DP26, contact@canabal.fr, 0603974189, English spoken, swimming pool.) A longer off-road stretch follows, ascending back to another ridgeline and then making a steep descent. If sunflowers are in bloom, you'll be rewarded with a brilliant view of Lauzerte. Pass a fountain, then finally turn right on **D54** (**5km**, ⌂ Gîte Fleuri du Tuc de Saint-Paul 🅾 Do Pf Dr K R W S, 2/8, €15/-/40/-, DP20, m.bourrieres@laposte.net, 0632146495, camping €6/person, no wifi). Fork right through a roundabout onto **D2** at the entrance to Lauzerte. Turn right on a footpath (**0.7km**). Turn right onto a paved road, then fork left. Turn left, then immediately right, on D73 (**0.4km**). Continue straight into Place des Cornières in

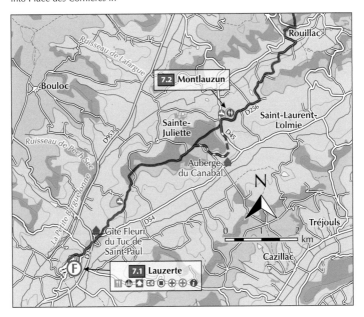

143

7.1KM LAUZERTE (ELEV 210M, POP 1455) 🚉 ⊕ 🏠 🄫 ◎ ⊕ ⊕ ❶ (356.2KM)

WC and fountain outside church. Markets on Wednesday and Saturday mornings.

Raymond V, the Count of Toulouse, already had a castle here in the late 12th century when a group of counts petitioned to develop a *castelnau* – a 200-home, planned community that anticipated the wave of bastides that would proliferate in the next century. Despite its admirable fortifications, it was taken by the English in the 13th century. Indeed, it had been legally granted to England in 1259, as part of the Treaty of Paris, but the proud residents fought this to the bitter end. Soon enough, though, Lauzerte would succeed in rejoining France. It was the site of significant acts of religious violence over the next few centuries, with a massacre of Jews conducted by shepherds in the 14th century and the slaughter of 194 Catholic clerics by Protestant forces in 1562.

A trailside fountain near Lauzerte

The arcaded town square, the Place des Cornières, features a charming recent embellishment. In 1988, a local artist, Jacques Buchholtz, sculpted the square's corner so that it appears to be curling upward, with a colorful geometric pattern beneath it.

🛌 Gîte Communal Do Pr Dr R W S, 1/6, €14/-/38/51, DP18, 15 Rue du Millial, corinne.segard6@orange.fr, 0619708949, open Apr–Oct, English spoken

🛌 Gîte Les Figuiers O Do Pr Dr Br R Cr W S Z, 3/16, €21/-/56/-, DP15, 25 Chemin du Coudounié, accueil@lesfiguiers-lauzerte.com, 0685317131

🛌 Gîte Chez Serge Do Dr K R S, 1/4, €15/-/-/-, DP17, 32 Rue de la Garrigue, serge.pradin@orange.fr, 0672241985, open Apr–Oct

🛌 Le Gîte des Carmes Do Pr K R W S, 1/12, €20/-/60/-, 4 Rue des Carmes, legitedescarmes@gmail.com, 0689877247, closed Jul–Aug, breakfast €5, camping €15/person, swimming pool

🛌 Gîte Tamba'kï Do Dr R S, 4/12, €16/-/-/-, DP19, 36 Rue de la Garrigue, tambaki36@gmail.com, 0761311122, open Apr–Oct

🛌 Gîte L'Abeille Lulu O Do K R W S, 3/7, €17/-/-/-, 1 Chemin de la Fontaine, abeillelulu82@gmail.com, 0687055360, reservation required in offseason, breakfast €5

STAGE 16

Lauzerte to Moissac

Start	Place des Cornières, Lauzerte
Finish	Abbaye Saint-Pierre, Moissac
Distance	27.8km (28.3km via high-level variant)
Total ascent	475m (555m via high-level variant)
Total descent	605m (695m via high-level variant)
Difficulty	Moderate
Time	7hr 30min (7hr 45min via high-level variant)
Percentage paved	62% (63% via high-level variant)
Gîtes	Parry 5.1km, Lesclapayrac 7.1+2.5km, Durfort-Lacapelette 12km, Saint-Hubert 13.4+1.2km, Saint-Martin 15.1km, Colibri d'Espis 21.5km, Moissac 27.8km

The stage begins with a pair of appealing, small sites: a perfect dovecote and a quaint Romanesque church. From there, though, notable landmarks are few and far between. The village of Durfort-Lacapelette offers a solid spot for a lunch break, but beyond that it's mostly agricultural country, primarily featuring stone fruits and apples, until your final destination. Moissac is a larger town with a vibrant pedestrian-only center, situated around the medieval abbey. The abbey's cloister is an exceptional work of art that demands an extended visit; make time as well to attend evening Vespers in the church, listening to the singing nuns. To bypass an unappealing final stretch on busy roads, consider the high-level variant, which offers lovely views of the river valley, but a steep descent into the center.

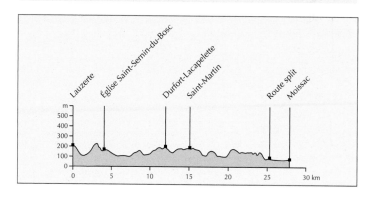

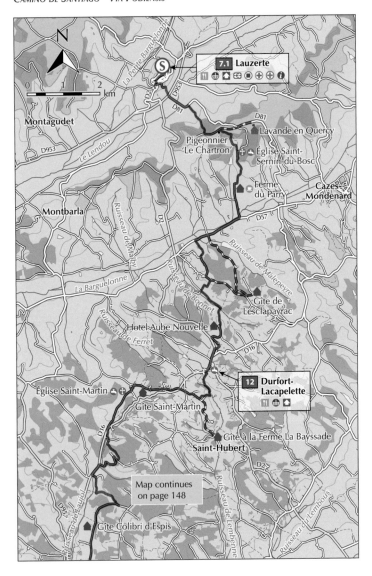

N

0   1   2
km

7.1 Lauzerte

Montagudet

Lavande en Quercy

Pigeonnier
'Le Chartron'

Église Saint-
Sernin-du-Bosc

Ferme
du Parry

Cazes-
Mondenard

Montbarla

Ruisseau de Malepeyre

Gîte de
Lesclapayrac

La Barguelonne

Hotel Aube Nouvelle

Ruisseau de Ferret

**12 Durfort-
Lacapelette**

Église Saint-Martin

Gîte Saint-Martin

Gîte à la Ferme La Bayssade

Saint-Hubert

Ruisseau de Lembous

Map continues
on page 148

Gîte Colibri d'Espis

Continue straight through Place des Cornières and onto Rue du Marché. Turn right on Grand Rue, then fork left onto a pedestrian walkway and steps descending from the old town. Cross Rue de la Brèche and continue straight downstairs. Cross a paved road (bakery) and descend Passage du Pélerin. Turn left, cross **D2**, then fork right (**0.6km**). Make a sharp right on a dirt track, then continue onto pavement. Cross **D953** and proceed straight on **D81** (**1.2km**).

Turn right, into the countryside, following a mix of paved roads and dirt tracks past the **Pigeonnier 'Le Chartron'** (**1.4km**). This exemplar of the classic Quercy dovecote was built in August 1789 to celebrate the abolition of privileges. (Continue straight here to reach ▲ Lavande en Quercy 🅿️ 🄳🄳 🄺 🅁 🅆 🅂, €-/35/55/90, DP25, marienoelle.turti@free.fr, 0563946619, open Apr–Oct, reservation required.) The GR65 turns right on a footpath, leading to **Église Saint-Sernin-du-Bosc**, a Romanesque church formerly under Moissac Abbey control (**0.8km**, fountain). Turn right and then

The Pigeonnier 'Le Chartron', near Lauzerte

left around ▲ Ferme du Parry (**1.1km**, snack bar, 🄳🄾 🅿️ 🄳🅁 🅁, 16/-/60/-, DP19, ginestet.mar@orange.fr, 0680644579, closed Dec–Jan, camping €7/person). Turn right onto **D57** (**1km**). (To detour to ▲ Gîte de Lesclapayrac 🄾 🄳🄾 🅿️ 🄳🅁 🄺 🅁 🅆, 6/15, €14/19/34/-, DP16, jcdgilbart82@gmail.com, 0984128518 or 0607997355, turn left 1km later and continue 2.5km.)

Proceed along a footpath, a paved road, and then a dirt track (**2.7km**). Wind through a series of fields, then emerge on a paved road, passing ▲ Hotel Aube Nouvelle 🅿️ 🄳🅁 🅁 🄲🄵 🅆 🅂 🅉, €-/56/71/86, DP30, aubenouvelle82@yahoo.fr, 0563045033, open Apr–Oct, donkey parking,(**1.9km**). Continue straight onto a dirt track, looping around a residential street, then emerging on **D2** (**1.1km**). Proceed through the roundabout, then fork right on **D16** in

12KM DURFORT-LACAPELETTE (ELEV 180M, POP 845) 🍴 ⊕ 🛏 (344.2KM)
Fountain below café. The Durfort family was based here in the Middle Ages, although their castle was destroyed by Simon de Montfort in 1213. The French language didn't become compulsory in schools here until between the two world wars.

▲ Gîte de Soleil Levant 🄾 🄳🄾 🅿️ 🄱🅁 🄺 🅁 🅆 🅂 🅉, 1/6, €20/-/40/-, 20 Rue des Pelerins, gitedusoleillevant@hotmail.fr, 0614960030

Turn left onto a dirt track, then turn right. Turn right on a minor paved road (**1.4km**). (Alternately, turn left to reach **Saint-Hubert** and ▲ Gîte à la Ferme La Bayssade   , 4/11, €22/-/-/-, DP15, earldebayssade@wanadoo.fr, 0563045147, open Apr–Oct, donkey parking.) Cross **D16** (**0.6km**). Pass ▲ Gîte Saint-Martin (, 5/14, €17/-/-/-, DP20, gite.saint.martin82@gmail.com, 0685357359, open mid Mar–Oct, English spoken, camping €6/person, swimming pool), then turn left (**1.4km**), skirting **Église Saint-Martin** (fountain). Cross **D16** and descend onto a footpath into the woods (**1.4km**). Turn right onto a minor paved road (**1.1km**) and follow it as it loops sharply back to the left. At a T intersection, turn left on **D16** (**0.9km**). Turn left and then right onto a footpath (**0.5km**). Make a sharp left, then an equally sharp right onto a paved road (**1.2km**). Pass ▲ Gîte Colibri d'Espis (, 2/12, €19/38/42/-, DP19.50, colibridespis@gmail.com, 0616480729, camping €6/person) and continue forward (**1km**). After a long stretch, turn left on **D957** (**3.5km**). Continue straight through the roundabout on D957, then join a footpath on the road's right side (**0.4km**). Soon after, you have a choice to make.

GR65 direct to Moissac (2.4km)

The recommended route continues straight on D957. Fork right on Chemin des Vignes, then merge with **D927** (**1km**). Fork right on Chemin du Ricard. Turn left at a T and pass under the railroad, then turn right back onto D927 (**0.7km**). Fork right through a roundabout on Rue Malaveille, then turn right on Rue de la République, leading to **Moissac**'s abbey.

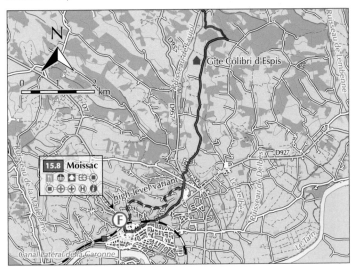

High-level variant to Moissac (2.9km)

Turn right off D957 onto a minor paved road, then turn left onto a footpath (**0.6km**), climbing steeply into the hills above Moissac. Merge back onto a paved road (**0.2km**), winding through a quiet neighborhood, with good views of the river valley below. Fork right, then left in quick succession (**1.4km**), then fork right onto a footpath, dropping sharply (**0.2km**). Turn left on Avenue de Brienne, then fork left through a parking lot and descend a flight of stairs to **Moissac**'s abbey.

15.8KM MOISSAC (ELEV 80M, POP 13,040) 🏨 ⊕ 🏠 🄲 ◉ ◉ 🄷 ⊕ ⊕ 𝒊
(328.4KM)

Markets on Saturdays and Sundays. WC behind tourism office.

Situated near the confluence of the Tarn and Garonne rivers, the Benedictines founded the **Abbaye Saint-Pierre** here in the seventh century, but Moissac really surged in influence when it became linked to Cluny. Moissac's abbot ultimately climbed as high as second-in-command in the Cluny order. The Église Saint-Pierre, the abbey's church, was consecrated in 1063, with its cloisters completed 35 years later. The south portal is one of the most impressive and elaborate Romanesque portals of the 12th century, offering a vision of the Apocalypse, with carved images occupying walls of the porch, door, and tympanum. The doorway is divided in half by the trumeau (supports lintel), which is decorated on three of its four sides. On the front are three pairs of lions/lionesses guarding the entry. On the east side is the prophet Jeremiah, holding a scroll, while the west side features St Paul. Across from Paul is St Peter, located on the door jamb, and across from Jeremiah is the Prophet Isaiah. The lintel is decorated with 10 rosettes. Above the lintel is the tympanum, which focuses on chapter four from the Book of

The Romanesque cloisters in Moissac's Abbey Saint-Pierre

Revelation. Jesus is enthroned with his right arm raised in blessing and left hand on the Book of Life; Matthew is the winged man, Mark the lion, Luke the bull, and John the eagle. The 24 elders of the Apocalypse fill the scene, each holding a musical instrument in one hand and a chalice in the other.

Inside, the walls appear to be covered with wallpaper, but this is original painting. The church once had dome vaults but was transformed in the 15th century into the typical French style, with a single nave. Meanwhile, the Romanesque cloisters (€4.50), accessed through the tourism office, are said to be the oldest surviving cloisters with narrative capitals. The 76 carved capitals and 12 large pillar reliefs depict a wide variety of themes (46 of them illustrate Biblical themes or the lives of the saints) and served as a model for many cathedrals. The distinctive capitals, shaped like upside-down pyramids, have carvings covering the entire surface, many with Latin inscriptions explaining the scene.

While stone fruits dominate the gentle hills leading into Moissac, the upcoming stages feature vineyards. Romans first brought viticulture to the region by Romans, but Moissac's monks introduced the Chasselas grape in the Middle Ages, and it remains a celebrated part of regional food and drink today.Every evening, a group of nuns sing Vespers in the church at 6pm: a service that is well worth attending.

♠ L'Ancien Carmel O Do Pr Dr K R Cf W S Z, 8/36, €16/-/56/-, DP20.50, 5 Sente du Calvaire, contact@lanciencarmelmoissac.com, 0563046221, camping €7/person, donkey parking

♠ Gîte Ultreia Moissac O Do Pr Dr Br R W S Z, 3/14, €22/46/62/84, DP14, 45 Ave Pierre Chabrié, info@ultreiamoissac.com, 0563051506 or 0671740314

♠ Gîte Les Etoiles Do Pr Dr R W, 5/13, €16/-/38/51, DP19.50, 4 Rue Falhière, contact@gite-moissac.com, 0625630016 or 0563942247, open mid Apr–Sept, English spoken

♠ La Petite Lumière Do Pr Dr K R W, 1/6, €16/28/40/-, DP20, Panorama du Calvaire, lapetitelumiere@free.fr, 0674681294 or 0662627372, open Apr–Oct, camping €8/person

♠ Gîte La Maison d'Aliénor O Do Pr Dr R Cf W S, 5/15, €20/-/45/-, DP20, 25 Rue Malaveille, lemee.moissac@gmail.com, 0787900721

♠♠ Auberge des Chemins O Do Pr Dr R W S, 1/5, €16/29/38/-, DP19, 17 Rue du Pont, aubergedeschemins@gmail.com, 0624348087, reservation required in offseason

♠ La Maison Lydia O Pr Br R W S, €-/60/70/140, 2 bis Quai Magenta, contact@lamaisonlydia.fr, 0749782202

Moissac

1. L'Ancien Carmel
2. Gîte Ultreia Moissac
3. Gîte Les Etoiles
4. La Petite Lumière
5. Gîte La Maison d'Aliénor
6. Auberge des Chemins
7. La Maison Lydia
8. Abbaye Saint-Pierre

high-level variant

D927

D9

N

0   300 m

Canal Latéral de la Garonne

D813

Tarn River

Place Roger Delthil, before the Abbey Saint-Pierre in Moissac

STAGE 17
Moissac to Auvillar

Start	Abbaye Saint-Pierre, Moissac
Finish	Office de Tourisme, Auvillar
Distance	19.8km (22km via high-level variant)
Total ascent	135m (405m via high-level variant)
Total descent	105m (370m via high-level variant)
Difficulty	Easy (easy-to-moderate via high-level variant)
Time	4hr 30min (5hr 30min via high-level variant)
Percentage paved	99% (72% via high-level variant)
Gîtes	Malause 11.2km, Espalais 18.7km, Auvillar 19.8km

While the Canal du Midi gets more of the fame, only with the construction of the Canal Latéral de la Garonne in the mid 19th century could boats travel seamlessly from the Atlantic to the Mediterranean through these twin canals (with help from the Garonne River). The bulk of today's walk, between Moissac and Pommevic, proceeds directly along the 18m-wide Garonne canal. After forking through Pommevic, the route crosses back over a pair of canals, leading through flat farm country. A second major crossing, over the Garonne River this time, and a short ascent leads to Auvillar, a lovely hybrid of red-brick and limestone. If all that flat pavement is too much, a variant is possible that deviates from the canal for a considerable distance.

With the abbey's elaborate south portal at your back, proceed through the pedestrian plaza and onto Rue de la République. Stick with it as it curves left and changes names, until turning right at an oval-shaped intersection (**0.5km**). Cross the **Canal Latéral**, continue straight through a roundabout, and then turn right onto a riverside footpath. Turn right, away from the river, and then left soon after, walking with the canal on your right (**1.1km**).

Continue straight onto a paved walkway along the canal (**0.3km**). At the **Pont Écluse** (**2km**) there are two waymarked routes to choose from.

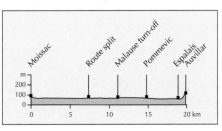

152

GR65 direct to Malause turn-off (7.3km)

Stick with the paved canal track, continuing straight for **7.3km**. At that point, the high-level variant rejoins and it's possible to detour across the canal into **Malause** and its services.

High-level variant via Boudou (9.5km)

Cross the canal, backtrack to the right on **D813**, then turn left, soon climbing a dirt track into the hills, along the treeline. From there, the route winds along mostly paved roads to **Boudou** (**4.4km**). The next section, by contrast, is primarily unpaved, descending to a turn-off for the 0.4km one-way detour to ⌂ Pugnal (Do Pr Dr Br R W, 1/3, €22/50/70/99, DP18, 1186 Route du Point de Vue, jennysmither@wanadoo.fr, 0963014021 or 0666593872, open Apr–Oct, swimming pool, English spoken) (**1.7km**) and then crossing another wooded ridge to reach **Malause** (**2.9km**). Take the second left at a roundabout towards the *mairie*, make a sharp right, then turn left. Cross the canal and turn right, rejoining the official route.

11.2KM MALAUSE TURN-OFF (ELEV 75M, POP 1160) 🍴 ⊕ 🏧 ◉ ⊕ (317.2KM)
The Durfort family ruled over Malause and the surrounding region for nearly four centuries.

⌂ Gîte Boudet O Do Dr K R W S Z, 4/12, €20/-/-/-, DP20, 11 Ave de Bordeaux, yolande.boudet@wanadoo.fr, 0679440977 or 0633299675

After another long stretch on the canal (**3km**), the reunited routes turn right across it and continue straight. Turn left on **D813** and proceed into

3.5KM POMMEVIC (ELEV 70M, POP 545) 🍴 ◉ (313.7KM)
A town with Gallo-Romanic origins, reflected in its name, which is Latin for 'apple village.' The Église de Saint-Denis preserves its original Romanesque apse and southern wall.

Turn left and cross the Canal Láteral, the **Canal de Golfech**, and the **D116**, continuing straight onto a minor paved road (**0.8km**), often with a footpath accessible just off to the side. Pass a seasonal farm stand (**1.5km**). Turn right in

4KM ESPALAIS (ELEV 60M, POP 390) 🏧 (309.7KM)
The 13th-century Église Saint-Orens is dedicated to a fourth-century hermit of the Gévaudan and subsequent Bishop of Auch.

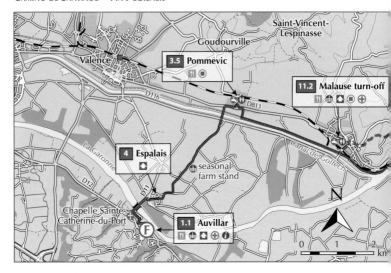

♠ Gîte Le Par'Chemin **O** **Do** **Dr** **K** **R** **W** **S**, 3/14, €15/-/-/-, DP19, 34 Ave Monplaisir, frederic.ceillier@gmail.com, 0666460903, campers welcome, reservation required Nov–Mar, donkey parking

♠ Château de Lastours **O** **Pr** **Dr** **Br** **R** **Cf** **W** **S**, €-/59.50/119/178.50, incl DP, 3 Route d'Espalais, reservation@chateaudelastours.eu, 0581780001 or 0624242466, swimming pool, English spoken

♠ Le Clos d'Espalais **Pr** **Dr** **Br** **R** **W** **S**, €-/48/96/144, incl DP, 8 Route de Timbrune, verozun64@yahoo.fr, 0581519287, open Feb–Nov, swimming pool

Turn left through a roundabout on **D11**. Cross the **Garonne River**, then turn left (**0.6km**), passing the **Chapelle Sainte-Catherine-du-Port** (rebuilt in the 14th century by order of Pope Clément). Take a sharp left, going uphill, and then emerge at the Office de Tourisme on Rue du Couvent in

1.1KM AUVILLAR (ELEV 110M, POP 920) ⛺ ⊕ 🛏 ⊕ ❶ (308.6KM)
Market on Sunday mornings. Another of the 'most beautiful villages' in France, Auvillar has ancient origins. However, its most striking sights are of more recent vintage, with both the circular market hall (Halle aux Grains) and the clock

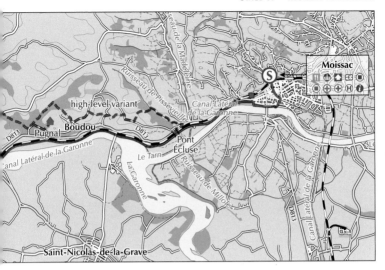

tower (Tour de l'Horloge) dating to the 16th century and distinguished by their mixture of brick and limestone. The Église Saint-Pierre, situated just outside the town walls, dates to the 12th century, although it has been extensively rebuilt. It features a highly regarded baroque altarpiece.

The promenade overlooks the Garonne River and is a lovely place to linger in the evening. While Auvillar is quite peaceful today, its history is even more troubled than that of many of its war-stricken peers; the town suffered from attacks in the 11th-century Norman invasion, the Albigensian Crusade, the Hundred Years' War, and the Wars of Religion.

⌂ Gîte Communal **O Do K R S**, 6/18, €15/-/-/-, ot-auvillar@cc-deuxrives.fr, 0563398982, check-in at tourism office

⌂ Gîte Le Baladin **Do Pr Dr K R**, 2/6, €16/45/60/80, DP22, 5 Place de la Halle, les-crapettes-dauvillar@wanadoo.fr, 0563397361, open Mar–Oct

⌂ Gîte Chez le Saint-Jacques **Do Pr Br K R W**, 4/8, €20/-/-/-, 14 Place de la Halle, gemijo@orange.fr, 0563291423, open Apr–Oct

⌂ Gîte Place du Château **Do Pr Br R W S**, 5/15, €26/36/52/-, auvillar.gite@gmail.com, 0604029836 or 066693074, open May–Oct

⌂ Hôtel de l'Horloge **O Pr Dr R Cr S**, €-/-/92/-, 2 Place de l'Horloge, restaurant@hoteldelhorlogeauvillar.com, 0563399161, breakfast €12

STAGE 18
Auvillar to Lectoure

Start	Office de Tourisme, Auvillar
Finish	Office de Tourisme, Lectoure
Distance	32.8km
Total ascent	590m
Total descent	535m
Difficulty	Easy-to-moderate
Time	8hr 15min
Percentage paved	46%
Gîtes	Saint-Antoine 8.4km, Flamarens 13km, Miradoux 17.1km, Castet-Arrouy 21.8km, Lectoure 32.8km

While this is a long stage, it benefits from an unusually large mix of towns and villages along the way. And those communities offer a similarly wide variety of appealing sights: regal châteaus, vibrant frescoes, skeletal ruins, fantastic beasts, and ancient remains. The *chemin* has overlapped with Roman history at many points already, but Lectoure marks the transition into some of the richest links to that past, beginning with the town's archaeological museum. And, if you are so inclined, Lectoure's municipal swimming pool is ideally situated on a terrace below the church, offering awe-inspiring views of the surrounding countryside.

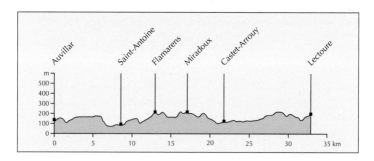

Proceed through the center on Rue des Nobles, forking right past the Halle Aux Grains, and then onto Rue de l'Horloge. Leaving the old town, continue straight on **D11**. Turn left on a minor road, then fork right onto a dirt track (**1km**). Turn left back onto **D11**

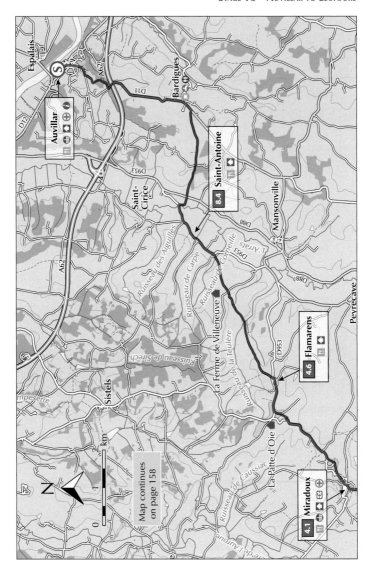

Map continues
on page 158

157

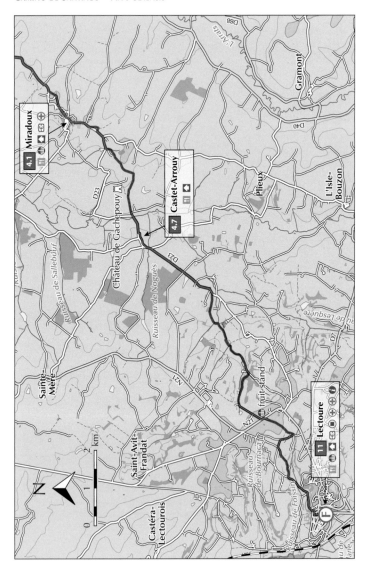

(**0.7km**). Skirt **Bardigues** (**2.3km**, fountain, WC, restaurant). Soon after, cross into the Gers department. Turn right off D11 (**0.4km**). At a T, proceed forward onto a footpath (**1.5km**). Rejoin pavement, cross **D88**, then turn left on **D953** (**1.3km**). Fork left on Rue des Pélerins (**1km**, fountain), then pass through the gate into

---

8.4KM SAINT-ANTOINE (ELEV 75M, POP 200) 🏠 📷 (300.2KM)

The village is linked to the Order of Saint Anthony, a congregation founded in 1095 to care for victims of 'St Anthony's Fire,' a medieval disease linked to leprosy. Members wore the Greek Tau letter as identification. In the 17th century, the French scientist Denis Dodart discovered the cause of the 'fire,' or ergotism, which involved the consumption of cereal products contaminated by the ergot fungus. While that discovery brought an end to the Antonine Order, it didn't eliminate ergotism altogether; indeed, a severe outbreak occurred in a French village in 1951.

The Église de Saint-Antoine has two 14th-century murals. One is devoted to St George and the Dragon, a famous dragon-slaying legend of pre-Christian origin that eventually was attributed to George. The other mural focuses on St Blaise, a bishop and doctor in fourth-century Armenia, known for helping patients with objects stuck in their throats (seriously). Over time, he became better known for his capacity to heal the soul, with many miracles attributed to him.

🛏 Gîte Le Figuier 🅾 Do Dr R W, 3/12, €16/-/-/-, DP19, 14 Chemin de Ronde, paysanmichele@yahoo.fr, 0641893764

🛏 La Maison du Bois 🅾 Pr Dr Br K R, €-/40/55/-, DP17, jonandpearl@hotmail. co.uk, 0562286815, no wifi

---

Leaving the old town, continue straight on **D953**. Fork right onto a dirt track (**0.7km**). Pass the turn-off for 🛏 🛏 La Ferme de Villeneuve Do Pr Dr Br R Gr W, 1/3, €42/65/99/148.50, incl DP, contact@la-ferme-de-villeneuve.fr, 0562282175 or 0610336799, open Apr–Jun and Sept–Oct, swimming pool (**1km**). Rejoin a paved road (**1.6km**). Turn right on **D953**, then left almost immediately after to enter

---

4.6KM FLAMARENS (ELEV 200M, POP 150) 🏠 📷 (295.6KM)

The impressive Château de Flamarens, built and then expanded between the 12th and 15th centuries, survived a rough 20th century that saw it neglected for four decades, during which it burned following a lightning strike. After significant restoration, though, some of its former glory has been regained. Meanwhile, the Église Saint-Saturnin is in even greater disrepair, only recently saved from collapse. Nonetheless, the ruins are evocative.

A tree-lined trail leads beyond Flamarens

🏠 Gîte Château de Flamarens **Do** **Pr** **Dr** **Br** **R** **S**, 2/11, €43/-/110/-, incl DP, a.gadel@orange.fr, 0620300352 or 0620444448, open May–Oct, no wifi

🏠 Gîte Les Artisans du Voyage **Do** **Pr** **Dr** **K** **R** **W** **S**, 1/4, €20/-/60/-, DP17, sandra.fillol@gmail.com, 0678935519, open Apr–Oct, camping €4/person

Continue through the village, rejoining **D953** soon after. Turn left on a minor paved road (**0.9km**). (Alternately, follow D953 for 0.2km to reach 🏠 Accueil Pèlerin La Patte d'Oie **O** **Do** **Dr** **Br** **R**, 1/5, €Donation, incl DP, 0562286113, no wifi.) Fork right on a dirt track, then turn left on a footpath parallel to D953. Fork left away from the highway, continuing straight on a dirt track, then merge back onto it (**2.7km**). Turn left at a T, remaining on D953, as you loop through the village. Pass the church and continue through

4.1KM MIRADOUX (ELEV 200M, POP 500) 🏨 ⊕ 🛏 🅒 ⊕ (291.5KM)
Market on Saturdays. The oldest bastide in Gers, founded in 1253. The 16th-century Église Saint-Orens-et-Saint-Louis was built from the old castle's remains and contains a modern statue of St James.

🏠 Gîte Bonte Divine **Do** **Pr** **Dr** **R** **W** **S**, 2/9, €16/22/40/-, DP20, 5 Rue Porte d'Uzan Nord, contact@bontedivine.net, 0620500970 or 0562683080, open Apr–Oct, camping €6/person, English spoken

🏠 Les Tournesols **Pr** **Dr** **Br** **R** **W**, €-/33/48/-, DP15, 4 Place de la Halle, josiane. wachill@wanadoo.fr, 0646248249 or 0562286853, open Apr–mid Nov, English spoken

🏠 Ailleurs **Pr** **Dr** **Br** **R** **W** **S**, €-/40/60/70, DP13, 12 Rue Major, chrystele. pommies@sfr.fr, 0572666287, open Apr–Oct, English spoken

Fork left and then turn right on a footpath (**0.8km**). Turn left on **D953**, then fork right onto a footpath parallel to **D23**. Turn left on a dirt track (**0.7km**). Note the ruins of the Château de Gachepouy to your right. Turn right at a T (**1.1km**), then continue straight onto **D23**, rejoining a footpath along it (**1.2km**). Turn left on a paved road through village outskirts (**0.6km**), then right soon after. Continue past the church in

---

4.7KM CASTET-ARROUY (ELEV 105M, POP 185) 🔲 🔼 (286.8KM)

The late-Gothic Église Sainte-Blandine is most notable for its choir murals, which is where you can find a fantastic bestiary.

🔺 Gîte Communal 🔲🔲 🔲 🔲 🔲, 4/20, €20/-/-/-, gitecomcastetarrouy0@orange. fr, 0684927396 or 0562292843, open Apr–Oct, English spoken

🔺 Albert Sala 🔲 🔲 🔲 🔲 🔲, €-/40/60/75, Place de l'Église, aumuseedalbert@ gmail.com, 0622184276 or 0562287397, English spoken, donkey parking, swimming pool

🔺 Chez Nat 🔲 🔲 🔲 🔲 🔲 🔲 🔲 🔲 🔲, 3/7, €22/30/52/72, DP16, 10 Rue des Glycines, nat.arnulf@orange.fr, 0622395407, kitchen and dorm beds available outside summer only

---

Continue straight on D23, then join a parallel footpath (**0.4km**). Cross D23, switching to a footpath on the other side. Cross again, then gradually veer away from D23, now on a dirt track (**2km**). An extended stretch on unpaved roads eventually leads over **N21** (**4.5km**, fruit stands in summer) and then back onto paved roads just outside of Lectoure (**3.2km**). Turn right at a roundabout. Turn left on Rue de la Barbacane and then take the next right (**0.6km**). Turn left on Rue Saint-Gervais and arrive at the cathedral and Office de Tourisme in

---

11KM LECTOURE (ELEV 165M, POP 3665) 🔲 ⊕ 🔼 🔲 ◉ ⊕ ⊕ ❶ (275.8KM)

Market on Friday mornings. Pilgrim welcome in the cathedral 4–6pm daily. The stunningly located public swimming pool, behind the cathedral, is open July/ August (€3.50). If you prefer your water hot, the ValVital thermal spa is open June–October and costs a bit more (€12) for access to its thermal swimming pool, sauna, and jacuzzi.

Built on a rocky outcropping, Lectoure has prehistoric origins, established as an oppidum (fortified settlement) in the Iron Age. Lectoure flourished under Roman rule; its Archaeological Museum (€3), located in the town hall's cellar, preserves some of the area's finest Roman remains, including mosaics, sarcophagi, and altar stones. Its collection of 20 taurobolic altars, devoted to bull sacrifices, is unique. The museum also details the stories of Lectoure's most famous residents, Boué de Lapeyrère (a WWI admiral) and Marechal Jean Lannes (one of Napoleon's most talented generals). The quality of Lectoure's fortifications – well tested over its many years – earned a callout from Victor Hugo in *The Hunchback of Notre-Dame*. The Lectoure-Nérac melon, first introduced to the region in 1950, is a refreshing summer treat.

The Cathédrale Saint-Gervais et Saint-Protais dates from 1488. The bell tower provides sweeping views, although it was once even taller, one of the tallest steeples in all of France. The cathedral preserves the relics of Saint-Clair-d'Aquitaine, Lectoure's first bishop, who was martyred along the town's ramparts. Behind the cathedral, the ramparts offer another compelling vantage point. Downhill, the Fontaine Diane ou Hountélie is a 13th-century fountain built upon Roman remains.

⬥ Presbytère de Lectoure `Do` `Pr` `Dr` `Br` `R` `S`, 2/10, €Donation, incl DP, 100 Rue Nationale, delor.v@gmail.com, 0649168584, open Easter–Sept, campers welcome

⬥ Gîte L'Etoile Occitane `Do` `Pr` `Br` `K` `R` `W` `S`, 2/14, €21/-/52/-, 140 Rue Nationale, isabelfournier@hotmail.fr, 0674451117, open mid Mar–Oct

⬥ Gîte Le Boudoir `Do` `Pr` `Dr` `K` `R` `W` `S`, 1/6, €18/44/56/-, DP25, 17 Rue du 14 Juillet, patricia.fourniat@gmail.com, 0675903281, open Mar–Oct, reservation required, breakfast included with rooms, English spoken

⬥ Gîte Le Pas Sage `Do` `Dr` `K` `R` `W`, 2/8, €16/-/-/-, DP14, 29 Rue des Frères Danzas, aurelienduc63@live.fr, 0762208983, open Apr–Oct, English spoken

⬥⬥ Gîte Le Résidence du Marquisat `O` `Do` `Pr` `Br` `K` `R` `W` `S`, 3/6, €31/45/62/-, 2 Chemin du Marquisat, contact@lemarquisat.com, 0562687127

⬥⬥ B&B A2 PAS `O` `Do` `Pr` `Br` `K` `R` `W` `S`, 1/4, €26/58/68/93, 56 Rue Nationale, contact@a2-pas.fr, 0670993779, English spoken

⬥ Hôtel de Bastard `Pr` `Dr` `Br` `R` `Cr` `W` `S`, €-/-/93/-, DP40, 2 Rue Lagrange, info-booking@hoteldebastard.com, 0562688244, closed Jan, swimming pool

STAGE 19
Lectoure to Condom

Start	Office de Tourisme, Lectoure
Finish	Cathédrale Saint-Pierre, Condom
Distance	32.1km
Total ascent	610m
Total descent	695m
Difficulty	Moderate
Time	8hr 30min
Percentage paved	48%
Gîtes	Espazot 4.4km, Marsolan 8.8km, La Romieu 18.6km, Gîte de Beausoleil 19.7+0.7km, Le Maçon 22+1km, Castelnau-sur-l'Auvignon 23.4km, Condom 32.1km

The GR65 rarely moves in a straight line, but this stage stands out for being particularly indirect. That trajectory is shaped entirely by the goal of incorporating La Romieu, a small town founded by a former pilgrim nearly a millennium ago. Its collegiate church is an artistic marvel, particularly its octagonal tower. Take time strolling the town's main street, watching carefully for the many cat sculptures perched upon windowsills. The day's destination, Condom, is a large town also worth exploring. This is the center of the armagnac industry, so anticipate good options for both the aperitif and digestif.

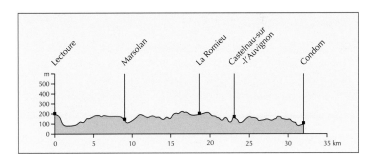

With the cathedral entrance at your back and the Office de Tourisme to your left, follow Rue Nationale. Turn right at the fountain, then left soon after. Arrive at Lectoure's western

163

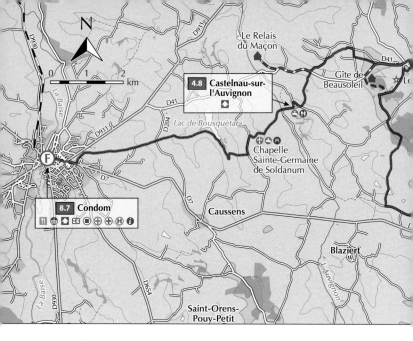

ramparts, descend the steps, then emerge from the northwest corner (**0.8km**). Make a sharp left, then right, then another left in quick succession, descending from the hill. Merge with another road and then turn right onto **D7**, crossing the Gers River (**0.7km**).

Make a sharp right on a dirt track, crossing the 18th-century **Pont-de-Pile** and the more recent **D36**, then fork left onto a paved road (**1.7km**). Curve left through a hamlet, then continue onto a dirt track. Turn left, then right, back onto pavement, passing ♠ Ferme d'Espazot (**Pr** **Dr** **K** **R** **S**, €-/-/40/-, DP25, peregrine32@orange.fr, 0637648980, open Easter–Oct) soon after (**1.2km**). Fork right on a dirt track (**2.6km**). Return once more to pavement, turning left onto it (**1.2km**). Fork left, then right, into

8.8KM MARSOLAN (ELEV 160M, POP 460) 🏠 (267KM)
The remains of the medieval Hôpital Saint-Jacques are at the town entrance.

♠ ♠ Gîte L'Enclos du Tabus **Do** **Pr** **Dr** **Br** **K** **R** **W** **S**, 5/15, €36/60/97/135, incl DP, mussetrichard@gmail.com, 0562687940, open mid Apr–June and Sept–Oct, bed-and-breakfast only €20

♠ Chemin de Tables **Pr** **Dr** **Br** **R** **Cr**, €-/-/99/-, incl DP, chemindetables@gmail.com, 0972507066, open Apr–Oct

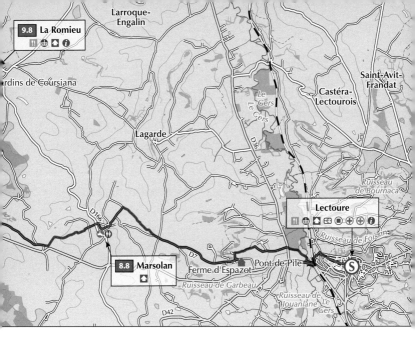

Loop downhill around the church, descend Marsolan's main street (WC on left), then fork left. Cross **D166** and continue forward (**0.5km**). Few notable landmarks exist on this next stretch, leading into gently undulating countryside. After starting on pavement, the bulk of what follows is on dirt tracks (**6.9km**). Turn right back onto pavement for the final approach to La Romieu, then left soon after. Pass **Les Jardins de Coursiana** (**1.5km**). This six-hectare botanical garden has 350 different varieties of roses. Turn right on a footpath, skirting around a small park (**0.4km**), then fork right around La Romieu's historic center. Finally, turn left into

9.8KM LA ROMIEU (ELEV 185M, POP 575) 🍴 ⊕ ⛺ ❶ (257.2KM)

WC and fountain in center. The town's name comes from medieval pilgrims (*romieux*), and specifically links to Albert, a German pilgrim, who is believed to have founded a Benedictine priory here in 1082. The 14th century brought the Collégiale Saint-Pierre, built by Arnaud d'Aux with support of Clement V, one of the Avignon popes. Unfortunately, the town suffered significantly in the Wars of Religion and Revolution, with much of the complex, including the priory church, destroyed by 1804. As a silver lining, the collegiate church survives, along with parts of the cloisters (€5). Two towers flank the church; the octagonal tower housing the sacristy is a highlight, with walls covered in tempera paintings. On the ceiling, between the ribbed vaulting, 16 angel musicians are depicted. The walls feature family and biblical figures, as well as decorative motifs. The bell tower contains one of Gers' oldest bells (1450). The Gothic cloisters still stand, although they were heavily damaged in a 1569 fire.

In 1342, multiple years of bad harvests culminated in famine and despair. Villagers ate whatever they could, including household pets. Legend holds that a local orphan, Angeline, hid a male and female cat in the attic of her home. Soon, every other pet in the village had been killed. The next year, the harvest was bountiful, but the crops were quickly threatened by rodents, loving life in a feline-free town. Angeline offered to give her cats to the village for protection, on the condition that townspeople promised never to harm a pet again. Her cats killed all the rodents and saved the crops. In the 1960s, a local sculptor who grew up with this story carved stone cats, still perched on buildings across town (hence, La Ro-meow!).

● Gîte Le Refuge du Pèlerin O Do K R W Z, 1/6, €15/-/-/-, Rue du Docteur Lucante, laurent.foltran@wanadoo.fr, 0643128101, breakfast €5

● Le Couvent de La Romieu Pt Br K R W Z, €-/35/54/-, leveupas@orange.fr, 0688473617, open Apr–Oct

● Maison d'Artiste O Pt Br K R S, €-/30/44/-, Blvd Quintilla, christineboisson0908@orange.fr, 0562282322

● L'Etape d'Angéline O Pt Dr Br R Cf, €-/52/68/81, etapeangeline@orange.fr, 0562281029, English spoken

▲ Le Camp de Florence Pt Dr R W, €-/65/117/157.50, DP26, info@lecampdeflorence.com, 0562281558, open May–Sept, camping €9/tent, swimming pool

Turn right out the back corner of Place Bouet, pass out of the historic center, and turn left onto **D41**. Initially, make do with the road's minimal shoulder, but once outside of town join a footpath alongside it. Turn right on a footpath (**1.1km**). (Alternately, remain on D41 and continue 0.7km to reach ● Gîte de Beausoleil O Do Pt K R W Z, 3/15, €20/44/68/-, iocoupey@club-internet.fr, 0671585021, breakfast €6, no wifi.) Turn right at a T on a paved road (**0.6km**). Turn left and then join a footpath (**0.5km**). Turn left at a T on pavement (**0.6km**). Turn left on **D41**, then right soon after on a dirt track (**0.6km**). (Or turn right on D41 and continue 1km to reach ● ● Le Relais du Maçon Do Pt Dr Br K R W, 5/14, €23/-/46/69, DP10, n.pillon80@laposte.net, 0616938470, open Mar–Nov, donkey parking, swimming pool.) Turn right onto a paved road (**1.1km**) and proceed into

4.8KM CASTELNAU-SUR-L'AUVIGNON (ELEV 165M, POP 145) 🛏 (252.4KM)
Fountain and WC near entrance. Castelnau was a hotbed of anti-Nazi resistance
in 1942, with George Reginald Starr, of the British Special Operation Executive,
establishing a base of operations here. Starr fled the continent in the Dunkirk
evacuation, but returned in 1942, before occupied rule was established in Vichy
France. Another acclaimed resistance fighter, Jeanne Robert, took up residence
here after fleeing the Gestapo, but was forced to escape once again after being
betrayed. Robert, a schoolteacher, would live to see Castelnau's school named
in her honor. That was much later, though; in the short term, the town suffered
greatly, being burned to the ground by Nazi forces.

🛏 Gîte Les Arroucasses 🅓🅞 🅟🅯 🅓🅯 🅑🅯 🅡 🅦 🅢, 3/9, €37/-/100/-, incl DP,
  jeaninne32@hotmail.fr, 0770039593, open Apr–Oct, camping €5/person,
  swimming pool

Turn left after the church onto a dirt track, descending quickly from the village.
Turn right (**1.4km**), passing **Chapelle Sainte-Germaine de Soldanum** (fountain). The
chapel is all that remains of a former monastery, destroyed by Normans in the ninth
century. Turn left through a small cluster of houses on a paved road, then right onto
a dirt track (**1km**). Turn left again, then make a hairpin turn to the right, alongside **Lac
de Bousquètara** (**0.7km**). Fork left away from the lake on a paved road (**0.8km**). Cross
D204, then fork right (**2.4km**). Continue straight on a dirt track, then fork left (**1.4km**).
Turn right on **D7** and cross the Ruisseau La Gèle, then turn left on **D931** (**0.7km**). Take
the next right on Rue Gambetta and proceed directly to the cathedral in

8.7KM CONDOM (ELEV 80M, POP 6530) 🏨 ⊜ 🛏 € ⊙ ⊕ ⊕ ❶ (243.7KM)
Markets on Wednesday and Sunday. Mass and pilgrim blessing in the cathedral
on Mon/Tue/Wed/Fri at 6pm. CAMINOLOC, the pilgrim-focused gear shop, also
has a location here (1 Place Souvenir, 0695338531).
    Situated on a spur between the Géle and Baïse Rivers, the town's notable
name comes from the Gallic *condate-o-magos*, which means 'market of the confluence.' Condom is the center of the Armagnac industry. Armagnac is the oldest
French brandy, distilled from white wine grapes and aged in black oak casks. A
14th-century cardinal claimed that it had 40 virtues. Try to identify them all at
Musée de l'Armagnac, or perhaps at a town café.
    The 16th-century **Cathédrale Saint-Pierre** was previously the site of a
Benedictine abbey. It exemplifies the southern approach to the flamboyant
Gothic, with its interior noted for complex vaulting and large gallery windows.
A few of the stained-glass windows are original, although most were replaced
in the 19th century. In 1569, during the Wars of Religion, the Huguenot army

threatened to demolish the cathedral, but Condom's citizens averted this by paying an enormous ransom: 30,000 francs.

Condom's most popular photo opp, other than the town sign, is the statue of d'Artagnan and his Three Musketeers outside the cathedral. Born as Charles de Batz de Castelmore in a nearby village in 1611, he later inherited his more notable title, the Count of Artagnan, before enlisting in the Musketeers of the Guard, a military company of the French royal household. Alexandre Dumas's novel, published in 1844, cemented his historic immortality.

The Three Musketeers and d'Artagnan circle together just outside Condom's cathedral

⌂ Gîte L'Ancien Carmel **Pr Dr Br R W S Z**, €-/25/50/-, DP12, 35 Ave Victor Hugo, accueilcarmel@gmail.com, 0562294156, open Apr–Oct

⌂ Le Champ d'Étoiles **O Do Pr Dr Br R W S**, 3/14, €17/-/49/-, DP17, 18 Ave Joffre, lechampdetoiles@gmail.com, 0608052684 or 0760557829, camping €7/person, English spoken

⌂ Gîte La Halte du Kiosque **Do Pr Dr Br R W**, 3/10, €35/-/82/105, incl DP, 2 Square Salvandy, contact@lahaltedukiosque.fr, 0684323001, open Apr–Oct, bed only €19, English spoken

⌂ Gîte Le Relais St Jacques **O Do Pr Dr Br K R W S**, 1/4, €20/45/60/90, DP15, 2 Ave du Maréchal Joffre, laurent_crassous@orange.fr, 0613285266 or 0621784786

⌂ Gîte de Gabarre **Do Dr K R W S Z**, 2/40, €17/-/-/-, DP20, 42 bis Ave des Mousquetaires, contact@gitedegabarre.com, 0686415839, open mid Apr–Oct

⌂ ⌂ Gîte Au Plaisir d'Etape **Do Pr Dr R W S**, 3/10, €20/-/90/120, DP20, 37 Blvd Clemenceau, contact@auplaisirdetape.fr, 0642318417, open mid Mar–Oct, breakfast included with private room, swimming pool

⌂ Les Trois Lys **O Pr R Cr S**, €-/61/82/150, 38 Rue Gambetta, info@lestroislys.com, 0562283333, breakfast €10, swimming pool

Condom's Cathédrale Saint-Pierre is a Gothic feast for the eyes

Condom

- 🏛 Cathédrale Saint-Pierre
- 🏠 1 Gîte L'Ancien Carmel
- 🏠 2 Le Champ d'Étoiles
- 🏠 3 Gîte La Halte du Kiosque
- 🏠 4 Gîte Le Relais St. Jacques
- 🏠 5 Gîte de Gabarre
- 🏠 6 Gîte Au Plaisir d'Etape
- 🏠 7 Les Trois Lys
- ① Musée de l'Armagnac

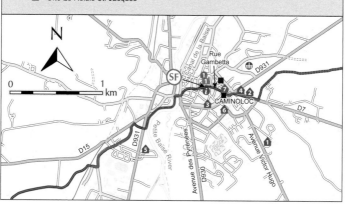

STAGE 20
Condom to Éauze

Start	Cathédrale Saint-Pierre, Condom
Finish	Cathédrale Saint-Luperc, Éauze
Distance	33.8km (35.6km via Seviac)
Total ascent	460m
Total descent	390m
Difficulty	Easy
Time	7hr 30min
Percentage paved	44%
Gîtes	Larressingle 5.3+1km, Montréal-du-Gers 16.3km, Lamothe 25.8km, Éauze 33.8km

While Lectoure marked the transition into Rome country, this stage immerses you in the heart of it. After Montréal-du-Gers, a detour makes it possible to visit a well-preserved Roman villa at Séviac. Meanwhile, just outside of Éauze the old Gallo-Romanic capital of Elusa has also been excavated; within the town center is an archaeological museum featuring an extensive collection of Roman coins. Séviac isn't the only detour to consider on this lengthy stage, as another short variant swings northward to Larressingle, perhaps the most adorable fortified village you'll ever see. To take everything in, you may need to split this stage in two, with an overnight in beautiful Montréal.

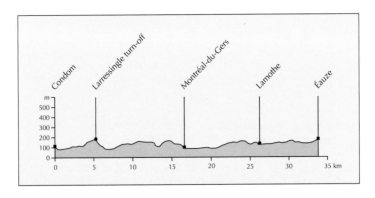

Watch for circular, bronze waymarks in the road through Condom's center. With the cathedral's entrance at your back, fork right on Rue Charron. Fork right on Rue des Armuriers, then left on Rue Roques. Turn right to cross the Petite Baïse River, then left onto a riverside walkway (**0.4km**). Curve right, cross **D931**, and join a dirt track (**0.5km**). Turn left on a paved road, right at a roundabout, then carry on through Condom's outskirts. Turn left onto a dirt track (**3.4km**), then transition back onto pavement soon after (**0.6km**). When that road curves right, continue straight on a dirt track past the

---

5.3KM LARRESSINGLE TURN-OFF (ELEV 130M, POP 200) 🏢 🛏 ❶ (238.4KM)
You can reach Larressingle, France's smallest fortified village, by following the paved road to the right for 1km. The medieval fortress of Condom's bishops is one of the few Gascon villages whose walls have survived. From the walled village and cemetery, follow D507 1.4km to return to the GR65. This adds 1.2km to the stage.

⌂ La Halte de Larressingle ⬛Do⬛ ⬛Pr⬛ ⬛Dr⬛ ⬛Br⬛ ⬛R⬛ ⬛W⬛ ⬛S⬛ ⬛Z⬛, 1/5, €38/54/86/-, incl DP, lahaltedelarressingle@gmail.com, 0766851675, open mid Apr–mid Oct, camping €6/person, English spoken

⌂ Accueil à la Ferme de Tollet ⬛O⬛ ⬛Do⬛ ⬛Pr⬛ ⬛Dr⬛ ⬛K⬛ ⬛R⬛ ⬛W⬛, 6/12, €20/-/40/-, DP16, ferme.tollet@gmail.com, 0562280245

If not visiting Larressingle, continue forward on the dirt track, cross **D278** and join a paved road, as the detour returns from the right (**1.2km**). Cross the **Pont d'Artigues** soon after. This was originally a five-arched Roman bridge, with an adjacent pilgrim hospital in the Middle Ages. Turn right and then left onto a dirt track (**1km**). Turn right to rejoin a paved road, then turn left at a T (**2.5km**). To the right, 0.1km off-route, is the **Église de Routges** (fountain), the oldest church in the region.

Note the small side-door, which would have been the entrance for **Cagots**. Known historically as Europe's 'untouchables,' this was a persecuted minority group that was forced to live on town outskirts and severely restricted in their professional pursuits. They could receive the Eucharist, but only at the end of a very long spoon. The historical record is unclear about this discrimination; while Cagots were often scorned as lepers, heretics, cannibals, and evil, there is no definitive answer to the animus's roots.

Merge onto **D254**, then fork right off it (**0.9km**). Pass ⌂ ⌂ Agapè du Gers ⬛Do⬛ ⬛Pr⬛ ⬛Dr⬛ ⬛K⬛ ⬛R⬛ ⬛Gr⬛ ⬛W⬛ ⬛S⬛, 2/8, €18/-/70/-, DP20, agape.du.gers@gmail.com, 0622786880, open Apr–Oct, camping €10/person, English spoken (**1.2km**). Fork left onto a dirt track. Briefly rejoin a paved road, then fork left back onto a dirt track (**2km**). Turn left and transition back onto pavement, moving into Montréal's outskirts (**0.8km**). Merge onto

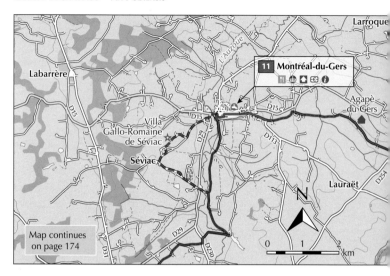

D113, then turn left on **D15** (**0.6km**). Fork right on D113 towards Montréal-Centre. Turn left into Place Centrale in

11KM MONTRÉAL-DU-GERS (ELEV 120M, POP 1170) 🏠⊕🏠🄲ⓘ (227.4KM)
Fountain in Place Centrale. Market on Friday mornings.

A 13th-century bastide, built upon the remains of an Iron Age settlement, and featuring a lovely arcaded central plaza. Montréal was a Catholic stronghold in the Wars of Religion but suffered terribly consequently; it was razed to the ground by Protestant forces in 1565. The fortified, 13th-century Collégiale Saint-Philippe-et-Saint-Jacques has an impressive Gothic portal.

⌂ **Gîte La Halte du Rempart** Do Dr K R S, 1/10, €16/-/-/-, DP16, 11 Place de l'Hôtel de Ville, lahalteudurempart@hotmail.fr, 0615153438, open Apr–mid Oct

⌂ **Gîte Compostela** Do Pr Dr R W S, 2/13, €17/-/78/-, DP18, 10 Rue du 14 Juillet, anitadann@hotmail.com, 0562286736, open 20 Mar–10 Oct, DP included with private room, English spoken

⌂ **Gîte Napoléon** Do Pr Dr K R W S Z, 2/12, €19/-/110/-, DP29, Blvd des Pyrénées, armagnac.zago@gmail.com, 0632155928, open Apr–Oct, washing machine included, no wifi

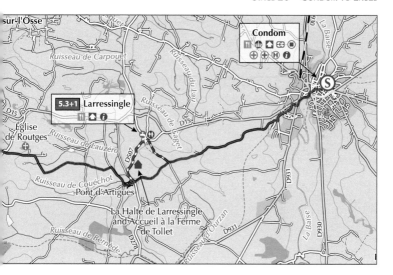

🏕️ ⛺ Le Couloumé **Pr** **Dr** **R** **W** **S**, €-/-/65/-, DP28, lecouloume@orange.fr, 0685355126, open Mar–Oct, camping €10/tent, swimming pool

🏕️ Carpe Diem **Pr** **Dr** **Br** **R** **W** **S**, €-/55/75/95, DP20, Quartier Bitalis, mimibertin@wanadoo.fr, 0688495719, open mid Mar–Nov, English spoken

With the Office de Tourisme on your left, continue through Place Centrale, passing to the right of the church. Turn right on Boulevard des Pyrénées. Fork right, looping around the historic center (**0.3km**). The detour to Séviac is worth considering at this point; otherwise, to stay on the GR65 direct to Lamothe, make a sharp left, descending from town. Turn right on **D15**, then make another sharp left. Continue straight on a dirt track (**1.1km**), then turn left at a T back onto pavement (**1.2km**). The Séviac variant rejoins from the right here.

Optional detour to Séviac (4.1km)
Instead of following the waymarks left, descend the steps from Montréal, merge with **D29**, then fork right to remain on D29. Turn left, again sticking with D29 (**0.2km**). Take the next right, then fork right soon after. Turn right (**1km**) at the sign for Séviac. Arrive at the **Villa Gallo-Romaine de Séviac** (**0.4km**), which features a sparkling new visitor center (€5).

A classic example of a **Roman country villa**, dating from the second to seventh centuries, Séviac features multiple rooms radiating out from a square courtyard, lined with marble columns. There are more than 450m square meters of preserved mosaics.

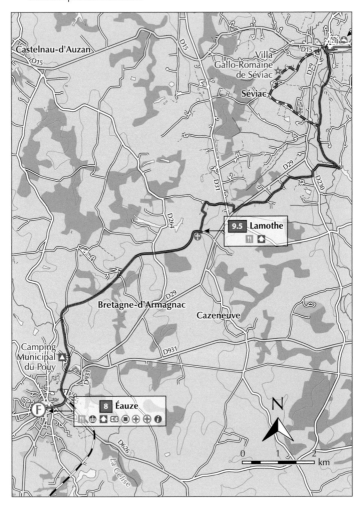

To rejoin the GR65, continue straight along a dirt road, forking left on a smaller track. Turn left in the middle of **Séviac village** (**0.4km**). Turn right at a T on a paved road. Turn left at the next T, then fork left (**0.7km**). Cross **D29** (**1.1km**), then rejoin the official route as the road curves right (**0.3km**).

Routes reunited, fork right, then continue straight on a dirt track. Pass under a road, then loop back around to the left to join it (**1.4km**). Turn left on **D230**, then turn right off it (**1km**). Wind along a series of tracks through vineyards, crossing (and briefly joining) **D29** (**2.3km**) and **D31** (**0.7km**), and finally making a sharp right into

9.5KM LAMOTHE (ELEV 150M, POP 80) ⏚ 🏕 (217.9KM)
Le Mille Bournes offers a snack bar, just before the church.

⌂ Gîte Le Mille Bornes ☒☒☒☒☒☒☒☒, 3/11, €16/-/-/-, DP21, gitemillebornes@gmail.com, 0650621346, open Apr–Nov, camping €5/ person

Make a sharp right, pass the Église à Lamothe, and continue onto a dirt track. Cross **D264** (**1.7km**) and follow a converted rail trail – paved initially, but later becoming a dirt track – through wooded terrain (**5.3km**). Emerge on a paved road, then turn right on **D931** (**0.3km**). Continue straight on Rue Saint-July, arriving at the cathedral in

8KM ÉAUZE (ELEV 155M, POP 3920) ⏚ 🖀 🏕 🅲 ◉ ⊕ ⊕ ❶ (209.9KM)
Market on Thursday mornings. A former Gallo-Roman capital (Elusa), that was conquered by Crassus on behalf of Julius Caesar in 56BC. The town's Musée Archéologique (€5) was founded near the site of a major Roman discovery and features more than 28,000 Roman coins, along with an extensive collection of ancient tools. The actual historic site of Elusa has been excavated and can be visited (€5), although it's a kilometer east of the center. Éauze's central Place d'Armagnac is lovely, filled with medieval, half-timbered houses. The Cathédrale Saint-Luperc stands on the north end. Built in the late 15th century in the Gothic style, it was significantly restored in the 19th century.

⌂ Gîte Communal ☒☒☒☒☒☒, 3/15, €11/-/-/-, DP29, Rue Leyral, qualite@ grand-armagnac.com, 0562098562, open Apr–Oct, check-in at tourism office, no wifi

⌂ ⌂ Gîte En Chemin ☒☒☒☒☒☒☒, 2/9, €18/-/50/96, DP22, 15 Allée du Fossé Neuf, gite.enchemin@gmail.com, 0663082191, open Apr–Oct, DP included with private rooms

🏠🏠 Gîte Chez Nadine ⓄⒹⓄⒻⒻⒹⒻⒷⒻⓇⓌⓈ, 5/11, €43/58/86/-, incl DP, 43-45 Ave de Sauboires, francis.corlaiti@orange.fr, 0562081837, donkey parking

🏠 Gîte l'Estanquet ⓄⒹⓄⒻⒻⒹⒻⓀⓇⓌ, 3/7, €12/17/30/-, DP13, 28 Ave des Fleurs, jeanpierred@ntymail.com, 0635192583, camping €8/person

🏠 La Grange de Marie-France ⓄⒻⒻⒹⒻⓀⓇⓌⓈⓏ, €-/-/40/-, DP20, 4 Ave de la Ténarèze, lagrangedemariefrance@gmail.com, 0661244804, reservation required in offseason

🏠 Au Posse Pèlerins La Grange ⓄⒻⒻⒹⒻⓀⓇⓌⓈⓏ, €-/40/60/-, DP20, 3 Blvd St Blancat, lagrangedemariefrance@gmail.com, 0661244804, reservation required in offseason, check-in at La Grange de Marie-France, English spoken

🔺 Camping Municipal du Pouy ⓄⒹⒻⓇⒼⒻⓌ aumoulindupouy@gmail.com, 0950757658, camping €6/person, swimming pool

A magnificent half-timbered building in the center of Éauze

STAGE 21
Éauze to Nogaro

Start	Cathédrale Saint-Luperc, Éauze
Finish	Collégiale Saint-Nicolas, Nogaro
Distance	21km
Total ascent	250m
Total descent	300m
Difficulty	Easy
Time	4hr 45min
Percentage paved	49%
Gîtes	La Hargue 7.2+0.5km, Manciet 11km, Relais du Haget 14.6+0.3km, Domaine de la Source 17.2+0.7km, Nogaro 21km

After a series of long stages, today's route offers a relaxing stroll through predominantly flat terrain. Manciet serves as a handy place for a snack, near the walk's midpoint, while the Église-Hôpital Sainte-Christie is a tranquil spot for rest and quiet reflection. What Nogaro might lack in atmosphere is offset by convenience, with all the facilities you might need situated in relatively close proximity – aside, perhaps, from the Gîte Communal, which is situated 800 meters outside the center.

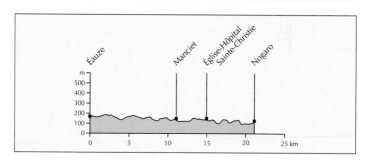

With your back to the cathedral, fork right on Rue Robert Daury. Cross D626 and continue forward on **D931**. Turn right, then left at a T (**0.9km**). Transition onto a dirt track, cross **N524**, then turn left on a paved road (**1.6km**). This becomes a dirt track, then dwindles to a footpath (**1.2km**). Turn left at a T onto a dirt track, then right on a paved

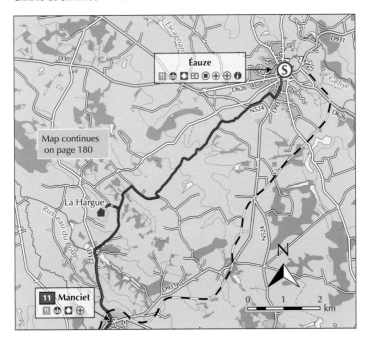

road soon after (**2km**). Turn left on a dirt track, then pass the turn-off for ⛺ ⛺ La Hargue Do Pr Dr R W, 1/4, €19/31/50/63, DP22, eric.texier0449@orange.fr, 0562085005 or 0665545589, open Mar–Nov, closed first half of Aug, swimming pool, English spoken (**1.5km**). Transition back to pavement (**1.1km**). Turn left on **D122** (**0.5km**). Fork right at the entrance to Manciet, passing a bull ring (**2km**). Turn right on a minor road parallel to **D931**, left on the highway overpass, and then right on Rue Centrale in

11KM MANCIET (ELEV 135M, POP 805) 🍴 ⛪ 🏠 ✚ **(198.9KM)**
An important stop on the Compostelle pilgrimage, due to its bridge over the Douze River, free of tolls for pilgrims. The Église Notre-Dame-de-la-Pitié, like others in the area, was forcibly converted to Protestantism in the Wars of Religion, before returning to Catholicism in 1685. Extensive restoration work followed. Note the rural bull ring at the town entrance. The bullfighting tradition here is called the Course Landais, a bloodless competition that uses 'athletic cows' (not an oxymoron), as opposed to bulls.

Manciet's bull ring

🏠 Gîte Le Chemin Enchantant **Do** **Pr** **Dr** **R**, 3/7, €18/-/36/-, DP22, lecheminenchantant@gmail.com, 0668877824, open Apr–mid Nov

🔺 Camping Sur le Chemin d'Escoubes **O** **Pr** **K** **R** **Gt** **W** **S**, €-/-/50/-, sas. hies32@gmail.com, 0638176081, camping €10/person, swimming pool

Leaving town, continue straight on **D931**. Turn left on **D153** (**0.9km**). Fork right on a footpath (**0.9km**). Curve right, emerging parallel to a paved road, then turn left away from it (**1km**). The trail then zigzags through fields, passes the turn-off for 🏠 🏠 Relais du Haget (**Do** **Pr** **Dr** **K** **R** **W** **S**, 2/8, €15/-/64/-, DP22, stephanie.brud@ wanadoo.fr, 0611661398, open Apr–Oct, camping €8/person, breakfast included with private rooms, no wifi), and forks left past **Église-Hôpital Sainte-Christie** (**1.1km**, fountain). This formerly belonged to the Knights of Malta. Curve left on a footpath parallel to **D522** (**0.5km**), then veer south of D522 on a series of unpaved tracks. Pass the turn-off for 🏠 🏠 Domaine de la Source (**O** **Do** **Pr** **Dr** **K** **R** **W**, 2/10, €15/25/50/-, DP20, domainedelasourcegers@gmail.com, 0610783522) (**1.6km**). Turn right on a paved road (**0.6km**). Turn left, then fork right back onto a dirt track (**1.5km**). Turn left on a paved road, then left again onto **D522** (**0.6km**). To reach Nogaro's Gîte Communal, turn right on D931 (0.7km); the gîte is just after the ALDI on the left. To continue into Nogaro, proceed ahead on **D931**. Cross D147 and continue straight into the center. Finally, arrive at the church in

10KM NOGARO (ELEV 105M, POP 2010) 🏨 ⊕ 🔼 🄲 ⊛ ⊕ ⊕ ❶ (188.9KM)
Markets on Wednesdays and Saturdays. WC behind church.

The town's name comes from the Latin for 'place of walnut trees,' although the current incarnation dates to the 11th century, when it was founded by the Archbishop of Auch. In 1660, Louis XIV stayed here, en route to his wedding, accompanied by d'Artagnan and his Musketeers. Today it has a thriving flying club, the Aéro Club du Bas Armagnac. Its 11th-century Collégiale Saint-Nicolas, one of the region's oldest fortified churches, features one of the earliest representations of pilgrims in a fresco, telling the story of St Laurent's martyrdom.

⌂ Gîte Communal 𝐃𝐨 𝐏𝐫 𝐊 𝐑 𝐖 𝐒 𝐙, 1/10, €12.50/20/31/-, 18 Ave des Sports, bac.gite.nogaro@gmail.com, 0562690615 or 0631593472, open mid Apr–Oct, camping €8.50/person, breakfast €3.50

⌂ Gîte du Pied Levé 𝐃𝐨 𝐏𝐫 𝐊 𝐑 𝐖 𝐒, 3/9, €15/-/40/-, 7 Ave de Daniate, gitedupiedleve@gmail.com, 0671237326, open mid Mar–Nov, camping €6/person, breakfast €5

⌂ Manuel Acacio 𝐎 𝐏𝐫 𝐑 𝐒, €-/32/60/90, 12 Rue Nationale, acacio.manuel@wanadoo.fr, 0682246735

⌂ Hôtel Le Commerce 𝐎 𝐏𝐫 𝐃𝐫 𝐑 𝐆𝐫, €-/61/71/-, DP24, 2 Place des Cordeliers, info@hotelrestaurantnogaro.com, 0562090095

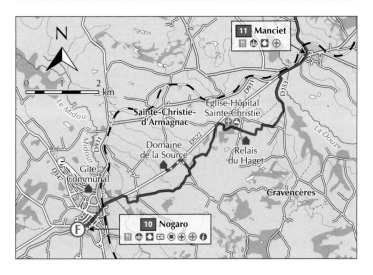

STAGE 22

Nogaro to Aire-sur-l'Adour

Start	Collégiale Saint-Nicolas, Nogaro
Finish	Cathédrale Saint-Jean-Baptiste, Aire-sur-l'Adour
Distance	27.6km
Total ascent	230m
Total descent	255m
Difficulty	Easy
Time	6hr 15min
Percentage paved	52%
Gîtes	Lanne-Soubiran 8.1km, Lelin-Lapujolle 15.4km, Arblade-le-Bas 12.9+4km, Barcelonne-du-Gers 25km, Aire-sur-l'Adour 27.6km

While longer, this stage is every bit as easy as yesterday's, at least physically. From a mental perspective, it can be challenging, with few landmarks to interrupt the extensive agricultural fields, and even fewer facilities. The lone hope for food before Barcelonne comes in Lelin-Japujolle, more than 15km into the stage, and if you're relying on that it's worth confirming the café's availability. Regardless, leave Nogaro well supplied. Aire-sur-l'Adour has a vibrant center and two impressive and moving churches. Be sure to visit Église de Saint-Quitterie, a long-time pilgrimage destination.

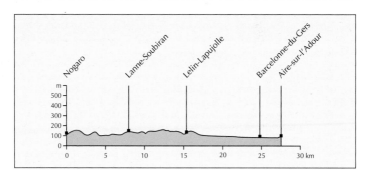

Fork right off Rue Nationale, shortly after the Collégiale, onto **D143**. Fork left, then right onto a dirt track (**1.1km**). Turn left at a T (**1.6km**) and then right on a paved road

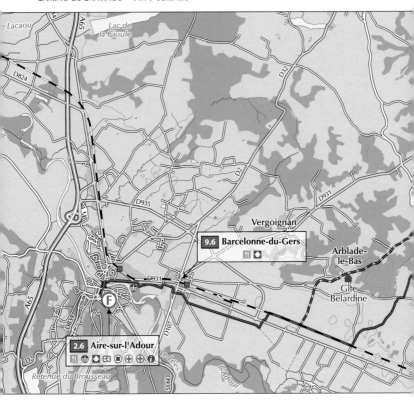

(**1km**). Turn left, then right on **D931** (**1.4km**). Join a footpath alongside the road, cross through a roundabout, then turn left on a dirt track (**0.8km**). Continue forward on a paved road into **Lanne-Soubiran**, passing ⬥ Gîte L'Âne Soubiran (O Do Pr Dr K R W S, 2/14, €16/-/50/-, DP21, l.ane.soubiran@gmail.com, 0666294455, camping €8/person) and its pilgrim rest area, then turn right on D152 (**2.2km**). The Église Lanne-Soubiran (fountain) and ⬥ Gîte La Presbytère (Do Pr Dr R W S, 3/12, €15/-/50/-, DP21, marinette.piret@gmail.com, 0643349945, open Apr–Oct, camping €5/person) are on the right. Turn left (**0.3km**).

A lengthy sequence follows through countryside with few landmarks (**4.5km**). Turn left at a T, or right to follow a detour to **Arblade-le-Bas** (**0.2km**, ⬥⬥ Gîte Belardine O Do Pr Dr Br K R W S, 2/8, €18/-/52/67, DP13, contact@belardine.fr, 0789573330). Finally, turn right on a paved road and proceed into

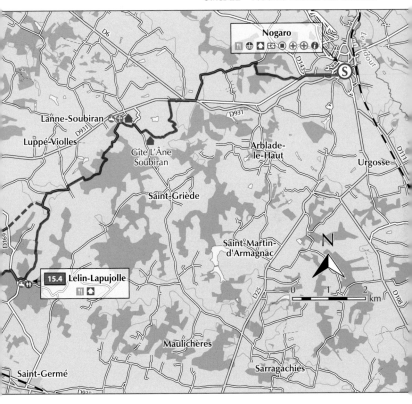

15.4KM LELIN-LAPUJOLLE (ELEV 140M, POP 280) (173.5KM)
Fountain and WC by church.

▲ Gîte La Grange à Dubarry 🔵 🔵 🔵 🔴 🔴 🔴 🔴 🔵 🔵, 3/12, €17/-/-/-, DP19,
lagrangeadubarry@gmail.com, 0627358413, camping €8/person, reservation
required in offseason

▲ Camping La Solanilla 🔵 🔵 🔵 🔴 🔴 🔴 🔵 🔵, €-/-/80/105, info@
campinglasolanilla.com, 0562696409, mobile homes, camping €13/tent,
breakfast €5, restaurant

Turn right on **D169**, then take the next two lefts. Turn right at a T (**1.5km**). Turn right alongside the railroad (**2km**), then cross **D935** (**2.8km**). Turn right on a dirt track, then right again at a T (**2.3km**). Fork left on **D107**, then continue straight as D107 curves left (**0.5km**). Take the next right, then turn left on Rue de l'Hôpital in

9.6KM BARCELONNE-DU-GERS (ELEV 80M, POP 1370) 🍴 🏠 (163.9KM)

Market on Sunday. Founded in 1118 by the Templars as a pilgrim hospital, the town didn't emerge until two centuries later, in 1316, when Philip the Fair ordered its construction, complete with a grid plan and city walls. In 1814, the Duke of Wellington attacked Napoleon's base here and took control. It suffered greatly in the world wars; in one notable event, 12 residents were killed for resisting Nazi rule on 13 June 1944.

🔺 Gîte L'Hospitalet du Cosset 🅾 🅳🅾 🅿🅁 🅳🆁 🅺 🆁 🆆 🆂, 4/12, €17/-/34/-, DP17, 11 Place de la Garlande, info@bastideducosset.com, 0633805095

Between Barcelonne and Aire-sur-l'Adour, you move into the Landes département in the Nouvelle-Aquitaine region. Just after merging with **D931**, turn left on Chemin de Beret. Turn right on Chemin des Moncaux, sticking with the road as it curves right (**1.1km**). Turn left on **D931**. Fork left towards the grassy riverbank, then ascend the Adour Bridge (**1km**). Cross the Adour River, then fork right into the center on Rue Carnot (**0.3km**). Turn left on Rue Duprat, breaking with the GR65 waymarks, and proceed to the cathedral in

2.6KM AIRE-SUR-L'ADOUR (ELEV 80M, POP 6130) 🍴 ⊕ 🏠 🅲 🅾 ⊕ ⊕ 🅸 (161.3KM)

Market on Saturdays. In 56BC, this was the site of a battle in the Gallic Wars, in which Rome's forces, led by Publius Licinius Crassus, the son of his fellow triumvar, the banker Marcus Licinius Crassus, enjoyed a clear victory. Afterward, the town was restructured under Roman rule and named Vicus-Julii ('Village of Julius'). In the fifth century, Aire became the residence of Visigothic kings; King Alaric II passed the Breviary of Alaric here, which served as the prevailing legal code until the 11th century.

Aire has two major religious buildings. The Cathédrale St-Jean-Baptiste reflects the town's history as the bishopric's seat for 1500 years. While founded in the 12th century, it was destroyed twice, and then fully rebuilt in the 19th century. Its organ is a historic monument. The 14th-century chapter house has recently been converted into a treasury. Meanwhile, the Gothic Église de Saint-Quitterie is a UNESCO World Heritage site. It was built near the location where the virgin martyr Quiteria, having failed to escape her father and his demands

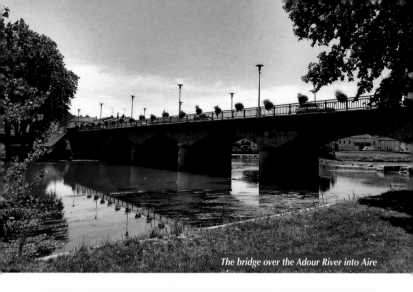
The bridge over the Adour River into Aire

that she renounce her faith, was beheaded. Her crypt has been frequented by pilgrims since the Middle Ages. The fifth-century sarcophagus, recently restored, can be visited through free guided tours offered on weekdays.

🔺 Chapelle des Ursulines **O Do Dr R W S**, 4/20, €15/-/-/-, DP19, 40 Rue Despagnet, chapelle-ursulines@outlook.com, 0670496526

🔺 La Maison des Pèlerins **Do Pr Dr Br K R W S**, 1/6, €34.50/-/73/109.50, incl DP, 4 Rue du Labat, lamaisondespelerins@gmail.com, 0780041140, open Mar–Oct, bed only €15.50

🔺 Hospitalet Saint-Jacques **Do Dr K R**, 1/6, €14/-/-/-, DP16, 21 Rue Despagnet, 0558523168, open mid May–Oct, no baggage transfers or cyclists, English spoken

🔺🔺 Hôtel de la Paix **O Do Pr Br K R W**, 1/9, €15/18/36/54, 7 Rue Carnot, hoteldelapaix.40@wanadoo.fr, 0558716070 or 0681395002

🔺 Gîte Au Passage de l'Adour **Do Pr Dr Br K R W S**, 1/4, €25/-/52/-, DP15, 30 Rue Daugé, aupassagedeladour@gmail.com, 0651436818, open mid Apr–mid Oct, English spoken

🔺 Camping Les Ombrages de l'Adour **Pr R W**, €-/16/22/-, contact@camping-adour.com, 0772136484 or 0558527928, open Jan–Oct, camping €7/person, English spoken

STAGE 23
Aire-sur-l'Adour to Arzacq-Arraziguet

Start	Cathédrale Saint-Jean-Baptiste, Aire-sur-l'Adour
Finish	Centre d'Accueil, Arzacq-Arraziguet
Distance	33.8km
Total ascent	485m
Total descent	330m
Difficulty	Easy
Time	7hr 30min
Percentage paved	71%
Gîtes	Latrille 11.9+2.3km, Miramont-Sensacq 17.7km, Gîte La Ferme de Marsan 23.7km, Pimbo 26.8km, Arzacq-Arraziguet 33.8km

It's worth pausing, as you advance deeper into the Nouvelle-Aquitaine region today, to reflect on how dramatically the landscape has changed since your pilgrimage began in Le Puy-en-Velay. While the transition from ranching to predominantly agricultural production occurred many stages past, the farming estates have grown larger as the GR65 has moved southward – a consequence of an intentional process of *remembrement*, or land consolidation. Efforts were made towards that throughout the modern era, but the process surged in the 1960s–1980s, in pursuit of greater efficiency and profitability. Today's stage highlights the impact of those changes, with circuitous navigation around smaller plots replaced by lengthier stretches along expansive fields. Don't expect any services prior to Miramont-Sensacq.

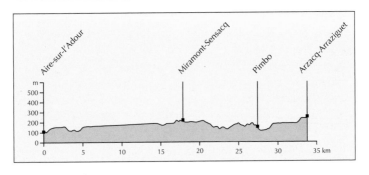

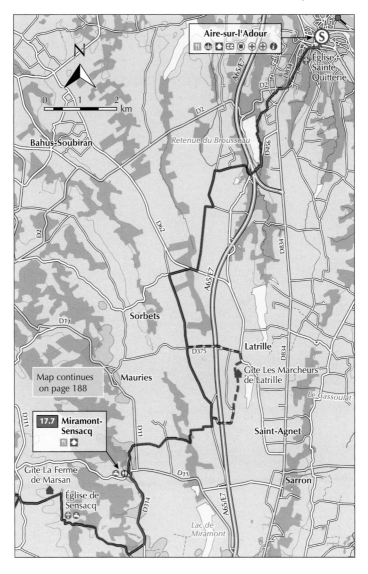

Aire-sur-l'Adour

Église Sainte-Quitterie

Retenue du Brousseau

Bahus-Soubiran

Sorbets

Latrille

Gîte Les Marcheurs de Latrille

Le Gassoulat

Mauries

Map continues on page 188

Saint-Agnet

17.7 Miramont-Sensacq

Sarron

Gîte La Ferme de Marsan

Église de Sensacq

Lac de Miramont

Backtrack from the cathedral to Rue Duprat, then turn left on Rue Carnot. Turn right at a T on Rue Labeyrie, then join Avenue des Pyrénées. Fork left on Rue Despagnet towards **Église Sainte-Quitterie** (**0.4km**). Continue straight on **D834** (**1km**). Turn right at a roundabout on **D2** (**0.3km**). Turn left through a parking lot and a residential neighborhood, making a series of quick turns (**1.5km**). Join a footpath, which later merges alongside **D456**. Turn left at a T on a paved road, then right onto D456 (**1.4km**). Pass under **A65/E7** then turn right on a dirt track (**0.2km**). After a mix of dirt and paved roads, turn right on **D62** (**4.2km**). A longer stretch exclusively on asphalt follows, briefly joining **D375** (**2.5km**). (Turn left on D375 to detour 2.3km to ⌂ Gîte Les Marcheurs de Latrille **Do Dr Br K R**, 2/4, €27/-/-/-, DP10, 589 Chemin de Lamenchaou, amandine.martocq@gmail.com, 0645371080, open Apr–Oct.)

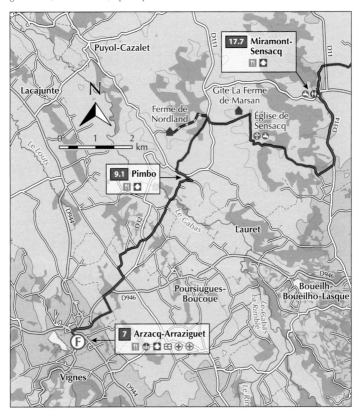

Eventually turn right on a dirt track (**2.7km**). Turn left at a T, then right at another T, transitioning back onto pavement (**1.4km**). Continue on a dirt track, then cross **D11**, rejoining a paved road (**1.3km**). Turn left at a T, then fork right. Pass Église Saint-Martin (fountain) at the entrance to

17.7KM MIRAMONT-SENSACQ (ELEV 205M, POP 360) 🏠 🏕 (143.6KM)
Miramont was one of the 12 baronies of Béarn.

🏠 Gîte Communal ⓞ 🅳🅾 🅳🆁 🅱🆁 🅺 🆁 🆉, 4/20, €13/-/-/-, DPDonation Apr–Oct, gite@miramont-sensacq.fr, 0558799406 or 0558799123

🏠 La Maison du Bos ⓞ 🅿🆁 🅳🆁 🅱🆁 🆁, €-/80/110/159, incl DP, 378 Chemin Dubos, info@maisondubos.com, 0558799318 or 0642798426, swimming pool

🏠 La Prade ⓞ 🅿🆁 🅳🆁 🅱🆁 🆁 🆆 🆂, €-/-/66/81, DP18, 1294 Route du Tursan, la.prade40@orange.fr, 0607757430

Turn left on Rue de Lescloupe, then right on Rue de la Mairie (WC by *mairie*). Leaving town, turn left onto **D314** (**0.3km**). Fork right (**2km**). Turn right at a T onto a road that transitions into a dirt track soon after (**0.9km**). Turn right onto a paved road at another T, arriving soon after at the **Église de Sensacq** (**2km**, fountain). This

Donkeys are the real stars of the chemin

11th-century church, formerly dedicated to Santiago, has a total immersion font in the corner.

Turn right soon after the church. Turn left onto a dirt track (**0.8km**), climbing steadily, just before 🏠 Gîte La Ferme de Marsan (ⓞ 🅳🅾 🅿🆁 🅺 🆁 🆆, 2/10, €14.50/-/40/-, contact@laferme-demarsan.com, 0558799493, breakfast €3.50, swimming pool, mini-épicerie). Turn right on **D111** (**1.2km**), then left onto a footpath soon after. (Alternately, take the next left to detour 1.2km to 🏠 Ferme de Nordland 🅳🅾 🅳🆁 🅺 🆁 🆆, 2/8, €22/-/-/-, DP22, contact@ferme-de-nordland.com, 0558444980 or 0675973423, open mid Apr–mid Oct.)

Descend sharply through dense woods, then emerge onto a dirt track (**1.5km**) that climbs right back up into

---

9.1KM PIMBO (ELEV 190M, POP 210) 🏛 ⛺ (134.5KM)

One of the region's oldest bastides, founded in 1268. Its church, the Collégiale Saint-Barthélemy, sits on the site of a former monastery established by Charlemagne.

🏠 Gîte Communal **Do Pr Dr Br K R Cf S**, 8/24, €17/30/55/-, DP13, 355 Rue de la Bastide, gitedepimbo@hotmail.fr, 0558444657, open Apr–Oct, camping €5/person

🏠 Maison Couhet **Pr Dr Br R W S**, €-/45/80/-, incl DP, 475 Rue de la Bastide, stheux@gmail.com, 0684982164, open Mar–Oct

---

In this next section, you cross into the Pyrénées-Atlantiques department, still in the Nouvelle-Aquitaine region. Follow paved roads away from the village, finally turning right on **D32** and then left on Chemin de Lassalle (**2.7km**). Turn left at a T, then right on **D32** (**1.6km**). Turn left on a dirt track (**0.8km**). Turn right at a T, rejoin a paved road, then fork left on **D946** (**1.1km**). Fork left through a roundabout on D944/D946 (**0.5km**). Fork left on D944, then fork right through a parking lot, leaving the GR65 waymarks. The Centre d'Accueil is on your right.

7KM ARZACQ-ARRAZIGUET (ELEV 235M, POP 1090) 🏛 ⊕ ⛺ 🄲 ⊕ ⊕ (127.5KM)

Market on Saturday. Another bastide, this distinguishes itself with two main squares, side by side, reflecting its prominent role as a medieval market town. The Place de la République is the more impressive square, lined with arcaded walkways. In one corner, the Tour de Peich hosted Louis XIII on an overnight visit in 1620. The 19th-century Église Saint-Pierre features a stained-glass window of St James. This once marked the Franco-Béarn border.

🏠 Centre d'Accueil Communal d'Arzacq **Do Pr Dr K R S**, 14/44, €13/25/40/-, DP16, Place du Marcadieu, centreaccueil@arzacq.com, 0559044141, open Feb–Nov, camping €5/person, English spoken

🏠 Maison Pantalou **O Pr Dr Br R W S**, €-/-/45/-, incl DP, 25 Chemin de Saint-Jacques, pdulucq@hotmail.com, 0698311282

🏠 Hôtel La Vieille Auberge **O Pr Dr R Cf W Z**, €-/64/66/-, DP21, 0559045131, English spoken

---

STAGE 24

Arzacq-Arraziguet to Arthez-de-Béarn

Start	Centre d'Accueil, Arzacq-Arraziguet
Finish	Église Saint-Étienne, Arthez-de-Béarn
Distance	30.2km
Total ascent	460m
Total descent	495m
Difficulty	Easy-to-moderate
Time	7hr 30min
Percentage paved	69%
Gîtes	Labalette 3km, Larreule 12.3km, Uzan 16.3km, Pomps 20.8km, Arthez-de-Béarn 30.2km

You are now deep in corn country; if you pass through this stage in the peak of growing season, you're likely to have walls of towering ears flanking you, as you stroll down quiet, paved roads. Combined with the mostly flat terrain, it's difficult to see much of the surrounding world; the past is quickly lost behind you and the future is obscured, perhaps spurring a deeply contemplative walk. While the route passes through villages regularly, these are quite small with few facilities. By comparison, modest Arthez-de-Béarn is a veritable metropolis, while its 200m elevation practically soars above the valley.

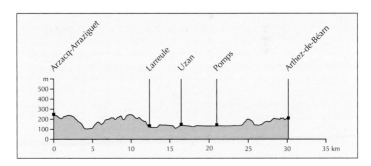

Backtrack from the Centre d'Accueil through the parking lot and continue straight into Place de la République. Turn left on Chemin de Larrouzé. Descend on a dirt track to **Lac d'Arzacq** (**0.7km**). Turn right, then left soon after, looping around the lake. Turn right uphill away from the lake (**0.9km**). Turn right at a T on a minor paved road, noting

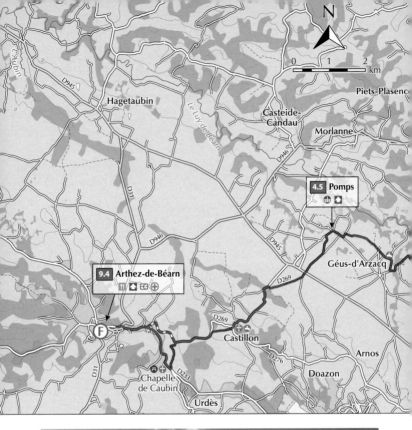

Gîte à Labalette, near Arzacq

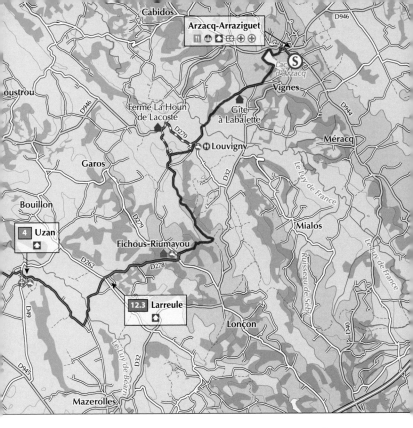

a much-decorated pilgrim tree on your right (**0.7km**). Pass ⛺ **Gîte à Labalette** 🅿️ 🏠 📶 🅺 🆁 🆆 🆂, €-/36/72/108, incl DP, ndupouts@gmail.com, 0608314856, open Apr–Oct, camping €5/person (**0.7km**). Transition back to pavement, then merge onto **D270** (**1.9km**). Turn left into **Louvigny** (**0.1km**, fountain, WC). Here there is a modern church and the remains of a castle and dungeons destroyed in the 20th century.

Turn right on Chemin de Lassoulade, then wind through minor tracks, passing the turn-off for the 0.8km detour to ⛺ ⛺ **Ferme La Houn de Lacoste** 🅾️ 🅳🅾️ 🅿️ 🏠 📶 🆁 🆆 🆂 🆉, 1/4, €25/50/84/-, incl DP, 1 Route d'Orthez, jeanmichel.lacadee@hotmail.fr, 0680426894, camping €5/person, swimming pool (**0.7km**). Fork left on Chemin de Pedebignes (**0.5km**). Fork right, then continue through a series of dirt tracks (**3.6km**). Turn left on **D279** in **Fichous-Riumayou** (**0.2km**, fountain, ⛺ **Bien-Hêtre Ecolodges** 🅾️ 🅿️ 🏠 📶 🆁 🆆, 3/7, €-/50/100/150, incl DP, contact@bien-hetre.fr, 0616897377). Turn right on **D278**. Fork right to remain on the highway (**1.4km**), then cross D262 in

12.3KM LARREULE (ELEV 125M, POP 180) ⬛ (115.2KM)

WC and fountain. This was the site of a Benedictine monastery (founded 995) and an important pilgrim stop in the Middle Ages.

⬥ Gîte L'Escale O Do Pr Dr K R W Z, 1/10, €15/55/70/90, DP18, alain. patricia64@orange.fr, 0559814924 or 0632022548, camping €5/person, swimming pool

Fork left on Route de Mazerolles. It's all pavement to Uzan. Turn left at the first T (**1.1km**), right at the second T on Route d'Uzan (**0.4km**), then right at the third T (**2.3km**), passing Église Sainte-Quitterie. Turn right on **D49**, then left in

4KM UZAN (ELEV 130M, POP 175) ⬛ (111.2KM)

Uzan's church, like Aire-sur-l'Adour's, is dedicated to St Quitterie.

⬥ Gîte Chez Darribère O Do Pr Dr Br R, 2/4, €35/-/70/-, incl DP, darribere_ cecile@hotmail.fr, 0671598468

Negotiate a series of turns on paved roads, eventually turning left on Cami de Compostelle, leading into **Géus-d'Arzacq** (**2.3km**, fountain). Fork right, transitioning onto a dirt track (**0.5km**). Turn left at a T back onto pavement (**1.1km**). Turn right at a T, then left to

4.5KM POMPS (ELEV 130M, POP 290) ⊕ ⬛ (106.7KM)

Its two notable landmarks are its 17th-century Église Saint-Jacques and a château with an octagonal tower.

⬥ Gîte Communal Do Dr K R W, 2/22, €13/-/-/-, DP17, reservationlahaltepompsoise@gmail.com, 0684919400, open mid Mar–Oct, camping €6/person, washer/dryer included, reservation requested

Turn left on Route de Brana, then right at a T on Rou dou Pebe (**0.8km**). Cross **D945**, then fork right on a dirt track (**0.9km**). Turn left on **D269** (**1km**). Proceed past Église Saint-Pierre in **Castillon** (**1.3km**, fountain), with its 11th-century pilgrim hospital ruins. Continue straight through a D269/D276 intersection onto a dirt track, then join D269 (**1km**). Arrive at an intersection with Chemin de Benicet (**1km**), where the GR65 forks left. Tired pilgrims can continue straight on D269, then turn right at Arthez's entrance onto D233, rejoining the GR65 there. This saves 1.2km.

Chapelle de Caubin, on the outskirts of Arthez-de-Béarn

Climb steadily, then turn right on **D233**, atop the ridgeline (**0.9km**). Soon after, arrive at **Chapelle de Caubin**. This restored Romanesque chapel sits on the site of a former command center for the Knights of St John. Continue straight on D233, taking care with the narrow shoulder on the winding road, as it navigates Arthez's extended outskirts (**2.3km**). Cross **D31** and continue on Rue la Carrère, arriving at the church in

9.4KM ARTHEZ-DE-BÉARN (ELEV 200M, POP 1860) 🔟 🏠 🄲 ⊕ (97.3KM)
Market on Saturdays. Fountain in front of *mairie*. A long and narrow town strung along the ridgeline. Arthez developed around an Augustinian commandery, which was destroyed during the Wars of Religion. The transition to Basque-style architecture accelerates here. Consider a break on the benches behind the church, where splendid views of the Pyrenees can be enjoyed on clear days.

🔺 Gîte Boulangerie Brousse ⓄⒹⓄⒹⓇⒷⓇⓀⓇⒸⓇⓌⓈ, 3/14, €31/-/-/-, incl DP, 13 Rue la Carrère, bertrand.brousse@wanadoo.fr, 0559677446

🔺 Gîte La Maison des Pelerins ⒹⓄⓀⓇⒸⓇⓌⓏ, 5/24, €12/-/-/-, 52 Rue la Carrère, mairie.arthezdebearn@wanadoo.fr, 0559677052, open Apr–Oct, camping €6/person, donkey parking, no wifi

🔺 Gîte Domi ⒹⓄⒹⓇⓀⓇⒸⓇⓌⓈ, 3/7, €16/-/-/-, DP17, 14 Chemin Diserane, gitedomi-arthez@orange.fr, 0770093265, open Apr–Oct

🔺 Camping L'Orée du Bois ⒫ⓇⒸⓇⓌ, €-/-/-/41, mairie.arthez@orange.fr, 0559677656, open Jun–Sept, camping €8/person, swimming pool

195

STAGE 25
Arthez-de-Béarn to Navarrenx

Start	Église Saint-Étienne, Arthez-de-Béarn
Finish	Office de Tourisme, Navarrenx
Distance	31.6km
Total ascent	475m
Total descent	550m
Difficulty	Easy-to-moderate
Time	8hr
Percentage paved	74%
Gîtes	Argagnon 7.8+0.6km, Maslacq 9.5km, Sauvelade 17.7km, Navarrenx 31.6km

A long but easy walk, primarily following paved roads, that breaks cleanly into thirds. Maslacq, at the end of the first third, is the best chance of supplies. Sauvelade, which marks the second third's conclusion, preserves a lovely 12th-century church and is a good spot for a picnic. The day's major highlight is unquestionably Navarrenx, with its impressive, Italian-style town walls, which are perfect for an evening stroll.

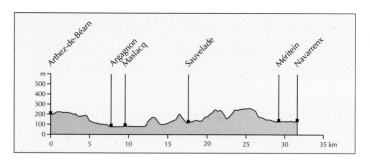

Follow Rue la Carrère out of **Arthez**, then join **D946**. As the highway curves right, continue straight. Fork right on Chemin du Bosc (**1km**). Transition onto a dirt track (**1.1km**), then fork left just after rejoining a paved road (**2.5km**). As the route approaches D817, fork left along a parking lot and past a **cemetery** and church (**2.7km**), skirting the edge of **Argagnon** (fountain, bakery, restaurant, ⬥ Gîte du Cambarrat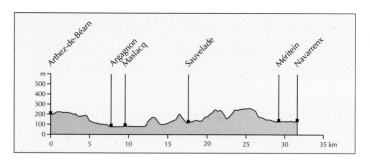

R W S, 3/10, €15/-/50/-, DP15, 350 Chemin de Baraten, giteducambarrat@yahoo.fr, 0559676598, donkey parking, English spoken), ▲ ▲ **Arrêt et Aller** O Do Pf Df Br R W S, 1/4, €25/-/75/-, DP12, 190 Route de Pedauque, glyn34@hotmail.com, 0559093735 or 0679569837, camping €15/tent, English spoken). Follow a footpath alongside D817, then cross the highway and turn right. Backtrack along a footpath on the other side, then turn left on **D275** (**0.6km**). Cross the **Ousse River**, then join a footpath along D275 (**0.7km**). Turn left at a T on Rue du Fronton in

---

9.5KM MASLACQ (ELEV 75M, POP 890) 🏤 ⊕ 🏠 (87.8KM)

First documented as Marzlag in 1110, the village's current incarnation dates to the 14th century, when an abbey was founded on the banks of the River Gave by Gaston Phoebus, the Count of Foix. Its most famous resident, Bertrand d'Abbadie, founded the Maison Abbadie over the abbey's remains in the 16th century, only to have it destroyed and rebuilt in the 17th, with a bell tower added in the 19th. Castle Maslacq was the abbot's residence before the French Revolution, but today it is in private hands.

▲ **Gîte L'Estanquet** Do Pf Df K R W S Z, 2/5, €20/-/50/-, DP20, 12 Route de Lagor, babeth.malherbe@orange.fr, 0672720779, open Apr–Oct, camping €10/person, no wifi

▲ **Gîte Méziat** Pf Df K R W S, 3/5, €-/24/45/-, DP20, 6 Chemin de la Tour, martinehautbois@sfr.fr, 0602390930, open Mar–Jun and Sept–Oct

▲ **La Ferme de Bicatou** O Pf Df Br R W S Z, €-/50/95/-, incl DP, 8 Rue de l'Ecole, lafermedebicatou@gmail.com, 0559676217, camping €5/person

---

Fork left on **D9**. Turn left on Quartier Laubadère, then fork left on a gravel track (**1km**). This winds first through fields, then alongside the **Ousse River**, and then into the woods. As you approach a clearing (**2.5km**), it's possible to make a short detour to the left to visit the Neo-Byzantine **Sanctuaire de Notre-Dame de Muret**.

A **church** built here in 1059 endured extensive turbulence, caught in a power struggle between local powers and religious leaders. And then things got worse, when the church was destroyed during the Reformation. By contrast, this contemporary sanctuary is quite placid, with 360-degree views.

Continuing on the *chemin*, cross **D9**, then turn left on a paved road. Turn right on Chemin Saubade, which leads into **Lacoume** (**1.9km**). Curve left behind a house, then join a dirt track through woods. Turn right on a paved road (**0.8km**, fountain). Cross Camin de Causet (**0.9km**), then descend through woods into

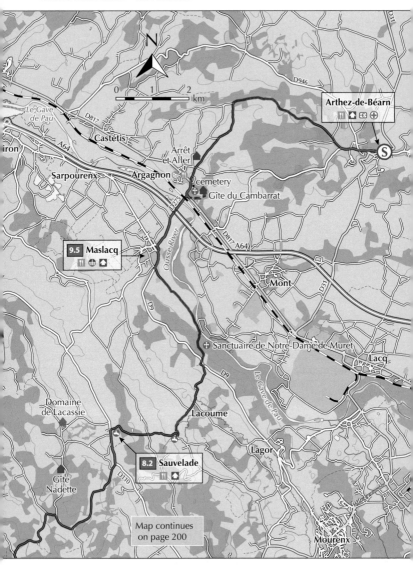

N

0   1   2
km

Arthez-de-Béarn

Le Gave
de Pau

D946

D817

Castétis

A64

S

iron

Arrêt
et Aller

Sarpourenx

Argagnon

cemetery

Gîte du Cambarrat

D225

D817 A64

9.5   Maslacq

Ousse River

Mont

D31

D9

✝ Sanctuaire de Notre-Dame de Muret

Lacq

D9

Le Gave de Pau

Domaine
de Lacassie

Lacoume

Lagor

Gîte
Nadette

D110

8.2   Sauvelade

Map continues
on page 200

Mourenx

8.2KM SAUVELADE (ELEV 120M, POP 270) 🍴 🏠 (79.6KM)

Fountain. The church is all that remains of a former Benedictine monastery, founded in 1128. It was sacked by Huguenots in 1569, restored in 1630, then sold off during the French Revolution. A video history is accessible in the church.

⌂ Gîte Le P'tit Laa 🅾 Do Pr Dr K R Gr W, 5/15, €12.5/-/-/-, DP22, 0760679468, restaurant/*épicerie*, donkey parking

⌂ ⌂ Gîte Nadette Do Pr Dr Br R W, 2/8, €45/75/138/160, incl DP, gitenadette@laposte.net, 0559384879 or 0687291370, open mid Apr–mid Oct, 2km outside Sauvelade but shuttle available

⌂ La Maison du Grillon Do Pr Dr Br K R Gr W S Z, 1/10, €25/30/60/90, DP15, 1559 Route deu Lavarth, oustau.grigt@gmail.com, 0684381421 or 0676273638, open Apr–Oct, camping €7/person

Turn left on a footpath alongside **D110**. Turn right on a minor paved road, then fork left on Camin de Compostela (**1.2km**). Fork right on Cami de Berduqueu (**2.2km**). Fork left towards Bugnein (**0.6km**) and then again towards Le Hameau de Bugnein (**0.3km**). Continue to follow a series of minor paved roads, leading through the **Fôret Communale de Méritein** (eclectic pilgrim rest stop, fountain) and eventually turning left on **D947** in **Méritein** (**7.3km**). Soon after, fork left on Chemin de la Biasse. Fork left again to pass under **D67**, continuing straight (**1.1km**). Turn right on **D111** (**0.4km**). Cross **D947E** and proceed on a minor paved road. Turn right on D2947 into Navarrenx's historic center, arriving at the Office de Tourisme on your left.

The view of the Gave d'Oloron from Navarrenx's imposing fortifications

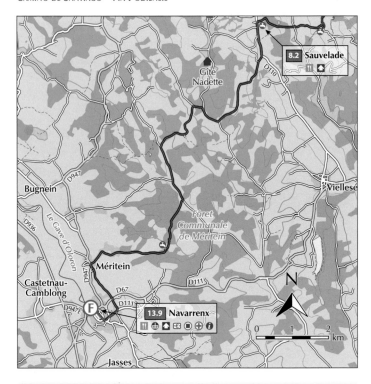

13.9KM NAVARRENX (ELEV 125M, POP 1050) 🍴 ⊕ 🔺 ⓒ ◉ ⊕ ❶ (65.7KM)
Market on Wednesdays, plus Sundays in July/August.While inhabited since the
first century, the current town likely dates to the 10th. The stone bridge, critical for the pilgrimage, was built in 1289, and its original main arch survives.
Navarrenx was the first French town to be fortified with Italian-style ramparts,
inspired by Lucca, between 1542 and 1549. The walls can be freely visited
today and are perhaps best enjoyed near the Porte Sainte-Antoine, alongside
the Gave d'Oloron River.

The Église Saint-Germain, built in 1562, experienced a turbulent first century, as it – and the town as a whole – converted to Protestantism soon after
its opening, when the French Wars of Religion erupted. The Queen of Navarre,
Jeanne d'Albret, played the key part in this, as she converted to Calvinism in 1560

Colorful illustrations introduce Navarrenx's merchants

and declared it the official religion of her kingdom. She also had the New Testament translated into Euskera (the Basque language) and Béarnese. Her Protestant loyalties led to a plot hatched by Pope Pius IV to have her kidnapped and moved under control of the Spanish Inquisition, although this never materialized. Jeanne helped to broker a peace settlement in 1570, winning Protestants the concession of being eligible to hold office in France. Two years later, hostilities resumed, and Jeanne died of natural causes. Her home in Navarrenx still stands, privately owned today, with a hair salon on the ground floor.

In 1620, Louis XIII (Jeanne's grandson) came to Navarrenx as part of his journey to unify Navarre and Béarn and to pull them forcibly back under French rule, imposing the French language in the process. He was welcomed peacefully into the town. While he preserved freedom of worship for Protestants, he restored Catholic worship in Navarrenx.

⬟ Gîte L'Alchimiste **O** **Do** **Dr** **Br** **K** **R** **W** **S**, 5/12, €Donation, incl DP, 10 Rue de l'Abreuvoir, alchimistesurlechemin@hotmail.fr, 0967032684, campers welcome

⬟ Gîte de l'Arsenal **Do** **K** **R** **W** **S**, 8/32, €12.50/-/-/-, 41 Rue St Germain, mairie. navarrenx@wanadoo.fr, 0550661022, open Apr–Oct

⬟ ⬟ Gîte Le Cri de la Girafe **O** **Do** **Pr** **Dr** **Br** **R** **W** **S**, 1/8, €23/30/43/-, DP12, 12 Rue du Faubourg, contact@lecridelagirafe.fr, 0559662422, washer/dryer included

⬟ Gîte En Chemin Vers Soi **Do** **Dr** **K** **R** **W** **S**, 2/6, €18/-/-/-, DP17, 3 Chemin de Bérénenx, encheminverssoi64@gmail.com, 0626308124, open mid Mar–mid Nov, sliding-scale pricing

⬟ Le Relais du Jacquet **O** **Pr** **Dr** **Br** **R** **W** **S**, €-/50/65/-, DP15, 42 Rue St Germain, regis.gabastou@orange.fr, 0675728933

⬟ Hôtel Le Commerce **O** **Pr** **Dr** **R** **Gf** **Z**, €-/70/81/-, contact@hotellecommerce. fr, 0559662254, breakfast €8

▲ Camping Beau Rivage **Pr** **Dr** **R** **W** **Z**, DP16.50, Le Pont de l'Est, contact@ beaucamping.com, 0676809844, open Apr–mid Oct, camping €6–10/tent, mobile homes, swimming pool

STAGE 26
Navarrenx to Aroue

Start	Office de Tourisme, Navarrenx
Finish	Gîte Municipal, Aroue
Distance	19.5km
Total ascent	275m
Total descent	290m
Difficulty	Easy
Time	4hr 15min
Percentage paved	51%
Gîtes	Castelnau-Camblong 2km, Aroue 19.5km

An easy, mellow stroll through quiet French countryside, as the Pyrenees gradually lay claim to the horizon. Plan for few resources along the way (including water), aside from an ideally positioned pâté factory (pack a baguette!), and little more from the destination, outside of demi-pension options in your accommodation. Note that the GR65 bypasses Aroue's center and the Gîte Communal, so this stage concludes just off-route.

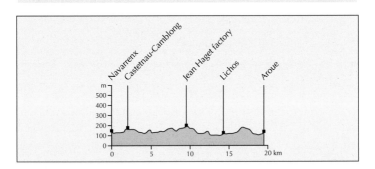

Turn left immediately after the Office de Tourisme on Rue Saint-Germain and proceed through the gate beneath the town walls. Cross **D947** and turn left on a footpath. Rejoin the road and cross the Gave d'Oloron, then fork right on **D115** (**0.3km**). Cross a roundabout, then turn right (**1.4km**), sticking with D115. Fork left on a footpath, then continue straight onto a paved road, merging with Rue de l'Église (**0.3km**). Proceed into

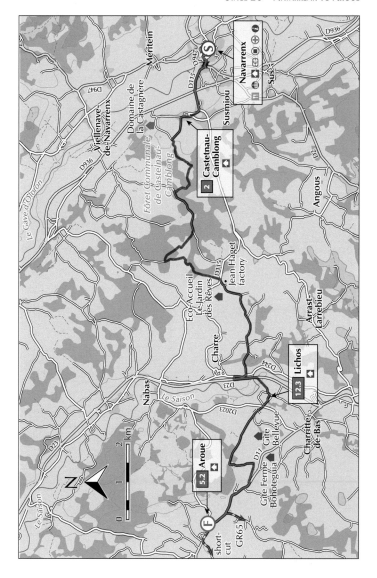

2KM CASTETNAU-CAMBLONG (ELEV 140M, POP 450) ⬛ (63.7KM)
The village's annual mid-August festivities feature *belote* (a 32-card game) and *pétanque* (like bocce ball) tournaments.

⬥ Gîte Aux 2 Anes **O Do Pr Dr Br K R W S**, 5/11, €Donation, incl DP, 6 Chemin des Pyrénées, aux2anes64190@gmail.com, 0620552792, campers welcome

⬥ Gîte Chez Bouju **O Do Pr Dr K R W S**, 1/4, €20/-/40/-, DP20, 2 Cote Perisse, montane.francis@neuf.fr, 0632092326, camping €5/person, donkey parking

⬥ Domaine de la Castagnère **O Do Pr Dr Br R W S**, 2/5 €20/-/55/-, DP20, 9 Chemin de la Castagnère, la-castagnere@hotmail.com, 0644310597, campers welcome

Turn left on Rue des Debantets (**0.3km**). Turn left on a gravel road (**0.7km**), beginning a lengthy stretch on dirt tracks and footpaths through the **Fôret Communale de Castelnau-Camblong**. Cross **D115** (**6.6km**), passing the **Jean Haget factory**, where it's possible to buy pâté, and ⬥ Eco-Accueil Le Jardin des Rêves (**Do Dr K R W S**, 2/9, €12/-/-/-, DP18, cigrandrosan@hotmail.fr, 0613290219 or 0610420235, open May– Oct, camping €5/person, no wifi). Fork right on Route de Saint-Jacques. Join a paved

Pâté for pilgrims at the Jean Haget factory

road (**1.5km**), then fork left (**0.6km**). Turn right on **D244** (**1km**), then turn left (**0.4km**). Just before reaching **D23**, turn right on a footpath, then fork left under a highway. Turn left on a dirt track, then continue on a footpath alongside D23 (**0.5km**). Cross the **Saison River**, then fork right onto a footpath, descending to a minor paved road and forking away from the highway. Turn left at a T in

12.3KM LICHOS (ELEV 110M, POP 135) 🏠 (51.4KM)
The birthplace of St Grat, Bishop of Oloron, in the fifth century. A small pilgrim rest stop is situated in the village center.

🛏 Jaury **Pr Dr Br R Cr W**, €-/50/85/-, incl DP, chris.jaury@gmail.com, 0682508244, open Mar–Nov

🛏 Cléromilo **O Pr Dr Br K R Cr W S**, €-/35/70/-, DP10, laurence.pouthier@orange.fr, 0782976544 or 0680656030

A waymark calls for a right turn in Lichos

Fork right, then turn right at a T. Cross **D2023** (**0.5km**) and proceed along a series of minor paved roads, until turning right at a T on a dirt track (**2.6km**). Turn right on **D11** (**0.6km**). **1.1km** later, having passed the turn-offs for Gîtes Bohoteguia and Bellevue, the GR65 turns left, just before the stage end at Aroue. If you plan to continue walking today, check the next stage to consider whether to turn here or carry on, as a short-cut is possible from Aroue. To reach Aroue, continue straight to the Gîte Communal (**0.4km**).

5.2KM AROUE (ELEV 110M, POP 240) 🏠 (46.2KM)
Its 12th-century Église Saint-Etienne has a Santiago Matamoros statue in its sacristy doors.

🛏 Gîte Ferme Bohoteguia **Do Pr Dr R W Z**, 2/11, €12/-/36/-, DP20, bohoteguia@aol.com, 0675838261, open Mar–Nov, camping €6/person, English spoken

🛏 Gîte Bellevue **O Do Pr Dr R W S Z**, 5/15, €12/-/24/-, gegubellevue@yahoo.fr, 0559657019 or 0616486365, camping €5/person, breakfast €4

🛏 Gîte Communal **Do K R W**, 4/12, €10/-/-/-, gite.aroue@wanadoo.fr, 0559659554, open Apr–Nov, mini-*épicerie*, camping €5/person

STAGE 27
Aroue to Ostabat-Asme

Start	Gîte Municipal, Aroue
Finish	Église Saint-Jean-Baptiste, Ostabat-Asme
Distance	24km (30.6km via Saint-Palais, 21.7m via Uhart-Mixe)
Total ascent	645m (770m via Saint-Palais, 610m via Uhart-Mixe)
Total descent	585m (710m via Saint-Palais, 550m via Uhart-Mixe)
Difficulty	Moderate-to-strenuous
Time	7hr (9hr via Saint-Palais, 6hr 15min via Uhart-Mixe)
Percentage paved	56% (64% via Saint-Palais, 51% via Uhart-Mixe)
Gîtes	Landaco 2.5+0.7km, Larribar-Sorhapuru 14.7km, Saint-Palais 19.3km (alt), Harambeltz 20.5km, Ostabat-Asme 24km

This stage is filled with options. Leaving Aroue, the official approach is longer and more strenuous, while an alternative approach from the town center is shorter and paved. From there, the official route offers a good mix of surfaces and a reasonably short length. If you're craving a town and can handle a longer stage, though, the Saint-Palais detour is for you; it's your only chance to restock supplies in this section. Alternatively, it's also possible to shave off a couple of kilometers and bypass the most significant ascent in many days by cutting through Uhart-Mixe.

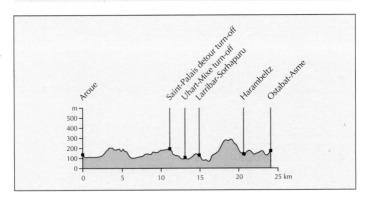

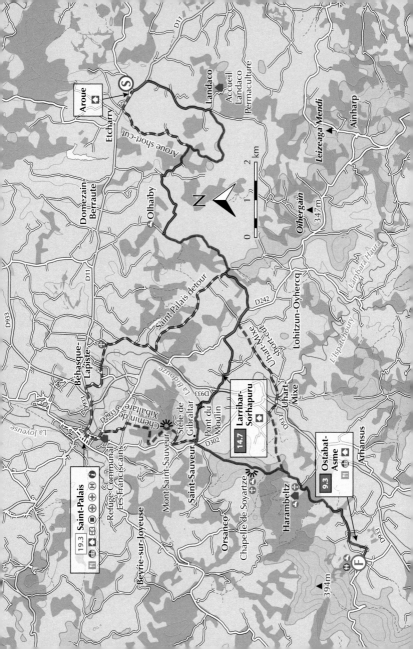

Right from the start, there are two options.

GR65 omitting Aroue center (5.3km)

The recommended official route of the GR65 turns off D11 before Aroue center, so you'll need to backtrack (**0.4km**) if you've visited there or stayed in the Gîte Communal. Turn onto a minor paved road towards Lohitzun-Oyhercq. Pass a signposted turn-off for **Landaco** (**2.1km**, ⌂ Accueil Landaco Permaculture O Do Pr Dr Br R W S, 4/6, €Donation, incl DP, landaco64@gmail.com, 0987889845, campers welcome, reservation required in offseason, no wifi), where there's a rest area and fountain 0.7km off route. Turn right onto a dirt track and ascend into the hills. Finally, make a sharp left, rejoining the direct approach from Aroue (**2.9km**).

Short-cut through Aroue center (3.1km)

For a shorter walk, continue straight on D11 past the Gîte Communal through Aroue, forking left at the roundabout soon after. Turn left on a paved road (**0.6km**). Fork left, then turn right at a T (**1.8km**). Fork right on a dirt track (**0.7km**) and rejoin the official route.

Routes reunited, fork right on a paved road, then make a sharp left (**1.3km**). Alternately, proceed straight 0.3km to the village of Olhaïby and the Église Saint-Just, where there's a fountain. Continue through a series of minor paved roads (**2km**), then dirt tracks, ending in a sharp right turn (**2.5km**). Soon after (**0.1km**), you have two more waymarked options: to stick with the GR65 or take a detour to Saint-Palais.

GR65 via Larribar Sorhapuru (5.8km)

Follow the GR waymarks left, onto a paved road. Fork left, then turn right on **D242** (**1.3km**). Another waymarked variant, through Uhart-Mixe, is accessible by turning left soon after (**0.5km**); for clarity's sake, it is described later in this stage. Continue following D242, then fork left towards Larribar (**0.5km**). Fork right past Gîte Ametza (**0.8km**), then fork left to skirt

---

14.7KM LARRIBAR-SORHAPURU (ELEV 120M, POP 190) ▣ (31.5KM)

The two municipalities merged in 1841, after previously falling under the power of the Uhart family in the late medieval era. The Église de l'Assomption features a 16th-century wooden statue of St Martin, the patron saint of France.

⌂ Gîte Terra Sylva Do Dr K R W S, 4/9, €12/-/-/-, DP14, zb.hicaubert@gmail.com, 0680447408, open Apr–Oct, camping €9/person

---

Cross **D933** and continue forward (**0.6km**). Fork left on Chemin Saint-Jacques, then right through a cluster of houses (**0.5km**). Cross **Pont du Moulin**, join a dirt track, then fork left in **Saint-Sauveur** (**1.3km**). The Saint-Palais detour rejoins from the right.

Saint-Palais detour (12.4km)

Continue straight on a minor paved road, ignoring side streets, as it winds through quiet terrain. Waymarking is subtle, consisting mostly of small stickers, so watch carefully. Turn right at a T (**3.2km**), then fork left onto a footpath (**1.5km**), crossing beneath Chapelle à Béhasque-Lapiste. Pass through the village of **Béhasque-Lapiste** (**0.7km**). Turn left at a T on **D11** (**1km**), taking care on the busy road. Skirt the left side of a large roundabout, continuing forward on **D933** (**0.7km**). Turn left on Rue du Palais de Justice in

19.3KM SAINT-PALAIS (ELEV 50M, POP 1840) 🏪 ⊖ 🛆 🄲 ⊙ Ⓗ ⊕ ⊕ *❶*
(33.5KM)

The capital of the Kingdom of Navarre in the 16th century, today Saint-Palais is a pleasant market town, with a regular Friday market, a 'Force Basque' festival in August (in which 'feats of strength' are performed), and a horse fair on Easter Monday. A pilgrim hospital was established here in 1784, by royal decree.

⬥ **Refuge Communal Les Franciscains** Do Pr Br K R W S, 1/14, €10/15/30/-, 2 Impasse du Prieuré, caminopa@hotmail.com, 0768977525, open mid Apr–mid Oct

⬥ **Soretena** O Pr Dr Br R W, €-/24/48/-, DP12, 2 Ave Frédéric de Saint-Jayme, lduploye@hotmail.fr, 0610107397, English spoken

⬥ **Hôtel du Midi** O Pr Dr R Ci W S Z, €-/56/64/-, DP23, 12 Place du Foirail, hotmidi@sfr.fr, 0559657064

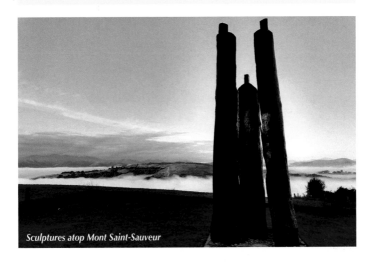

Sculptures atop Mont Saint-Sauveur

Turn left at the Refuge Communal Les Franciscaine (**0.4km**), on **D2933** towards Saint-Jean-Pied-de-Port. Turn right on Rue du Mount Saint-Sauveur (**0.2km**). Turn left at a T and then right onto a pedestrian track (**0.8km**), the Chemin de Xibaltare. A steep climb follows, winding through dense tree cover, until finally emerging at lovely oak sculptures, designed by Christian Lapie, atop **Mont Saint-Sauveur** (**2km**). Descend a steep footpath, then turn right onto a paved road and left at a T (**0.6km**). Wind into the **Saint-Sauveur** neighborhood and rejoin the official route (**0.7km**).

The routes reunite at the **Stèle de Gibraltar**. The Stèle is a small monument that marks the convergence of three of the Chemins de Saint-Jacques (Le Puy, Vézélay, and Paris). Cross **D302** and continue straight towards Orsanco (**0.1km**). Fork left onto a dirt track, climbing sharply. Fork left by **Chapelle de Soyartze** (fountain), enjoying the sweeping views (**1.8km**). Descend through a series of dirt tracks, with the Uhart-Mixe short-cut rejoining along the way (**0.9km**).

The Stèle de Gibraltar

Uhart-Mixe short-cut (4.6km)
This waymarked variant turns left off D242 1.7km before the GR65 reaches Larribar-Sorhapuru, then right almost immediately after. Continue straight onto a dirt track, then transition onto pavement (**2.1km**). Turn right on D302 (**0.2km**), leading into

13.4KM UHART-MIXE (ELEV 85M, POP 210) (28.3KM)
The Église Saint-Pierre dates to the 19th century.

Cross **D933** and continue straight on a minor road past the *mairie*. Turn left, then fork left immediately after onto a dirt track (**0.3km**). Stick with it until rejoining the official route (**1.9km**).

All routes reunited, turn left at a T, then transition back onto pavement at the entrance to **Harambeltz** (**0.6km**, fountain, ⌂ Gîte Etchetoa Do Df K R W S, 3/12, €14/-/-/-, DP20, marie.etchetoa@laposte.net, 0766024010, open Apr–Oct, camping €5/person).

Ascending towards Chapelle de Soyartze

This is the site of the **former Benedictine priory-hospital of St Nicholas**, although only the 1000-year-old chapel remains. Since its closure in 1784 by Louis XVI, the local Basque community has taken responsibility for its preservation.

Fork right onto a dirt track (**0.1km**). Rejoin a paved road (**2km**), then turn left onto a footpath (**0.6km**). Join another paved road, then turn right (**0.6km**). Fork right between buildings uphill, arriving at the church in

9.3KM OSTABAT-ASME (ELEV 170M, POP 195) 🍴 ⊕ 🏠 **(22.2KM)**
WC before church. In the Middle Ages, Ostabat could accommodate 5000 pilgrims in its 20 inns. Its central church, the Église Saint-Jean-Baptiste, is a newer, 19th-century structure.

🏠 Gîte Ospitalia Do K R, 3/10, €15/-/-/-, 0559378317, open Apr–Oct, no wifi

🏠 Gîte Gaineko Etxea Do Pr Dr Br R Cf W S Z, 2/14, €38/-/96/132, incl DP, lucie.eyharts@wanadoo.fr, 0559378110, open Apr–Nov, donkey parking, swimming pool

🏠 Gîte Aire-Ona Do Pr K R W S Z, 3/8, €16/-/42/-, gite.aire-ona@live.fr, 0633657715, open Apr–Oct, breakfast €5

🏠 🏠 Auberge Ametzanea Do Pr Dr Br R S, 1/3, €38/-/76/-, incl DP, danielantxo@wanadoo.fr, 0559378503 or 0559378156, open 25 Apr–10 Oct

STAGE 28
Ostabat-Asme to Saint-Jean-Pied-de-Port

Start	Église Saint-Jean-Baptiste, Ostabat-Asme
Finish	Pilgrim Office, Saint-Jean-Pied-de-Port
Distance	22.2km
Total ascent	325m
Total descent	310m
Difficulty	Easy
Time	5hr
Percentage paved	83%
Gîtes	Lacarre 12.3km, Saint-Jean-Pied-de-Port 22.2km

Depending on your plans, today might mark the completion of this pilgrimage, or the unofficial halfway point to Santiago. Even if the latter applies, though, today remains a day of closure – your last full stage in France (unless you're diverting to the Norte), probably your last night in a gîte, and almost certainly your last day spent as part of a small pilgrim community. From the moment you pass through the Porte Saint-Jacques into Saint-Jean-Pied-de-Port, you'll find yourself immersed in a much larger cohort. Now a veteran, you have a great deal of wisdom to share, while also benefiting from the enthusiasm of so many fresh-faced (and shiny-shoed) new pilgrims! This stage's walk is not, admittedly, very interesting, and it's largely road-bound. But if the skies are clear, you can admire the towering Pyrenees as you reflect on your pilgrimage thus far.

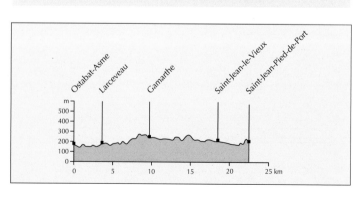

From the church, backtrack one block and turn right. Fork right onto a paved road, sticking with it through fields and woods, until turning left at a T (**2.6km**). Turn right on **D933** (**0.2km**). Turn right and then left soon after (**0.5km**). Fork right to continue walking, or turn left to access

3.7KM LARCEVEAU (ELEV 160M, POP 410) ▮▮ ▯ (18.5KM)
Note that all services are located off-route, on the D933.

🛏 Maison Oyhanartia ◯ ▯ ▯ ▯ ▯, €-/73/78/103, DP30, contact@oyhanartia.com, 0559378816

🛏 Hôtel Espellet ▯ ▯ ▯ ▯ ▯, €-/42/70/-, contact@hotel-restaurant-espellet.fr, 0559378191, breakfast €8, closed Jan

Wind through a series of turns; after passing a cluster of houses, fork right onto a dirt track (**0.9km**). Transition back onto a paved road (**1km**). A series of three left turns lead back to dirt (**0.5km**). Soon after (**0.6km**), pass **Ospital de Utxiat**, a pilgrim shelter that offers a pair of bunkbeds and fountain, but no toilet or shower. Continue roughly parallel to D933, until turning left across it onto **D522** towards Gamarthe (**2km**). Make a sharp left into the village (**0.8km**), then a pair of rights leading to the church in

6KM GAMARTHE (ELEV 230M, POP 125) ▯ (12.5KM)
Fountain at church gate. Gamarthe's Église Saint-Laurent is dedicated to Lawrence, one of seven Roman deacons martyred under the Roman Emperor Valerian's persecution in 258. Following Pope Sixtus II's death, Lawrence was ordered to gather the Church's wealth and relinquish it to the city's prefect. Lawrence took three days, studiously distributing that wealth in safe places, and then assembled a group of destitute, crippled, and suffering Christians. He delivered these people to the prefect, declaring them the Church's true treasures. Lawrence's martyrdom followed, in which he was placed on a gridiron to burn to death. Legend holds, he declared midway: 'I'm well done on this side. Turn me over!'

🛏 Iturria ▯ ▯ ▯ ▯ ▯, €-/-/45/45, DP22, 705 Route de Lacarre, valessential@gmail.com, 0766392402, open Mar–Dec, accommodation in teepee

From here, the walk is exclusively on pavement. Turn left on D522, then left again on **D933** (**0.9km**). (Alternately, cross D933 and proceed 0.2km to reach **Mongelos** and 🛏 Domaine de Schiltenea ◯ ▯ ▯ ▯ ▯ ▯ ▯ ▯, €-/40/70/-, DP20, Route de l'Église, albanne.t.sandras@gmail.com, 0559372256, reservation required). Climb into the hills, curving left (**0.6km**). Pass 🛏 Gîte Ferme Xokoan ◯ ▯ ▯ ▯ ▯ ▯, 1/7, €15/-/-/-, DP21, xokoan@wanadoo.fr, 0680157125, camping €8/person (**1.1km**). Follow minor

213

roads to **Bussunarits** (**3.3km**, fountain, ▲ Ferme Etxekonia 🄾 🄿🅵 🄳🅵 🄱🅵 🅁, €-/50/65/90, DP18.50, 0559370040, no wifi). Continue straight on **D120** (**0.8km**). Fork left, then turn left at a T (**1.5km**). Turn right on **D18**, then cross **D2933** in

---

8.6KM SAINT-JEAN-LE-VIEUX (ELEV 200M, POP 850) 🍴 ⊕ 🅰 (3.9KM)

Fountain and WC next to church. Pilgrims originally went straight to Saint-Michel from here; only from the 13th century onward did the route shift through Saint-Jean-Pied-de-Port. Its Église Saint-Pierre is a good example of a typical Basque church.

▲ Hotel Mendy 🄿🅵 🄳🅵 🅁 🄶🄴 🅉, €-/-/65/100, DP28, contact@hotel-mendy.com, 0559371181, open Apr–Nov

---

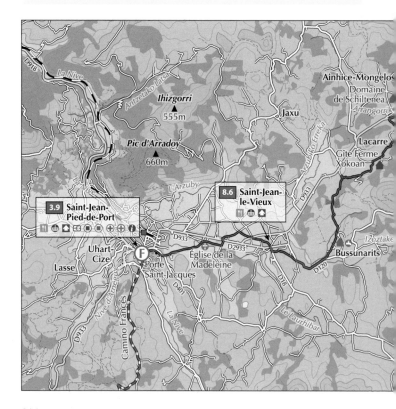

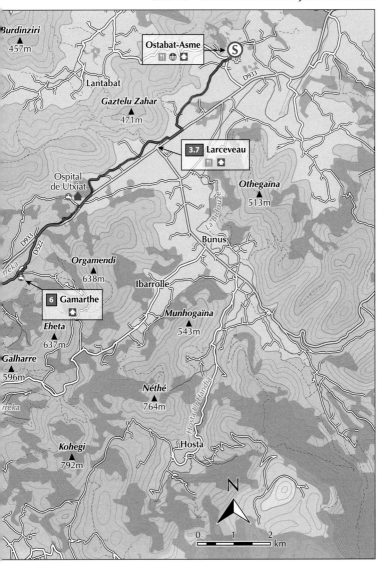

Proceed out the plaza's back-left corner. Turn right at a T, cross under **D933**, then fork left immediately after (**0.6km**). Turn left, then right onto **D933** (**0.9km**). After passing through a parking lot, turn left, passing to the right of **Église de la Madeleine** (**0.8km**). Fork right, then cross **D401** (**1.2km**). Walk through the **Porte Saint-Jacques** into the old town of Saint-Jean, descending to the Pilgrim Office, on your right. Your journey along the Via Podiensis is at an end.

3.9KM SAINT-JEAN-PIED-DE-PORT (ELEV 180M, POP 1585) 🍴 ⊕ ⌂ Ⓒ ⊙ ⊙ ⊕ ⊕ ❶ 783.6KM TO SANTIAGO DE COMPOSTELA
Market on Mondays. Daily mass at 7pm, except for Sundays at 11am. The Pilgrim Office is an invaluable first stop, as the volunteers can help you find a bed and offer current information on the Pyrenees crossing and beyond.

Porte Saint-Jacques

After Saint-Jean-le-Vieux was razed to the ground by Richard the Lionheart in 1177, the Kings of Navarre re-founded it here. Pilgrims enter through the 15th-century Porte Saint-Jacques and then follow the cobblestone Rue de la Citadelle downhill, through the Porte d'Espagne, and across the Nive River. The citadel, near the gate, was significantly remodeled in the 17th century, following the Wars of Religion, and offers dramatic views of the looming Pyrenees. The 14th-century **Église Notre-Dame** is a Gothic structure built out of red schist, and it succeeds an earlier church that was built by Sancho the Strong of Navarre to commemorate the Battle of Las Navas de Tolosa, the pivotal battle of the Reconquista.

The Basque cultural resurgence is on full display in Saint-Jean, with their red, green, and white national colors featured everywhere. Espadrille shops are prominent in the center. The canvas footwear was inextricably linked with Basque and Catalan nationalist movements in the 19th century, although it spread worldwide in the 20th. If you prefer to eat what you buy, look for the Gâteau Basque in the town's bakeries; it makes a great snack when you're sitting atop the Pyrenees.

🔷 **Gîte Communal Ospitalia** 🄾 🄳🄾 🄿🅁 🄱🅁 🄲🅁 🅂 🅉, 3/32, €12/-/30/-, 55 Rue de la Citadelle, contact@terresdenavarre.fr, 0617103189, simple breakfast

🔷 **Gîte Beilari** 🄳🄾 🄳🅁 🄱🅁 🅁 🅂, 4/14, €40/-/-/-, incl DP, 40 Rue de la Citadelle, info@beilari.info, 0630028667, open 15 Mar–Oct, no wifi

🔷 **Gîte Chemin Vers l'Etoile** 🄾 🄳🄾 🄿🅁 🄺 🅁 🄲🅁 🅉, 4/36, €18/-/42/-, 21 Rue d'Espagne, eric.viotte@gmail.com, 0559372071, breakfast €5

🔷 **Gîte Esteban Etxea** 🄾 🄳🄾 🄿🅁 🄳🅁 🅁 🄲🅁 🅆 🅂, 1/16, €17/-/59/-, DP18, 29 Rue de la Citadelle, esteban.etxea@yahoo.com, 0638228005

🔷 **Gîte Ultreia** 🄳🄾 🄿🅁 🄱🅁 🄺 🄲🅁 🅆 🅂, 1/7, €23/-/56/-, 8 Rue de la Citadelle, gite.ultreia@vertesmontagnes.fr, 0680884622, open Mar–Oct

🔷 **Gîte Le Lièvre et La Tortue** 🄳🄾 🄿🅁 🄳🅁 🅁 🅆 🅂, 2/9, €20/-/60/-, DP20, 30 Rue de la Citadelle, gite.lelievreetlatortue@gmail.com, 0663629235, open Apr–Oct

🔷 **Gîte La Vita è Bella** 🄳🄾 🄿🅁 🄳🅁 🅁 🅆 🅂, 2/8, €17/-/40/-, DP17, 4 Place du Trinquet, patrizia.giardini67@gmail.com, 0768234007, open Mar–Oct

🔷 **Hôtel Itzalpea** 🄿🅁 🄳🅁 🅁 🄲🅁, €-/65/89/-, 5 Place du Trinquet, itzalpea@wanadoo.fr, 0559370366, open Mar–Oct, breakfast €10

🔷 **Hôtel Ramuntcho** 🄿🅁 🄳🅁 🅁 🄲🅁, €-/-/92/-, 1 Rue de France, hotel.ramuntcho@wanadoo.fr, 0559370391, closed Dec, breakfast €11, English spoken

🔺 **Camping Plaza Berri** 🅁, Ave du Fronton, contact@saintjeanpieddeport.fr, 0559370092, open Easter–Oct, camping €11/tent, no wifi

Saint-Jean-Pied-de-Port

- Église Notre-Dame
- Gîte Communal Ospitalia
- Gîte Beilari
- Gîte Chemin Vers l'Etoile
- Gîte Esteban Etxea
- Gîte Ultreia
- Gîte Le Lièvre et La Tortue
- Gîte La Vita è Bella
- Hôtel Itzalpea
- Hôtel Ramuntcho

train station

N

0   100
              m

La Nive

D933

Pilgrim Office

Rue de la Citadelle

D401

Porte
Saint-Jacques

La Citadelle

GR10 / Voie
Nive Bidassoa

Pont Notre-Dame

Porte d'Espagne

GR65 to
Roncesvalles

Rue d'Espagne

La Nive

CÉLÉ VALLEY VARIANT

Pilgrims leave the gîte in Espagnac (Stage C1)

STAGE C1
Figeac to Espagnac-Sainte-Eulalie

Start	Pont d'Or, Figeac
Finish	Gîte Communal, Espagnac-Sainte-Eulalie
Distance	25.7km
Total ascent	475m
Total descent	510m
Difficulty	Easy-to-moderate
Time	6hr 30min
Percentage paved	53%
Gîtes	Lacassagnolle 4km, Béduer 12.3km, Corn 19km, Sainte-Eulalie 23.1+0.4km, Espagnac-Sainte-Eulalie 25.7km

The first 11.6km of this stage remain on the GR65 and include an opportune second-breakfast stop in Faycelles. In Mas de la Croix, though, the Célé Valley variant, the GR651, begins. A short descent from Béduer deposits you directly into the narrow valley, with cornfields squeezing in between the wooded hills and riverbanks. The aptly named village of Corn offers another chance for a snack, before the final push to Espagnac, where the historic monastic complex has been converted into a comfortable gîte and café. The large, grassy field beneath the towering cliffs provides a thoroughly pleasant space to laze away the afternoon.

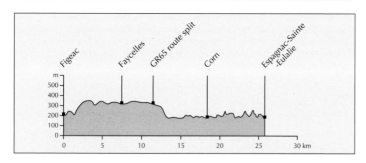

See Via Podiensis, Stage 11 for the route description from Figeac to Mas de la Croix. This is where the GR651 splits from the GR65. From **Mas de la Croix**, continue straight on D21 for the GR651. Merge onto **D19**. While the route turns right on D21, detour ahead a short distance to access services in

0.7KM BÉDUER (ELEV 260M, POP 720) 🚻 🛏 (495.2KM)
WC and fountain next to church. War broke out between Béduer and neighboring Cambouliat in 1819. Paul Valéry, the great poet, spent much of World War II here, after refusing to cooperate with Vichy. The town was historically owned by the Barasc, one of Quercy's most powerful families; their château, the largest in the region in the Middle Ages, survives, albeit extensively modified.

🛏 Gîte Le Bédigas Ⓞ Do Pr Dr Br R W S, 5/15, €24/55/70/93, DP15.50, gite.bedigas@gmail.com, 0950123357, reservation required in offseason, swimming pool, donkey parking, English spoken

▲ Camping Pech Ibert Do Pr Dr K R Gr W Z, €14/20/40/57, DP22, camping. pech.ibert@orange.fr, 0565400585 or 0671154272, open Apr–Sept, accommodation in chalets and mobile homes, camping €8.50/person, swimming pool, English spoken

Continue on D21, then fork right onto a footpath, descending through woods. Join a dirt road (**0.9km**) and proceed through corn fields in the river valley. Cross **D21**, then later transition onto pavement (**2.9km**). Turn right onto **D48**, cross the **Célé River**, then fork right onto D41 (**0.7km**). Turn left onto a minor paved road, just before **Boussac** (🛏 Mas Del Lum Ⓞ Pr Br K R, €-/-/90/140, contact@mas-del-lum.fr, 0565400663, swimming pool). The pietá in the Église Saint-Jean-Baptiste is worth a look, while the Grotte de Palabres, an Iron Age funereal cave, has been discovered below town. Follow a dirt track until rejoining D41 (**1.4km**). Shortly after the tea salon, turn right into

6.7KM CORN (ELEV 185M, POP 225) 🚻 🛏 (488.5KM)
Only ruins remain of the 15th-century Château de Roquefort. The story here surrounds the young widow Delphine Othon, who bemoaned the loss of her home in Camboulit. She wedded the owner of Roquefort and engineered a 23-year battle with Camboulit's new residents, finally winning it back. More than a century later, the two families took to arms once again in the Wars of Religion, with Catholic Roquefort facing off against Protestant Camboulit for 15 more years. The battle ended in a duel between the squabbling clans' two young leaders. Once again, Roquefort came out on top.

🛏 🛏 Gîte L'Antiqui'Thé Do Pr Dr K R W S, 2/5, €22.50/27.50/55/82.50, DP20, antiquithe@orange.fr, 0565400684 or 0565338327, open Apr–Sept, breakfast included with private rooms, donkey parking

🛏 La Maison de Cécile Pr K R W S, 2/4, €-/22/44/57, raymonde.roques123@ orange.fr, 0679427736, open Mar–Oct, breakfast €5, no wifi

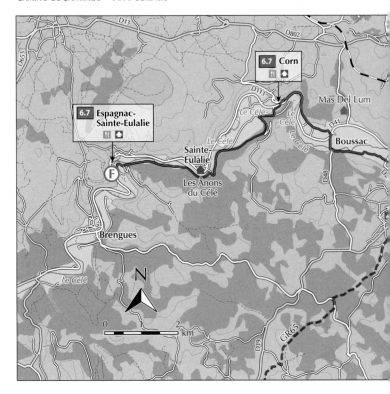

Cross **D113**, turn right, and then immediately back to the left on a footpath. Cross D41 and join a dirt track (**0.3km**). From here, it's all quiet, country tracks, often skirting the edge between forest and field (**3.5km**). Fork left onto a footpath to follow the GR651 (although you might consider a short detour, following the dirt road across the Célé into **Sainte-Eulalie** and ♠ ♠ Les Ânons du Célé Pr Dr Br R W S, €-/45/70/96, DP25, lesanonsducele@orange.fr, 0565502657, open mid Mar–mid Nov, English spoken).

Sainte-Eulalie's church dates to 974 and once hosted pilgrims to Compostela. Built above a cave with prehistoric paintings (no visits, unfortunately), the church includes a small resurgence into which villagers would once toss the clothes of sick children, hoping for a cure.

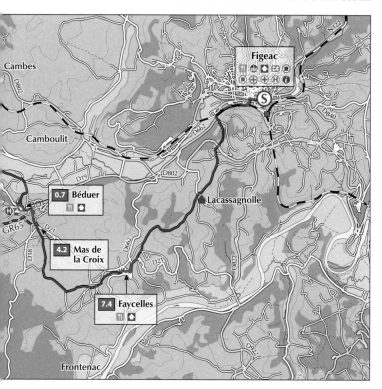

Soon after transitioning back onto a paved road, turn right at a T downhill. At a hairpin turn to the right, arrive at the Gîte Communal in

6.7KM ESPAGNAC-SAINTE-EULALIE (ELEV 160M, POP 90) ▯▯ ▯ (481.8KM)
WC and fountain behind the Gîte Communal.

Founded as a male monastery by Augustinian monk Bertrand de Griffeuil in 1130–40, then rebuilt after its destruction by the English in 1160, this area became fittingly known as Paradise Valley. After the monastery fell into disrepair, Aymeric, the Bishop of Coimbra, who originated in the area, converted it into a convent in 1293. It survived until the French Revolution. The Flamboyant Gothic church, which suffered greatly in the Hundred Years' War, has tombs, including that of Aymeric, who died in 1295. There's a massive, 17th-century painting of the Assumption inside; outside the fortified gate one can find ruins of the old priory.

Eulalia of Mérida was an adolescent Christian living during Diocletian's persecution. After her mother tried to hide her, Eulalia charged into the governor's court and declared her faith, rejecting his authority to punish her. She was tortured and ultimately burned at the stake, but she railed against her tormentors throughout. As she died, it is said a dove flew from her mouth. Her body was subsequently moved to Oviedo in Spain, and her tomb remains there in a cathedral's chapel.

⌂ **Gîte Communal** Do Pr Dr K R Gr W S Z, 2/12, €14/30/35/45, DP21, giteespagnac@orange.fr, 0565114266, open Apr–Oct

⌂ **La Maison du Passant Pélerin** Do K R W S, 1/4, €Donation, gabysenac@wanadoo.fr, 0565400524, open Jun–Sept

⌂ ⌂ **Célézen** Do Pr Dr R W S, 1/2, €25/-/64/79, DP24, jpduvauchel@gmail.com, 0565389009 or 0625155218, open Apr–Dec, jacuzzi, English spoken

The old monastic center in Espagnac-Sainte-Eulalie, now a gîte and café

STAGE C2
Espagnac-Sainte-Eulalie to Marcilhac-sur-Célé

Start	Gîte Communal, Espagnac-Sainte-Eulalie
Finish	Abbaye Saint-Pierre, Marcilhac-sur-Célé
Distance	15.9km
Total ascent	535m
Total descent	555m
Difficulty	Strenuous
Time	5hr
Percentage paved	20%
Gîtes	Brengues 4km, Marcilhac-sur-Célé 15.9km

While yesterday's walk offered an agreeable introduction to the Célé Valley, today's stage begins the highlight reel. It also marks a transition to some demanding terrain, with frequent ups-and-downs through the limestone cliffs. Indeed, the morning kicks off with a sharp ascent to the clifftop. The dramatic views of the valley below and opposing cliffs are to be savored. Two small villages offer breaks, with restaurants requiring small detours from the GR651, but the day's destination, Marcilhac-sur-Célé, is truly exceptional. Its compact medieval core offers evocative abbey ruins, and the shady, riverside park coaxes many into taking an afternoon dip. Don't miss the patisserie!

Cross the Célé, turn right at the T, then turn left onto a dirt track. Turn left again soon after, then transition onto a footpath (**0.6km**). After ascending through a series of switchbacks, emerge onto the clifftop (**0.8km**) and then pass the **Fontaine du Causse** (**0.8km**).

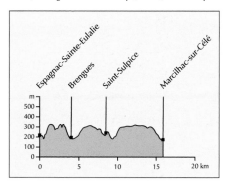

Briefly turn left onto a dirt track before returning to a footpath that runs parallel to the cliff face, passing **Château des Anglais**, a medieval fortification built into the cliff face (**0.5km**). Turn left onto **D38** (**0.9km**), then fork left off it. To access Brengues' restaurant/bakery, continue straight downhill to a small roundabout. Turn right, passing through a small cluster of houses in

4KM BRENGUES (ELEV 190M, POP 210) 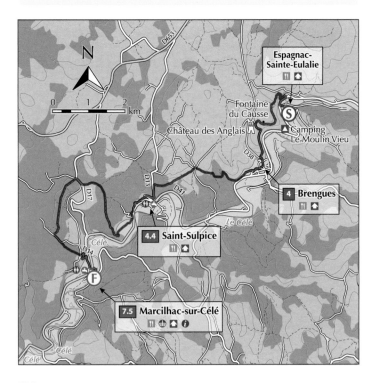 (477.8KM)

Exiting town, a private home offers drinking water. Market on Thursday evenings in July/August. The village dates to the 13th century, but the church features pre-Romanesque elements.

- ♠ Gîte La Brenguoise **Do Pr Dr R W S**, 2/8, €15/-/40/-, DP25, contact@labrenguoise.fr, 0630206806, open Apr–Oct, swimming pool

- ♠ Gîte Le Ricochet **Do Pr K R W S**, 3/6, €20/-/40/-, lericochetducele@gmail.com, 0565397883, open Mar–Jun and Sept–Oct, mini-*épicerie*

- ▲ Camping Le Moulin Vieux **Do Dr R W**, 2/6, €19/-/-/-, lemoulinvieux@outlook.com, 0606493325, open mid Apr–Oct, camping €8.60/person, swimming pool, restaurant/*épicerie*

Cross D38 and transition back to dirt tracks soon after, ascending to the cliffs (**0.2km**). From a complicated intersection (**2km**), turn left, then right, then left again, all in quick succession. After another long stretch, continue straight on **D13** (**1.5km**). Fork left onto a footpath, cross D13, then emerge on a paved road through a residential neighborhood. The *chemin* continues straight, but turn left to detour into

4.4KM SAINT-SULPICE (ELEV 205M, POP 145) 🏚 🔼 (473.4KM)

WC and fountain at church. The old castle guards the cliff face, owned by the Hébrard family. The Hébrards were the dominant family in the Célé in the Middle Ages, funding both abbeys. The town preserves a 19th-century mill. St Sulpice was Bishop of Bourges in the seventh century; his tomb became a minor pilgrimage site.

⬥ Gite Le Chant de la Falaise 🄳🄾 🄿🅁 🄳🅁 🄺 🅁 🅆 🅂, 1/7, €17/-/40/-, DP22, Barry du Four, severinevelien@mailo.com, 0652703028, open Apr–Oct

▲ Camping Le Célé 🄳🄾 🄿🅁 🄳🅁 🅁 🄲🅁 🅆, campinglecele@gmail.com, 0604089688, open Apr–Sept, restaurant, swimming pool

Returning to the track along the cliffside, pass a series of 'troglodyte houses' built into the rock. After another ascent, turn right on **D17** (**3.4km**). Return swiftly to a footpath (**0.2km**) for another extended off-road stretch (**2.9km**). Turn left on **D14** and descend towards town. The GR65 bypasses the center; instead fork left in town, away from the waymarks and towards the river. Then, take the next left as well (**0.7km**). This leads to a park. Join the riverside walkway, then turn right through a small gate in the wall. The Abbaye Saint-Pierre is on your right in

7.5KM MARCILHAC-SUR-CÉLÉ (ELEV 140M, POP 200) 🏚 ⊕ 🔼 ❶ (465.9KM)

WC and fountain by the river, near the *épicerie*. Markets on Tuesdays and Sundays.

The medieval town was surrounded by a square wall, of which one gate survives (along with a 16th-century house, the Maison du Roi). The Romanesque portion of the church from the Benedictine Abbey is largely in ruins, a consequence of damage done in the Hundred Years' War, but the 10th-century door is well preserved, portraying the Last Judgment. The Gothic portion is in better shape and includes a 16th-century pietà. During World War II, the town was briefly held by the resistance leader, Jean-Jacques Chapou. Stalactites were removed from nearby caves to adorn Catherine de Medici's castle. Wild rumors exist that Marcilhac's church was a hotbed of heresy in the eighth century; it's said that a local saint, Namphaise (a former general under Charlemagne), was sent to investigate claims of cannibalism and child sacrifice. No word on what he discovered!

An increasingly popular option for the next stage is to give the feet a rest and instead kayak along the Célé River. Numerous companies offer rentals and coordinate pack transportation, making it easy to do; book online or through your gîte. While your feet will appreciate it, don't expect to just coast lazily down the river – your arms will be getting quite a workout.

⌂ **Accueil Saint-Pierre** Do Pr Dr R Cf W S, 3/12, €18/38/42/54, DP19, 3 Route de Compostelle, gitemarcilhac@gmail.com, 0634365460, open Apr–20 Oct, camping €6/person

⌂ **Gîte de Galance** Do Pr Dr K R Cf W S Z, 6/15, €18.50/-/49/-, DP21, contact@gitedegalance.fr, 0615949197 or 0565342397, open Mar–Oct, English spoken

⌂ **La Ferme de Cazals** O Pr Dr Br K R W S, €-/45/75/105, DP25, fabiennebos2017@gmail.com, 0565500789 or 0615755434

⌂ **Le Picarel** Pr Dr Br R W, €-/-/72/-, DP25, lepicarelbandb@gmail.com, 0626462963, open May–Oct, English spoken

The riverside walkway in Marcilhac-sur-Célé

STAGE C3
Marcilhac-sur-Célé to Cabrerets

Start	Abbaye Saint-Pierre, Marcilhac-sur-Célé
Finish	D13 intersection, Cabrerets
Distance	18.3km
Total ascent	585m
Total descent	605m
Difficulty	Strenuous
Time	5hr 45min
Percentage paved	6%
Gîtes	Sauliac-sur-Célé 8.4km, Gîte La Flèche Bleue 12.4+1.3km, Cabrerets 18.3km

Another spectacular and strenuous day awaits. Soon after departing Marcilhac, you're back atop the limestone plateau, winding through rocky fields, with pavement a genuine rarity. The *Quercus pubescens*, or downy oak, thrives in this challenging terrain, although blackthorn and juniper are prevalent as well. While cliff-top views remain impressive, the walk along the cliff face after Sauliac may be even more memorable, courtesy of the Châteaux des Anglais built into the rock. For something completely different, an 'ecomuseum' offers a window into the region's heritage. The final approach into Cabrerets is a dramatic descent with some of the most spectacular vistas thus far.

With the abbey ruins at your back, pass out of the old town and turn right, away from the river. Fork left through an alley and cross **D41**. Turn right at the T, then take the next left, reuniting with GR651 waymarks. Proceed uphill, onto a dirt track (**0.4km**). Turn

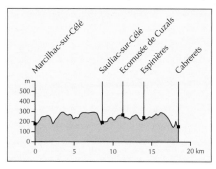

left at the cliff top and then, at a complicated intersection, follow a footpath between two roads (**0.7km**). Turn left onto a dirt track (**1.2km**). After a lengthy off-road stretch atop the plateau, turn left onto a paved road (**4.2km**). At the turn-off for Aux Lodges Mas de Nadal (**0.5km**), continue straight onto a footpath, beginning the descent towards Sauliac-sur-Célé. Soon after

(0.1km), it's possible to visit the Dolmen du Pech de Gadal by making a short detour to the left. The GR651 skirts the edge of Sauliac. To visit the center, make a sharp left before the Châteaux des Anglais.

8.4KM SAULIAC-SUR-CÉLÉ (ELEV 200M, POP 120) 🍴 ⛺ (457.5M)
Some 700 people lived here in the late 19th century, but less than 100 do now. This is one of the best places in the Célé Valley to see the Châteaux des Anglais. They generally date to the 11th/12th centuries and were utilized in the Hundred Years' War to protect civilians from attacks along the river. The village is situated in the *triangle noir du Quercy*, where there is no light pollution at night.

⌂ Gîte O Coeur des Sens **O Do Dr K R W S**, 2/10, €17/-/-/-, DP18, nathalievabre1@gmail.com, 0631052802, reservation required in offseason, no wifi

⌂ Château de Geniès **Pr Dr Br R**, €-/25/50/75, DP15, ch.genies@orange.fr, 0618277900, open late Apr–mid Sept, closed Aug, donkey parking

A house built into the cliff face near Cabrerets

Continue straight along the footpath alongside the **châteaux**. Turn left at a T (**2.6km**) and then, as you make a hairpin turn to the left, arrive at

2.9KM ECOMUSÉE DE CUZALS (ELEV 250M)(454.6KM)

This is a surprise: an impressive open-air museum (€5), seemingly stashed in the middle of nowhere. It offers an authentic 19th-century experience, sharing what life in the region was like between the French Revolution and World War II, complete with a practicing blacksmith, farmworkers, bakers, shoemakers, and even a 1900-era dental surgery.

Descend along the dirt track (**0.8km**), turn right, and then ascend once again. Pass the turn-off (**0.3km**) for ♦ Gîte La Flèche Bleue **Do Dr K R W S Z**, 11/32, €15/-/-/-, DP21, laflechebleue46@gmail.com, 0565233672, open mid Apr–mid Oct. Turn right and then cross **D40** (**1.5km**). Pass through the village of **Espinières** (**0.1km**). Turn left at a T (**1.6km**). The final descent to Cabrerets begins soon after. Take care, as this is steep in places and the footing is sometimes poor. Emerge onto a paved road (**2.1km**), then

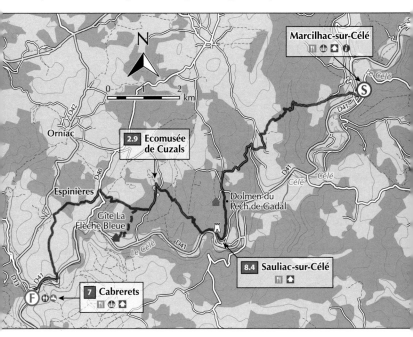

join **D41** (0.3km). Fork right onto a minor road between houses (0.2km), then proceed to an intersection with **D13**. Continue straight if you wish to keep walking, or turn right to enter

---

7KM CABRERETS (ELEV 140M, POP 230) 🍴 ⊕ 🛏 (447.6KM)
WC and fountain by the *mairie*.

The name means 'land of the giants.' One castle, built here in 1380 by Bastard of Albert, still exists. Another, Château de Diable, now in ruins, is much older, dating to the eighth century and credited to the Duke of Aquitaine. The English conducted a guerrilla campaign from this castle in 1390. Legend holds that a shepherdess, seeking to escape the duke's advances, jumped out of the window and drowned in the Célé. Enemies stormed the castle the next day, beginning an era of terror and famine in the region. Ultimately, the duke followed the shepherdess to his own watery death.

An excerpt from a Cahiers, a document of grievances submitted by Cabrerets residents to the Estates-General prior to the French Revolution, reads as follows: 'This community is situated in the most atrocious and abominable corner of the world. Its only possessions – if they can be called that – are rugged rocks and mountains that are almost inaccessible.'

⛺ Le Refuge du Célé ⬜ ⬜ ⬜ ⬜ ⬜ ⬜ ⬜ ⬜, 4/8, €17/-/34/-, DP30, refugeducele@gmail.com, 0565312015, open Apr–Sept

⛺ Gîte du Barry ⬜ ⬜ ⬜ ⬜ ⬜ ⬜ ⬜ ⬜, 2/9, €17.50/-/40/-, DP22, larouelot@yahoo.com, 0668145956, open Apr–Nov, English spoken

⛺ L'Auberge de la Sagne ⬜ ⬜ ⬜ ⬜ ⬜, €-/-/95/-, DP25, 663 Route Grotte du Pech Merle, aubergedelasagne@orange.fr, 0565312662, open Apr–Oct, English spoken

⛺ Hôtel des Grottes du Pech Merle ⬜ ⬜ ⬜ ⬜ ⬜ ⬜ ⬜, €-/-/75/100, reservation@hoteldesgrottes.com, 0565312702, open Apr–Sept, restaurant, swimming pool

---

Start	D13 Intersection, Cabrerets
Finish	Office de Tourisme, Saint-Cirq-Lapopie
Distance	10.7km (9.6km via train bridge short-cut, 11.4km via scenic alternative)
Total ascent	330m
Total descent	240m
Difficulty	Strenuous
Time	3hr 30min (3hr 15min via train bridge short-cut, 3hr 45min via scenic alternative)
Percentage paved	25%
Gîtes	Pech-Merle 1.4+0.7km, Conduché 6km, A La Source 9.2km, Saint-Cirq-Lapopie 10.7km

This unusually short stage serves several purposes. First, it gives the body a break – walking through the Célé Valley is rewarding, but also demanding. It also ensures ample time to enjoy Saint-Cirq-Lapopie, recently hailed as the most beautiful village in France, as well as a morning visit to the Pech Merle cave, which is situated just 1km after Cabrerets. The prehistoric paintings preserved in Pech Merle are some of the finest you'll see – just make sure to schedule your visit in advance. While Saint-Cirq-Lapopie is technically off-route and will likely necessitate some backtracking, there are a couple of alternative approaches to consider.

From the D13 intersection in **Cabrerets**, proceed uphill, following signs for Pech Merle. Fork right twice, pass the church, and turn left. Join a footpath, proceeding sharply uphill to

1KM PECH MERLE (ELEV 285M) ▦ (446.6KM)
WC near entrance, snack bar.

In 1922, three local teenagers went caving, as they had done on occasion for years. This time, though, they made an incredible discovery – a chamber full of prehistoric art. Some 15,000–25,000 years old, the paintings include a fish, bison, mammoths, a bear's head, and numerous human hands. Pech Merle is most famous, though, for its horses, and particularly its spotted horse, which masterfully capitalizes on the wall's curvature. While the paintings dominate the headlines, and justifiably so, the walk through the cave is worth the price of admission (€14), as the rock formations are other-worldly.

Reservations are essential (https://booking.pechmerle.com), as group sizes for the mandatory tours are strictly limited. If pausing here mid-walk, the proprietors provide a safe place to stash your pack.

Pass to the right through one parking lot, then back to the left through another, continuing out the back corner and onto a dirt track. Turn left (**0.4km**). (Alternately, continue straight 0.7km to reach ⛰ Ferme Équestre du Pech Merle O Do Pr Dr K R W S, 2/6, €25/-/50/-, DP23, randocheval@gmail.com, 0611932523, camping €5/person, no wifi). At a T, turn left again (**2km**). Descend to **D662** (**2.4km**). From there, you have three options for reaching Saint-Cirq: the official approach through Bouziès, a short-cut that bypasses Bouziès, or a scenic alternative that offers impressive views but a lot of pavement.

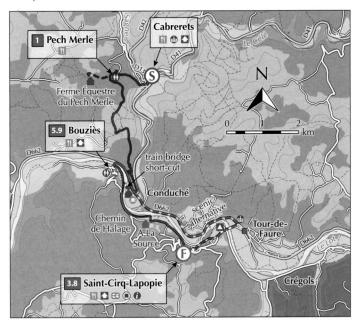

Saint-Cirq-Lapopie

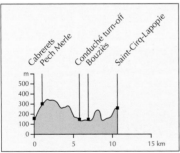

GR651 to Bouziès and GR36 to Saint-Cirq-Lapopie (4.8km to Saint-Cirq)

Turn right on D662. Turn left across the **Lot River** (**1km**). The GR651 concludes here; between Saint-Cirq and Cahors you'll primarily follow the GR36. If you don't wish to visit Saint-Cirq, turn right at Bouziès' church and pick up the directions in Stage C5. To continue towards Saint-Cirq, as recommended, turn left immediately after crossing the Lot in

5.9KM BOUZIÈS (ELEV 140M, POP 85) ◫ △ (440.7KM)

The Église Saint-Léger dates to 1847.

🛏 Hôtel Les Falaises Pr Dr R Gr S Z, €-/-/75/102, DP30, 245 Route Touristique, hotelfalaises@gmail.com, 0565312683, open Apr–Oct

Pass a riverside café and WC, continuing straight on a footpath (**0.2km**). After passing through a riverside park, the trail leads onto the **Chemin de Halage**, a historic towpath that was carved into the limestone cliff between 1843 and 1847. This is one of the most memorable stretches encountered on any part of the pilgrimage. After the

235

towpath concludes (**1.9km**), turn right briefly onto a dirt track (**0.1km**) and then left onto a paved road. (Alternately, to reach ⌂ A La Source ◯ ℙ Bʳ Ⓚ Ⓡ Ⓦ Ⓢ, €-/-/60/-, bclaquin@hotmail.com, 0621724356, campers welcome, no wifi, turn right on the paved road.) Finally, turn right onto a footpath and climb sharply through a wooded hillside, emerging at the Office de Tourisme in **Saint-Cirq-Lapopie**.

Short-cut to Saint-Cirq via train bridge (3.7km to Saint-Cirq-Lapopie)
This unmarked approach saves some distance and adds a bit of adventure to your day. Soon after turning right on D662, turn left onto a dirt track. Find a footpath at the base of the train bridge and scramble up. Cross the retired Eiffel bridge, then take the second footpath down from the right side. Turn right to join the GR36 just before the **Chemin de Halage**; pick up the directions from there above. Both bridge access points are steep and need to be managed with care. For that reason, this short-cut is not for everyone.

Scenic alternative to Saint-Cirq (5.5km to Saint-Cirq-Lapopie)
There are two reasons to consider this unmarked variant: first, it means you don't have to follow the exact same route back to Bouziès tomorrow; second, it offers a spectacular view of Saint-Cirq from across the Lot. Turning left on D662, pass through **Conduché** (⌂ Les Deux Vallées Dᵒ Dʳ Ⓚ Ⓡ Cʳ Ⓦ Ⓢ Ⓩ, 4/10, €17/-/-/-, DP23, 0565245892, open Mar–Oct, bar/restaurant) and continue straight. Take care – this requires you to pass through an auto tunnel; consider having your flashlight on and pointed towards traffic as you proceed. Skirt **Toure de Faure** (grocery), then turn right to cross over the **Lot**

A commanding view of the Lot River from the hill atop Saint-Cirq-Lapopie

(**3.4km**). Pass ▲ Camping de la Plage (details below) and then fork right (**1km**), joining a riverside road. Fork left onto a footpath (**0.5km**), the old Passage des Anglais, which English troops used to seize Saint-Cirq in the Hundred Years' War. Hopefully with more peaceful motives, ascend into town.

3.8KM SAINT-CIRQ-LAPOPIE (ELEV 230M, POP 200) ▯ ▢ ⓒ ◉ ❶ (436.9KM)
Market on Wednesday nights in July/August. WC behind tourism office.

Situated on a ledge above the Lot, this is indeed a particularly beautiful village. Originally, a Roman villa named Pompéjac stood here. The current town is named for St Cyr (also Cyricus, Quiricus), a child martyr who was killed in Roman Antioch in 304. His remains were brought here by St Amator (Amador), the Bishop of Auxerre and rumored founder of Rocamadour. One legend holds that three-year-old Cyr and his mother, Julitta, both Christians, were apprehended. As the governor oversaw Julitta's torture, Cyr scratched his face in protest, only to be thrown down a flight of stairs and killed. Julitta was executed soon after.

Pepin the Short oversaw a period of systematic devastation here in the 750s, with houses destroyed and land burnt. Inhabitants who survived owed it to subterranean retreats, hiding in caves all along the Célé. Richard the Lionheart tried to take it in 1198, but failed; however, the English would succeed in the 14th century. Three feudal families (the Lapopies, Gourdons, and Cardaillacs) dominated the town, contributing to the development of several fortified houses/castles. The ruins of the old fort, built by Oldoric, Viscount of Saint-Cirq in the 10th century, are still accessible, although it was destroyed in 1471 by King Louis XI for the town's betrayal in the Hundred Years' War. Henri of Navarre put an end to Saint-Cirq's strategic importance in 1580 when he had its remaining walls flattened. It has long been popular with artists and writers, including post-impressionist Henri Martin, Catalan painter Pierre Daura, and writer André Breton. Breton was one of Surrealism's founders, having produced a manifesto on the subject, and it's possible to visit his former home here, Maison André Breton. The Rignault Museum (€2) preserves a typical village home, with a spectacular garden and a collection of curios from around the world. The church preserves its Romanesque apse and 16th-century fortified tower, although much of it is newer.

🏠 Gîte de St-Cirq Lapopie **Do Dr Br R Gr Z**, 3/15, €43/-/-/-, incl DP, Place des Oules, gitelapopie@gmail.com, 0687436264, open mid Mar–mid Nov

🏠 Maison Lapopie **O Pr Dr Br R Gr W S**, €-/-/115/-, DP25, Chemin Neuf Lebourg, maison.lapopie@gmail.com, 0665306883

▲ Camping de la Plage **Do Pr Dr R W Z**, 1/6, €14/25/40/-, camping-laplage@wanadoo.fr, 0565302951, camping €8–12/tent, restaurant and *épicerie*, 1.3km from village, open late Apr–Sept

STAGE C5
Saint-Cirq-Lapopie to Cahors

Start	Office de Tourisme, Saint-Cirq-Lapopie
Finish	Cathédrale Saint-Étienne, Cahors
Distance	33.2km (36.8km via high-level alternative)
Total ascent	575m (870m via high-level alternative)
Total descent	675m (970m via high-level alternative)
Difficulty	Moderate (moderate-to-strenuous via high-level alternative)
Time	9hr (10hr via high-level alternative
Percentage paved	29%
Gîtes	Pasturat 15.2km, Vers 19+1.9km, Cahors 33.2km

This is the most complicated stage in the book, due primarily to an abundance of alternative routes. Note that if you adhere strictly to the recommended approach you will not encounter a single store or café between Bouziès and Cahors, although a bakery in Arcambal requires only a short detour. After backtracking through Bouziès, you'll continue westward on the GR36. When the route veers inland from the Lot, a possible short-cut (involving a challenging ascent and descent) follows a retired train bridge over the Lot and past Saint-Géry. The two approaches rejoin shortly before Pasturat, then carry onward to near the village of Béars. At that point, it's possible to detour into Vers on the GR46, and from there another variant loops back south to the recommended route. Soon after Béars, this guide recommends breaking with the GR36 and following an unmarked approach to a riverside path, which is both shorter and easier. Eventually the GR36 briefly rejoins the riverside path, before turning southward to climb into the hills prior to entering Cahors, where Mont Saint-Cyr offers stunning views. However, once again, the recommended approach here is to stick with the river, continuing a flat and relaxing stroll towards Cahors, one of the largest towns encountered on this pilgrimage.

Note that instead of proceeding directly to Cahors along the GR36 and the Lot River, it's possible to follow the GR36 southward through Concots to join the GR65 near Bach and Vaylats. This approach may be appealing to those interested in bypassing Cahors entirely; it is described in Via Podiensis, Stage 13.

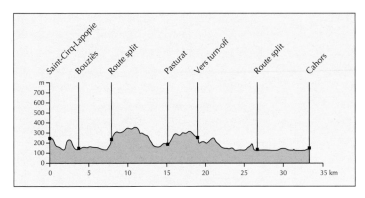

From the Office de Tourisme, backtrack **3.8km** to **Bouziès**, following the GR36 and the Chemin de Halage, and then continue straight past the church out of town. Fork right onto a dirt road, descending to a riverside track (**2.6km**). After a further **1km** you have a decision to make.

Official route on the GR36 (7km)
Turn left, through a train tunnel, and proceed inland on a dirt track. Climb sharply into the hills, eventually turning right onto a footpath (**2.8km**). Briefly join a paved road then fork right onto another footpath for another extended off-road sequence (**3.2km**). Descend to a riverside path. Intersect the **D10** (**1km**) at the **Saint-Géry turn-off**.

Alternative via train bridge (3.1km direct or 5.5km via Saint-Géry)
This route offers a possible short-cut and resupply point, but it's not for everybody. The climb to a retired train bridge is steep, on loose ground, and the descent can be even trickier. In addition, the tracks on the other side can be overgrown with sticker bushes, making it thorny to traverse. If you're comfortable managing those challenges, though, it's worth considering.

From the split with the GR36, continue straight along the riverside. Just before reaching the **train bridge** (**0.6km**), scramble up the hillside to your left. Follow the railroad to its second road crossing, descending to **D662** and turning left onto it (**0.5km**). After passing a car dealership (**1.6km**), continue straight to access **Saint-Géry**'s services (**1.2km**). Alternately, you could turn left to omit Saint-Géry and maximize the short-cut, saving 2.4km.

Continue straight, then turn left at the church. Fork right, pass under a railroad line, and then turn left (**0.3km**). At a T, turn right (**1km**), rejoining the direct short-cut as it crosses the **Lot**. Once on the other side, turn right to rejoin the GR36.

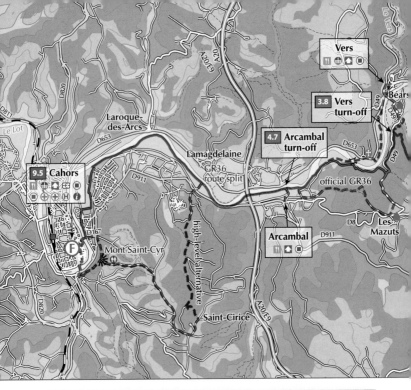

Vers

3.8 Vers turn-off

4.7 Arcambal turn-off

9.5 Cahors

Laroque-des-Arcs

Lamagdelaine

GR36 route split

official GR36

Arcambal

high-level alternative

Mont Saint-Cyr

Saint-Cirice

Les Mazuts

Béars

Le Lot

Le Vers

The bridge crossing on the alternative route to Saint-Géry

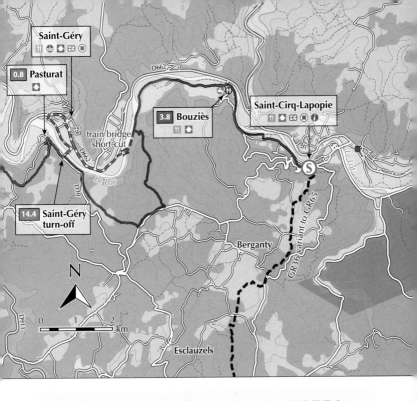

14.4KM TURN-OFF TO SAINT-GÉRY (ELEV 130M, POP 860) 🍴 ⊕ 🏠 ⓒ ◉
(422.5KM)

The town, located 1.6km off-route, is your best bet for services in this stage. The barebones campground is just across the river; the other services, including a fountain and WC, are clustered in the center. The town is named after Didier, the seventh-century bishop of Cahors. A small railway museum has been established in the defunct station, once part of the old Quercy Rail line.

🏠 Domaine du Porche ◎ Pr Br K R, €-/45/49/57, Ave de l'Europe, brumo@laposte.net, 0565314594, swimming pool, English spoken

Routes combined
Routes reunited, climb steadily along the paved road, looping sharply to the left, and then turning right at the church into

0.8KM PASTURAT (ELEV 220M) 🛏 (421.7KM)

🔺 Le Relais de Pasturat **Do Pr Dr Br R W S**, 4/15, €25/-/60/-, DP16, gitescharazac@hotmail.com, 0565314494, open Easter–Oct, camping €10/person, swimming pool

Turn left onto a footpath, then continue straight onto a paved road (**0.2km**). Proceed inland, through the hills, along a series of paved and unpaved tracks. When the GR36 makes a sharp left (**3.6km**), the GR46 from Vers joins from the right.

3.8KM TURN-OFF TO VERS (ELEV 160M, POP 420) 🏬 ⊕ 🛏 ◉ (417.9KM)

Vers is 2.1km away and offers a good place to split this stage in half. See the Rocamadour variant, Stage R6 for an alternative route back.

🔺 Gîte Le Monde Allant Vers **Do Dr R W**, 1/8, €18/-/-/-, DP19, Rue du Château, lemondeallantvers46@gmail.com, 0685653078, open Mar–Oct, no wifi

🔺 Hôtel La Truite Dorée **O Pr Dr R Gr S Z**, €-/75/90/116, DP32, Rue de la Barre, latruitedoree@wanadoo.fr, 0565314151, swimming pool

Merge onto **D49** as it curves right (**1.2km**). After **0.1km** you have another choice to make.

Recommended short-cut on riverside path (3.1km)

To make a useful, unmarked short-cut, instead of continuing with the GR36 on D49, turn right onto a minor paved road. Follow this **1.9km**. After passing through a small cluster of houses, turn right on a dirt track, crossing a defunct railroad and turning left immediately after. The train bridge short-cut from Vers joins here from the right. Fork right onto a riverside footpath (**0.3km**). Continue straight as the GR36 rejoins from the left (**0.9km**).

Official route via Les Mazuts (4.8km)

This approach is more strenuous, requiring a 100m up-and-down. Follow D49 for **1km**, then turn right onto a footpath. Briefly rejoin D49, then turn right on D8 and fork right immediately after on a minor paved road (**0.4km**). (Alternately, to reach 🔺 Les Mazuts **O Pr Dr Br R W S**, €-/45/55/65, DP15, carmenpierre@orange.fr, 0674859668, donkey parking, stay with D49.) Fork right onto an unpaved track (**0.4km**). Merge onto a paved road near **Arcambal** (**2.2km**) and continue straight through a neighborhood. Turn right at a T (to reach Arcambal center, turn left immediately after) and descend to the **Lot**, rejoining the recommended approach on a riverside track.

*Pilgrims follow the dirt track near the
lock on the Lot River in Arcambal*

Routes combined

Routes reunited, proceed to a three-way intersection (**0.3km**), from which Arcambal is accessible as a 0.4km detour to the left. Proceed inland, pass under the old railroad, curve right and then left, passing the bakery en route to the center.

> **4.7KM TURN-OFF TO ARCAMBAL** (ELEV 160M, POP 420) ⊞ 🛖 ◉ (**417.9KM**)
> The Château du Bousquet is a national historic monument.
>
> 🛏 Les 3 Cochons d'Olt 🅾 ᴘꜰ ᴅʀ ʙʀ ᴿ, €-/-/69/84, DP15, ulrikecurrie46@orange.
> fr, 0565212051 or 0642823054, English spoken

To proceed towards Cahors, continue straight on the riverside track, alongside a lock. Pass under the **A20/E9** (**1.2km**), then transition back onto a footpath, still on the riverside (**0.6km**). When the footpath intersects a minor paved road (**1.1km**), the GR36 splits.

Riverside GR36 (6.7km)

The main GR36 continues as a short, flat, and shady footpath along the riverside. After looping all the way around a bend in the Lot (**4km**), turn left onto a dirt track, then right soon after on a paved road. Turn right on Rue de la Guinguette, entering Cahors' outskirts (**1.1km**). Turn left on Rue de la Rivière, just before a sports complex, and then fork right onto a riverside walkway. Finally, turn right onto **D167** (**1.1km**), crossing the Lot into Cahors. You may see limited or conflicting waymarks from this point. Turn left after the bridge on D653, then fork right through Place Champollion onto Rue du Maréchal Foch. Turn left and arrive at the cathedral in **Cahors**.

High-level GR36 variant (10.3km)

A more strenuous variant is possible, which has its reward. Turn left onto a minor paved road off the riverside walkway. Cross the railroad and **D911**, forking right onto another paved road (**0.3km**). Climb steadily into the hills. Fork left onto a dirt track (**0.9km**). Fork right, remaining on the Route de Saint-Cirice, and then fork right again (**1.7km**). Fork left, following the dirt track as it curves sharply left (**0.9km**). Turn right at a T onto a paved road (**0.6km**), passing through **Saint-Cirice**. Fork right three times as you loop around the hillside (**1.4km**). Fork left onto a footpath parallel to the road (**0.9km**). Rejoin the paved road and arrive atop **Mont Saint-Cyr** (**2km**, WC), enjoying spectacular views of Cahors below.

For the final approach to Cahors, you have two options. Turn right to follow a footpath down to Cahors' eastern entrance. Then turn left on **D167** and rejoin the recommended approach above as it crosses the Lot. Alternately, turn left, also on a footpath (enjoying even better views along the way), emerging near Cahors' southern entrance. At a roundabout, fork left to cross Pont Louis-Philippe into Cahors. Proceed straight to the next roundabout, then take the second right onto Rue des Maures, a very minor street. Turn left at a T on Rue Nationale and proceed straight to the cathedral in

9.5KM CAHORS (ELEV 125M, POP 19,340) 🏠 ⊕ △ ⓒ ⊚ ⊙ ⊕ ⊕ ⊕ ❶
(403.7KM)
See Via Podiensis, Stage 13 for Cahors background information, town map and accommodation details.

To continue, see Stage 14 of the Via Podiensis.

ROCAMADOUR VARIANT

The sanctuary of Rocamadour as seen from the medieval village (Stage R3)

STAGE R1
Figeac to Lacapelle-Marival

Start	Pont d'Or, Figeac
Finish	Église de Notre-Dame de l'Assomption, Lacapelle-Marival
Distance	22.8km
Total ascent	560m
Total descent	375m
Difficulty	Moderate
Time	6hr
Percentage paved	58%
Gîtes	Planioles 3.5km, Lacapelle-Marival 22.8km

The first stage of the Rocamadour variant climbs steadily into the Causse de Gramat, a limestone plateau characterized by rocky terrain, scrubby bushes, and a medley of oak, maple, dogwood, and ash trees. The story behind today's walk is the Cardaillac family, one of the dominant influences in this region throughout the Middle Ages. Their historic base, the town of Cardaillac, stands near the midpoint of this stage, and preserves a spectacular – if compact – cluster of towers. Meanwhile, the destination, Lacapelle-Marival, was founded by the same family and boasts an impressive château. It's a rare day on the pilgrimage when the architectural highlights are predominately secular!

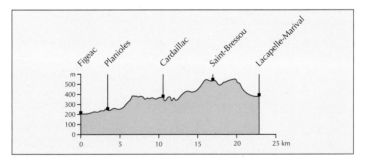

In **Figeac**, with the Pont d'Or behind you, turn left and proceed along the riverside. At the next pedestrian bridge (**0.2km**), turn right onto D840, transitioning at this point from the GR65 to the GR6. Turn left at the T on Rue des Maquisards (**0.3km**). Fork right

Anglars

D653

D653

F **12.4** Lacapelle-Marival
🍴 ⊕ ⌂ ⊕ ⊕ ⊕

D15

Sainte-Colombe

Le Bourg

D940

Saint-Bressou

D92

Le Bouyssou

Rabanal

10.4 Cardaillac
🍴 ⊕ ⌂

Saint-Perdoux

Issepts

Plan d'Eau des Sagnes 🍴 ⊕

D840

Fourmagnac

Fons

Reyrevignes

D15

Camburat

D840

Planioles

D802

Lissac-et-Mouret

N

Cambes

D802

Le Célé

Le Célé

Église Saint-Thomas

Figeac
🍴 ⊕ ⌂ ⊕ ⊙ ⊕ ⊕ Ⓗ ℹ

S

0   1   2
━━━━━━━━━━ km

Camboulit

D19

D662

D802

D662

D822

Following a grassy track towards Cardaillac

at **Église Saint-Thomas** onto Avenue Casimir Marcenac and then left soon after, towards La Curie (**0.3km**). Follow a series of minor roads away from Figeac, passing the turn-off for **Planioles** (**2.7km**) and 🔺🔺 Le Prieuré (◯ Do Pr Dr R Gr S, 1/4, €10/50/90/-, DP20, 27 Rue du Prieuré, pxm@garcette.fr, 0607569286), then fork left onto a dirt track (**1km**). Transition back onto pavement (**2km**), then turn right on **D15** (**0.4km**). Turn left towards Doulan, then right (**0.3km**). Rejoin **D15** (**1.4km**), pass through modern **Cardaillac**, then turn left into its historic center.

10.4KM CARDAILLAC (ELEV 370M, POP 600) 🍴 ⊕ 🛏 (518.2KM)
WC and fountain on left before historic core. Market on Sundays.

Another of France's 'most beautiful villages,' this bears the name of one of the region's most powerful families, as reflected in their motto: 'they were known in all the world.' The medieval fort, built in 1064 as a regional stronghold, is survived today by two square towers and a round one, the Tour de Sagnes, which offers panoramic views of the Drauzou Valley. The town was attacked by Richard the Lionheart in 1188, and then taken by the English in 1356 for three decades. It was established as a haven for Protestants by the Edict of Nantes in 1598. The Musée Eclaté has an eclectic mix of local history, including insights into the 19th-century phylloxera outbreak – an insect epidemic that wiped out viticulture in France and beyond for decades. Three youths were executed by Nazi occupiers here in 1944.

🔺 Le Relais de Conques ◯ Pr Dr Br R, €-/65/75/110, DP25, contact@relais-des-conques.fr, 0565401722 or 0642739644

Curve right, skirting the historic core, and join a footpath into the woods. Loop around a small lake, the **Plan d'Eau des Sagnes**, perfect for a relaxing break (**1.9km**,

The view of Cardaillac from atop the Tour de Sagnes

WC, fountain) and then turn left at a T (**1.1km**). After a series of turns on dirt tracks, leading through the day's lone significant ascent, turn left onto a paved road (**1.3km**). Pass by ⌂ Rabanal (Ⓞ Pr Dr Br R W S, €-/50/65/80, DP13, adecertaines@netc. fr, 0664888567), where there is a pilgrim rest stop (**0.7km**). Skirt the edge of **Saint-Bressou**; a fountain is accessible on the last building (**1.2km**).

After a brief stretch on **D92**, follow minor paved roads and dirt tracks for most of the remaining walk, with few notable landmarks. Finally, fork left onto **D15** (**6.1km**), then turn left at a T on **D653** (**0.1km**). Proceed to the château and Église de Notre-Dame de l'Assomption in

12.4KM LACAPELLE-MARIVAL (ELEV 380M, POP 1270) 🏠 ⊕ 🏕 Ⓒ ⊕ ⊕ (505.8KM)

WC on left after the château. Market on Mondays. Mass at 6pm.

Positioned on the old Roman road linking Lyon to Bordeaux, the modern town was founded by the Cardaillac family and is dominated by a 13th-century castle and its adjacent town hall. One original gate survives, the Porte l'Arbol, along with one original round tower and a 15th-century market hall. Its 15th-century Église Notre Dame features well-preserved stained-glass windows. The Das Reich (the 2nd SS Panzer Division) hit the town on 11 May 1944; all men between 16 and 60 were taken to Cahors and locked in coal cellars, then later moved to Montauban and tortured, with some executed. Ten days later, the survivors were shipped onward to concentration camps. A memorial to the 86 lost lives can be found on the château's wall.

▲ Camping Le Bois de Sophie Pr Dr R Cf W S Z, €-/20/40/-, DP17, Route d'Aynac, campingboisdesophie@gmail.com, 0680597986, open Apr–mid Oct, camping €8.50–15, reservations required

STAGE R2

Lacapelle-Marival to Gramat

Start	Église de Notre-Dame de l'Assomption, Lacapelle-Marival
Finish	Steps to D807, Gramat
Distance	24km (21.6 via historic GR6)
Total ascent	270m (185m via historic GR6)
Total descent	380m (275m via historic GR6)
Difficulty	Easy
Time	5hr 30min (5hr via historic GR6)
Percentage paved	57% (65% via historic GR6)
Gîtes	Thémines 10.6km, Gramat 24km

This is not a long stage, by any means, but it is chockablock with historically interesting sites: the fortified church in Rudelle, the medieval market hall in Thémines, the ruins of Hospital Beaulieu, and the Romanesque church in Issendolus. And that's without mentioning Gramat, a lively town and an excellent place to restock supplies. Tired legs can capitalize on a significant short-cut, following the historic GR6 from L'Hôpital directly to Gramat, shaving off a modest up-and-down in the process.

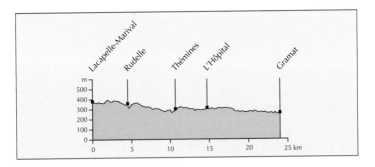

Follow D563 from the center, then turn left on **D940** (**0.3km**). Fork right on a minor paved road (**0.4km**), until finally forking right onto a footpath (**3.4km**). Rejoin a paved road through

4.3KM RUDELLE (ELEV 355M, POP 175)(501.5KM)

Its fortified, 13th-century Église Saint-Martial is more fort than church. St Martial was one of the most significant figures in French Christian history, known as the Apostle of the Gauls for his extensive evangelical work in the third century. His tomb in Limoges grew into a major pilgrimage site, leading to the construction of a Benedictine Abbey, although it was sadly destroyed in the 19th century. In 1593, Protestants seized the church during the Wars of Religion and the town members quickly surrendered to save it from destruction.

Turn left at a T, then take the next right. Soon after, fork right onto a paved road (**0.5km**). After a short ascent, the rest of this section trends downhill, on a mix of paved and dirt surfaces, winding through small communities. Brush against **D15** before forking left away from it (**3.4km**). Cross **D38**, then make a sharp left (**1km**). Finally, join **D40** and proceed into

6.3KM THÉMINES (ELEV 335M, POP 220) ▯▯ ▣ (495.2KM)

WC and fountain near the *mairie*. Multiple prehistoric caves have been found in the area with Bronze Age remains, although they aren't open to the public. Its medieval market hall is a good spot for a break.

🛏 **Gîte de la Halle** ▯▯ ▯▯ ▯▯ ▯ ▯, 5/14, €33/-/-/-, incl DP, daisyvo@hotmail.fr, 0616115297 or 0679051938, open Apr–Oct, camping €10/person, donkey parking

Fork right on C1 and keep forking right until transitioning onto a dirt track (**0.4km**). Continue through a series of quiet roads, finally turning right on **D840** (**3.4km**). Fork right on **D184** and proceed into

4KM L'HÔPITAL (ELEV 300M)(491.2KM)

The village contains the ruins of the Hospital Beaulieu, founded by the lords of Thémines in 1246 and then passed to the control of the Hospitallers of St John of Jerusalem in 1256, and dedicated to the care of pilgrims. Later, the Hospitallers passed authority to a group of nuns, a rarity for the order. After it was ravaged in the Hundred Years' War and then again by Protestants in the 16th century, Pope Pius IV ordered everything to be rebuilt. Soon after, the hospital achieved its peak, with 80 nuns in the convent administering a large area. Its buildings were fortified and surrounded by a 7m-high wall. However, all of that was destroyed during the French Revolution in 1793.

From L'Hôpital, there are two options for reaching Gramat.

GR6 through Issendolus (9.4km)
To continue on the 'official' GR6, take the next left, crossing back over **D840** (**0.2km**). At a T, turn left on **D20** (**1km**). Fork right into

1.3KM ISSENDOLUS (ELEV 330M, POP 515)(489.9KM)
Fountain outside church. The Romanesque church features Sainte-Fleur, who was a nun at L'Hôpital, known for her humility and for frequently experiencing religious ecstasy while taking Communion. Her name is invoked against lightning.

Turn right, then fork right again, away from the village (**0.2km**). Follow waymarks closely as the route makes many turns through this next stretch, mostly on dirt tracks.

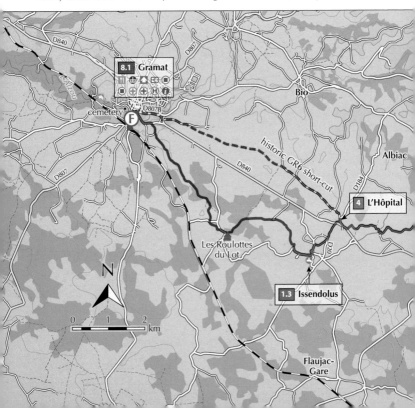

Walk past ⌂ Les Roulottes du Lot **O** **Pr** **Dr** **Br** **R** **W** **S**, €-/55/110/-, incl DP, lesrou-lottesdulot@gmail.com, 0681673854, camping €8/person, no wifi (**3.2km**). Finally, cross under **D807** (**4.7km**). To carry on into the next stage, continue forward. To reach Gramat's center and Gîte Associatif Les Petits Caillou du Chemin, climb the steps to D807 and turn left; the Grand Couvent requires a right.

Historic GR6 direct to Gramat (7km)
This alternative offers a significant short-cut, bypassing Issendolus. Continue straight through L'Hôpital, first on **D184**, and then leaving it when D184 veers right. Fork right, then left, then right – all in quick succession (**0.4km**). Fork left onto a dirt track (**1.8km**). After a long stretch, turn left onto a paved road (**3.1km**). Fork right, then turn right on **D840** (**0.8km**). Turn left at a large roundabout on **D807B**. Ahead, Gîte Associatif Les Petits Caillou du Chemin is on the left. Gramat's center is to the right. Continue straight, curving left and then descending steps on the right to rejoin the GR6.

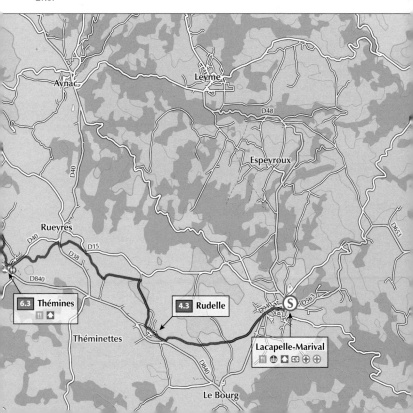

8.1KM GRAMAT (ELEV 270M, POP 3530) 🏨 ⊕ 🛆 🄴 ⊙ ⊙ ⊕ ⊕ ⊕ 🛈 (481.8KM)
Market on Tuesday/Wednesday mornings and Saturday nights.

Famous for its prehistoric remains, which include a complete human skeleton dubbed 'the man of Gramat,' it developed around a major Roman crossroads and later remained prominent with merchants and pilgrims. That also brought in plunderers, including Arabs in the seventh century and Normans in the ninth and 10th. In 1356, it was leveled in the Hundred Years' War, although the castle survived. A period of continued unrest followed throughout the Wars of Religion, ultimately seeing most residents departed or dead; at the low point, only five remained. The town lost many young men during World War I and then faced Nazi occupation in World War II, with massacres occurring south of here. Nazis occupied the town on 11 May 1944, rounding up all the men; all but the Jewish citizens were released at day's end. They were taken to Auschwitz.

🏠 Gîte Associatif Les Petits Caillou du Chemin O Do Dr R W S, 5/15, €17/-/-/-, DP15, 1 Ave Louis Mazet, gitegramat@gmail.com, 0565407936

🏠 Le Grand Couvent O Do Pr Dr R Cr W S Z, 5/64, €12/45/-/-, DP22, 33 Ave Louis Mazet, contact@grandcouventgramat.fr, 0565387329

🏠 Gîte l'Hospitalité de Béthanie d'Alzou Do Dr Br R, 2/14, €Donation, incl DP, 5 Rue Saint-Félix, bethanie.dalzou@gmail.com, 0781400002, open Apr–Oct, no wifi

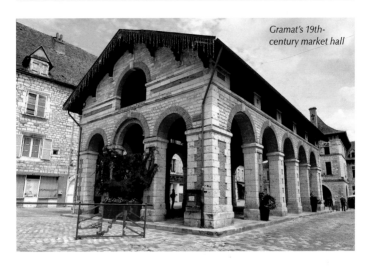

Gramat's 19th-century market hall

STAGE R3
Gramat to Rocamadour

Start	Steps to D807, Gramat
Finish	Le Grand Escalier, Rocamadour
Distance	12.4km
Total ascent	185m
Total descent	280m
Difficulty	Easy-to-moderate
Time	3hr 15min
Percentage paved	30%
Gîtes	Rocamadour 12.4km

Short and spectacular, this stage features a relaxing stroll along the Alzou River, often through dense tree cover. The ruins of medieval mills are wonderfully evocative and worth enjoying. It can be difficult to slow down, though, knowing that one of this pilgrimage's major highlights is just ahead: Rocamadour! It's a thrill to see the medieval shrine, clinging to the cliff, suddenly appear ahead, and even more rewarding to climb into the religious center and see it up close. A daytime arrival most likely means a very crowded shrine, but as the hours pass, so do the tour buses, allowing for a quiet and peaceful evening in one of France's most stunning settings.

Descend steps from the D807, rejoining the GR6, curving right, then left. Loop around a **cemetery** on Avenue des Cedres, cross Rue de Regardet, then fork left at the next intersection (**0.7km**). At the following intersection, take the middle of three roads. Curve left, then proceed straight onto a dirt track (**0.3km**). Turn right and then fork left onto a paved road (**0.4km**). Cross under a **railroad** and continue winding through a mix of paved and dirt roads. Fork right onto a footpath (**3.7km**).

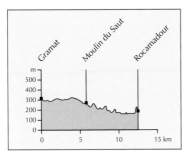

Cross the **Alzou River** and turn left (**0.4km**). Pass through a series of enchanting, ruined mills – **Moulin du Saut** (**0.3km**), **Moulin de Tournefeuille** (**1.3km**), and **Moulin de la Mouline** (**1.2km**) – but brace yourself for a jarring up-and-down between Saut and Tournefeuille. Cross the Alzou and

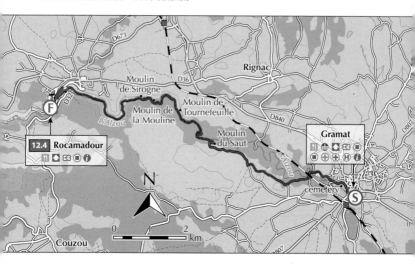

pass the last set of ruins, the **Moulin de Sirogne** (**0.3km**). Emerge onto a dirt track (**0.2km**), then transition onto a paved road for the final approach (**2.7km**). Fork left on **D32** (**0.2km**), then continue straight through a parking lot on D32B. Turn right and climb steps into **Rocamadour** (**0.4km**). Cross a road and climb more steps, then turn left (**0.1km**). Arrive in the Cité Médiévale and proceed to the Grand Escalier.

12.4KM ROCAMADOUR (ELEV 175M, POP 605) 🍴 🏠 ⓒ ◉ ⓘ (469.4KM)
Built into cliffs overlooking the Alzou Valley, Rocamadour has long been a major pilgrimage site in France. According to legend, Rocamadour is named after the ancient sanctuary's founder, St Amadour, sometimes identified with the Biblical Zaccheus of Jericho, who wiped Jesus's face on the way to his crucifixion. Driven out of Palestine, having witnessed the martyrdoms of Saints Peter, Paul, and his wife Veronica, Amadour/Zaccheus withdrew here, where he built a chapel to honor the Virgin Mary. In the chapel, Amadour placed a wooden statue of the Black Virgin, which he is sometimes reputed to have carved (although it dates to the ninth century). After Amadour's death, the double attraction of the saint's tomb and the Black Virgin drew pilgrims – and many reports of miraculous healings followed.

The site's early history has been lost. The first reference to the Virgin of Rocamadour's worship dates to 1105, with the first traces of pilgrimage following in 1112. Then, in 1166, an ancient grave containing an undecayed body,

Rocamadour, overlooking a field of wildflowers

believed to be St Amadour, was discovered in the cliffs. With this discovery, pilgrim traffic surged. A book of miracles was published six years later, highlighting 90 cases in which people were healed by the virgin. After peaking in the Middle Ages, the Hundred Years' War signaled Rocamadour's decline. By 1425, only 14 canons remained to oversee the church and the pilgrimage tailed off dramatically. In 1562, the oratories were pillaged and burned by Protestants, as was St Amadour's body. In the 18th century, the Abbot of Caillau was miraculously cured by the Virgin, and then committed himself to rekindling the pilgrimage. He was joined by Bishop Bardou of Cahors, who organized a national lottery in 1856 to raise funds.Rocamadour is made up of three levels: the Cité Médiévale is on the bottom, the Cité Religieuse sits mid-cliff, and L'Hospitalet is perched on top. The Grand Escalier, a stairway of 216 steps, links the first two levels; some devout pilgrims climb up on their knees. To continue higher, follow the Way of the Cross. The Cité Religieuse, also known as the Sanctuary of our Lady of Rocamadour, features seven chapels surrounding a square. The Basilique Saint-Sauveur provides the main place of worship. Built in the 11th–13th centuries, it has elements of both Romanesque and Gothic styles. To the basilica's left, follow steps to where a tomb is cut into the rock – this is where St Amadour's body was found. The Romanesque Chapelle Saint-Michel is built around the original cave on the left; inside are two 12th-century frescoes. To the right of the basilica, the Chapelle Notre-Dame is devoted almost exclusively to the Black Virgin. A ninth-century bell hangs from the vault; it announced miracles in the Middle Ages by ringing of its own accord, although it has remained silent since 1551. Votive offerings and memorial plaques line the room, declaring 'merci' for intervention. Above the door leading to the chapel is an iron sword (Durandal) that supposedly belonged to Roland, whose sacrifice is memorialized in the French epic poem, 'The Song of Roland', and in the village of Roncesvalles. The Chapelle Miraculeuse contains St Amadour's tomb. From the roof hangs one of the oldest known clocks, dating from the eighth century. Mass is celebrated at 11am daily at the sanctuary.

Up top, L'Hospitalet has several distinct highlights and many services. The medieval château offers impressive views, although more spectacular vistas can be enjoyed by following the road northwest, until the angle shifts to allow a complete view of the village. Along that road, you'll pass Grotte Préhistorique des Merveilles (€8, reservation required, 0788268478), a small cave system with prehistoric cave paintings. The ruined remains of the 11th-century Hôpital Saint-Jean are across the street. For something completely different, turn right and then left immediately after (passing a Proxi grocery store) onto D36, leading to the Forêt des Singes (€9.50), which houses more than 150 macaque monkeys, to which you are encouraged to feed popcorn.

Rocamadour's Cité Médiévale originally had 11 gates (seven survive) to control crowds. In the 14th century, up to 20,000 pilgrims would arrive in a single day. Some pilgrims performed acts of extreme penitence. Take, for example, the Knight of Bazas: 'When he was beside the rock, he took off his clothes, unafraid of exposing his miserable poverty to the eyes of all. He placed a rope about his neck and two of his companions dragged him like a robber, while others pushed him roughly before them with brooms.' In the Middle Ages, Dutch and Belgian prisoners were sent here on pilgrimage as punishment. In the 19th century, travel writers Davies and Christopher observed that the 'pilgrimage to Rocamadour is made chiefly by those childless wives who desire offspring.'

🛖 Centre d'Accueil Notre-Dame **Do** **Pr** **R** **Cr** **Z**, 3/19, €13/33/46/-, Le Château, centrendrocamadour@gmail.com, 0565332323, open Apr–Nov, breakfast €5

🛖 Gîte Lou Cantou De Nostro Damo **O** **Do** **Pr** **K** **R** **W**, 1/6, €12/20/30/-, Rue de la Mercerie, cantou.46@free.fr, 0565337369, donation-based breakfast

🛖 Le Terminus Hôtel des Pèlerins à Rocamadour **Pr** **Dr** **R** **Cr**, €-/69/79/89, Cité Médiévale, hotelterm.pelerinsroc@wanadoo.fr, 0565336214, open mid Apr–Oct

STAGE R4
Rocamadour to Labastide-Murat

Start	Le Grand Escalier, Rocamadour
Finish	Église Sainte-Catherine, Labastide-Murat
Distance	25.5km
Total ascent	745m
Total descent	460m
Difficulty	Moderate-to-strenuous
Time	7hr 15min
Percentage paved	43%
Gîtes	Montfaucon 20.1km, Labastide-Murat 25.5km

It will be hard to tear yourself away from Rocamadour, but it's important to be alert, nonetheless. Near the village's end, watch closely for waymarks indicating a split. From here, the GR6 continues in a wide loop towards La Romieu, which is beyond the scope of this guide. Most pilgrims instead turn left onto the GR46, following it to Vers as described here. And the GR46 welcomes you with a sharp ascent up the other side of the gorge – be sure to stop regularly to admire Rocamadour one more time, as it gradually disappears. No services are available until Montfaucon, some 20km away, so be prepared, and also note that a waymarked detour is necessary to enter Montfaucon proper. A lakeside park marks your final approach to Labastide-Murat, where you can restock supplies.

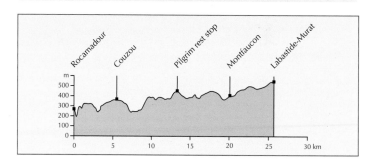

From the Grand Escalier, continue straight through a gate, a parking lot, and then a second gate. Leaving Rocamadour, the route leaves the GR6 and joins the GR46 – be sure to make this well-marked left turn near the village's end. Cross D32B and proceed along a minor road between houses. Cross the **Alzou River** and turn right onto a dirt track (**0.3km**). Cross **D32** and continue straight (**0.8km**). Fork right, then left, in quick succession. Turn left at a T onto a paved road, then right onto a dirt track (**1km**). Alternatively, continue straight to make a short detour to the Dolmen de Mages. After a sharp descent, turn left on D32 (**1km**). Make a sharp right, descending through woods on a dirt track. After a few turns along unpaved roads, emerge back on D32 (**1.9km**). Fork right into

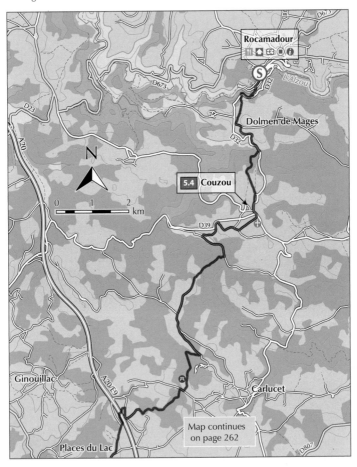

Map continues
on page 262

5.4KM COUZOU (ELEV 300M, POP 90)(464KM)
Its Église Saint-Cyr-et-Sainte-Julitte-de-la-Pannonie has the longest name of any church in this book.

Turn right at the church. A long stretch with minimal landmarks follows, with an even balance of paved roads and dirt tracks. After first swinging westward, roughly parallel to **D39**, the route plunges southward through wooded terrain, passing a pilgrim rest stop (**7.9km**). Pass under the **A20/E9**, then curve left (**3.3km**). Continue straight onto a paved road then turn right at a T (**0.8km**). Turn left in **Places du Lac**, then fork right soon after (**0.4km**). Cross **D801**, then fork left (**0.3km**). Turn left on **D10** (**1km**). After it curves right, and just before it bends back left, turn left onto a dirt track (**0.6km**). The GR46 bypasses Montfaucon center, but a waymarked right turn leads into town.

14.7KM MONTFAUCON (ELEV 310M, POP 590) 🏨 ⊕ 🛄 **(449.3KM)**
Fountain outside church. A bastide built by the English in 1292, it was taken over by a group of English soldiers-turned-bandits after the Hundred Years' War in 1370 and suffered badly over the next 80 years. The Église Saint-Barthélémy has three Baroque altarpieces and a 15th-century statue of the Virgin. The Château de Vaillac, built in 1470, is hailed as an exemplar of military architecture from the era following the Hundred Years' War.

🏠 Le Presbytère **Do** **Br** **K** **R** **W** **S**, 3/10, €16/-/-/-, 2 Rue Saint-Barthélémy, despierresenheritage@gmail.com, 0783514067, open Apr–Oct, washing machine included, no wifi

Descend from town back onto the GR46, passing a pond flanked by lush green lawns. Curve left on a minor paved road. Stick with it, ignoring multiple roads forking away, until finally turning left (**0.5km**). Turn right at a T (**0.5km**), then cross **A20/E9** (**0.7km**). Turn right at another T, fork left, then continue onto a dirt track (**1.1km**). Walk around **Lac de Boutanes**, which is surrounded by a pleasant public park, then emerge

Pond beneath the town of Montfaucon

back onto a paved road (**1.9km**). Fork left, briefly rejoining a dirt track, cross **D17**, and then follow a minor road into town. Join **D677** near the church in

5.4KM LABASTIDE-MURAT (ELEV 460M, POP 650) 🏠⊕⛺Ⓒ⊕🛈 (443.9KM)
WC and fountain near the *mairie*. Founded in 1238, it later changed its name to honor Joachim Murat, who was born here in 1767 and eventually became King of Naples. Murat met Napoleon in 1795 and quickly became his aide-de-camp. Consistently a key figure in Napoleon's military campaigns, he continued to gain honors and in 1800 married Napoleon's sister Caroline. After Napoleon fell, Murat was caught by Ferdinand IV of Naples; staring down his executioners, he declared, 'Save my face – aim for the chest. Fire!'

Note that no food is available during tomorrow's walk until Vers, so aim for Labastide-Murat's supermarket before leaving.

🏠 Gîte L'Auberge du Roy de Naples 🅳🅾🅺🆁, 3/7, €22/-/-/-, 8 Place Daniel Roques, mairie.labastide-murat2@wanadoo.fr, 0565311150, open Apr–Oct

🏠 Gîte Le Savitri 🅳🅾🅱🆁🅺🆁🆆, 1/13, €20/-/-/-, 64 Grande Rue du Causse, 0674401415, open Apr–Oct

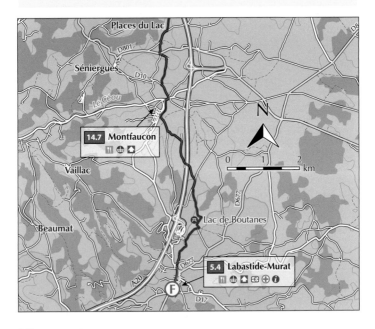

STAGE R5
Labastide-Murat to Vers

Start	Église Sainte-Catherine, Labastide-Murat
Finish	D653 roundabout, Vers
Distance	24.2km
Total ascent	280m
Total descent	580m
Difficulty	Easy-to-moderate
Time	6hr
Percentage paved	21%
Gîtes	Vers 24.2km

While departure from Labastide-Murat follows a moderately well-trafficked road, most of this stage enjoys tranquil, easy-going terrain. Footpaths wind through tree-covered hills during the first half, popping in and out of pocket valleys with green grass sparkling in their midst. A small climb delivers you into Cras, the lone village in this stage, before descending back through wheat fields into the woods. The last leg generally follows dirt tracks alongside the Vers River, heading due south. Note that, aside from a couple of water points, no other services are available, so stock up before leaving Labastide.

Follow **D677** out of Labastide, then fork left onto **D32**. Fork right onto a dirt track (**1km**). Continue straight onto D32 (**2km**). Turn right onto a dirt track, then left soon after. Follow mostly unpaved roads, making numerous turns, generally through narrow valleys between tree-covered hills (**4.7km**). Turn left on **D13**. Fork right onto a dirt track (**0.4km**), remaining off pavement until merging with **D7** (**1.4km**). Turn left onto a dirt

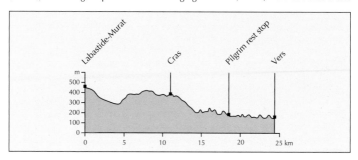

track (**0.5km**), then fork right, winding southward (**1km**). Fork right onto a dirt track and then left immediately after, climbing past a cemetery into

11KM CRAS (ELEV 355M, POP 100) (432.9KM)
The Bishop of Cahors donated Cras to the Knights Templar in the 13th century.

⌂ **Gîte Le Cayrou Mirabel** closed in 2021, planning to reopen in 2022 (emma. mourgues@orange.fr)

Follow the main road through town, then make a sharp left just before the *mairie* (fountain on right). Turn right onto a dirt road and then right again soon after. Fork left from the split just outside of Cras, then turn left at a T onto a paved road (**0.9km**). Turn right back onto a dirt track (**0.7km**), following a series of unpaved tracks first across the

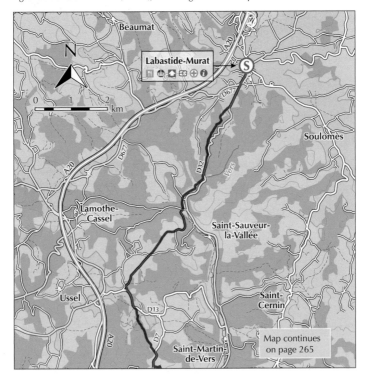

Map continues on page 265

Rauze River (**2.9km**), then back over it, turning right onto a paved road (**1.6km**). Fork left, then right on **D653** (**0.2km**). Fork left onto a footpath (**0.4km**), then turn left onto a dirt track (**0.5km**). A pilgrim rest stop (WC, fountain) is available soon after (**0.1km**). Another extended, unpaved stretch follows, leading past **Moulin de Bénédicty** (**3km**), then transitioning back onto pavement near Vers (**2.7km**). The GR46 forks right off the main road, crosses the Vers River, and leads to the roundabout at the center of

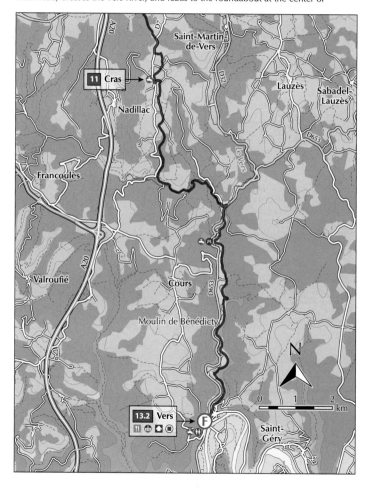

13.2KM VERS (ELEV 160M, POP 420) ⏸ ⊕ ⬆ ◉ (419.7KM)

Fountain by church, WC in riverside park. Vers has an extensive past, preserving a Bronze Age site and the remains of a Roman aqueduct. English forces made this a base during the Hundred Years' War.

⬤ Gîte Le Monde Allant Vers `Do` `Dr` `R` `W`, 1/8, €18/-/-/-, DP19, Rue du Château, lemondeallantvers46@gmail.com, 0685653078, open Mar–Oct, no wifi

⬤ Hôtel La Truite Dorée `O` `Pr` `Dr` `R` `Cf` `S` `Z`, €-/75/90/116, DP32, Rue de la Barre, latruitedoree@wanadoo.fr, 0565314151, swimming pool

The Vers River as it approaches the Lot

STAGE R6

Vers to Cahors

Start	D653 roundabout, Vers
Finish	Cathédrale Saint-Étienne, Cahors
Distance	16.3km (14.8km via train bridge short-cut)
Total ascent	160m (115m via train bridge short-cut)
Total descent	190m (145m via train bridge short-cut)
Difficulty	Easy
Time	3hr 30min (3hr 15min via train bridge short-cut)
Percentage paved	39% (or 22% via train bridge short-cut)
Gîtes	Cahors 16.3km

The bulk of this stage overlaps with Stage C5 of the Célé Valley variant. The route description here offers two options for traveling from Vers to join that. The official GR46 travels due south, crossing the Lot and passing through Béars before intersecting the GR36. An unmarked alternative stays on the north side of the Lot until crossing a retired train bridge over the river and joining the other route on a riverside walkway soon after; this offers an easier, shorter, and still quite pleasant way to link with the GR36.

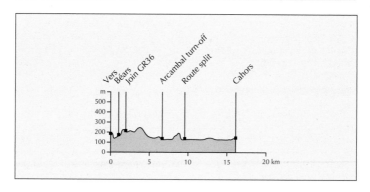

For route map see Célé Valley variant, Stage C5. Right from the start, there are two options.

*The footpath along the
Lot River near Arcambal*

GR46 to GR36, via Béars (1.9km)

Follow **D653** south of the roundabout. Fork left on **D49**, cross the **Lot**, and pass through **Béars** (1km, ⌂ Les Rives d'Olt Ⓞ Ⓓⓞ Ⓟⓡ Ⓓⓡ Ⓑⓡ Ⓡ Ⓢ, 1/4, €27/-/67/87, DP24, chambresdhotes.lesrivesdolt@gmail.com, 0674421213, English spoken). Turn left after the village, then fork right onto a dirt track (**0.1km**). Climb switchbacks and then intersect the GR36, forking right to continue towards Cahors. This rejoins the recommended approach to Cahors described in the Célé Valley variant, Stage C5, at the 19km mark. Cahors is 14.1km ahead.

Low-level short-cut via train bridge (3.9km)

From the roundabout, descend to the riverside park in Vers and cross a pedestrian bridge over the Vers River. Turn left and join a dirt track along the riverside. After looping inland, past a cemetery, cut behind the Église Notre-Dame-de-Vêles and fork left onto another unpaved road (**1.2km**). When this curves right and intersects **D653**, turn left onto the minor highway (**1.3km**). Just after passing a dirt road, turn left onto a retired railroad (**0.2km**). Follow this across the **Lot River** and continue a short distance on the other side, watching for a footpath on the right that allows you to join a parallel dirt road (**0.6km**). This rejoins the recommended approach to Cahors described in the Célé Valley variant, Stage C5, soon after (**0.6km**), at the 22.2km mark. Cahors is 10.9km ahead.

To continue, see Stage C5 of the Célé Valley variant.

CONNECTING TO THE CAMINO DEL NORTE

En route to Ascain on the Voie Nive Bidassoa

Views on the GR10 above Saint-Étienne-de-Baïgorry

Given that many pilgrims on the Via Podiensis have already walked the Camino Francés from Saint-Jean-Pied-de-Port to Santiago de Compostela, it's not uncommon for through-hikers to leave the GR65 in Saint-Jean and transition to the Camino del Norte in Irún, Spain. There are two primary options for accomplishing that: the high-level GR10 route through the Pyrenees, or the Voie Nive Bidassoa, which skirts the foothills. The two routes briefly converge in the town of Bidarray and just before arriving in Hendaye and Irún, but otherwise remain separate after their initial divergence. While a detailed description of both routes is beyond the scope of this guide, skeletal outlines follow.

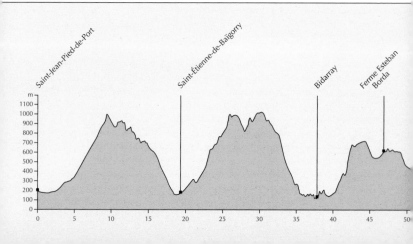

THE GR10

Start	Pilgrim Office, Saint-Jean-Pied-de-Port, France
Finish	Hendaye Plage
Distance	99.2km
Total ascent	5875m
Total descent	6065m
Difficulty	Very strenuous
Time	5 days
Percentage paved	34%
Gîtes	Saint-Étienne-de-Baïgorry 18.7km, Bidarray 36.7km, Ferme Esteban Borda 47.1km, Ainhoa 57.8km, Sare 69.1km, Olhette 78.2km

The GR10 follows the Pyrenees for 866km from the Mediterranean to the Atlantic, but you'll only experience a small chunk of it. The mountains are not quite as demanding here as they are further east, nor the peaks as high, but the walk is nonetheless quite strenuous – much more so than the Via Podiensis. It is also spectacular. Every stage involves a significant ascent that delivers marvelous views, followed by a descent to a charming Basque village. Make sure, though, that you are up for the challenge. As this is a GR, you will continue following red-and-white blazes. Express Bourricot may offer luggage transport (www.expressbourricot.com).

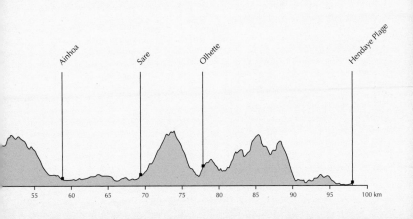

le Méhatché
720m

▲ **Iguzki**
843m

▲ **Itsusi**

GR10

Baztan

VNB

579m

Map continues
on page 275

▲ **Alkaxuri**
967m

Urritzate

Urritzateko Erreka

D918

La Nive

Osses

**Saint-Martin-
d'Arrossa**

▲ **Pic d'Iparla**
1045m

Abrakou Erreka

D918

Ruisseau d'Urdos

D948

Nive des Aldudes

Hotel-Restaurant Manexene

Bastidako Erréka

mehaka
·11m

Seasonal
spring

▲ **Astate**
1022m

▲ **Jarra**
812m

▲ **Pic de Buztanzelhay**
1030m

VNB

▲
Arrokamendi
730m

Ruisseau de Guermiette

D15

▲ **Irouléguy**

16 **Saint-Étienne-
de-Baïgorry**

Anhaux

▲ **Elhorriko
Kaskoa**
983m

D948

N

**Voie Nive
Bidassoa (VNB)**

▲ **Ohilarandoï**
933m

Nive des Aldudes

GR10

0   1   2
|———|———| km

▲ **Ixtauz**
1024m

Monhoa
1021m ▲

Banca

▲ **Urdiako Harria** ▲
996m

2.7KM LASSE (ELEV 210M, POP 330)
(96.5KM TO HENDAYE PLAGE)
WC and fountain next to Auberge.

⌂ Auberge Etchoinia Pr Dr K R Gr W S
Z, €-/-/70/-, DP21, aubergeetchoinia@
sfr.fr, 0559370157, open May–Oct, bar/
restaurant

The GR10 splits from the Voie Nive Bidassoa
(**2.1km**). Summit **Monhoa Peak** (**4.7km**, 1021m).
Pass a fountain, along a cement wall (**4km**).

16KM SAINT-ÉTIENNE-DE-BAÏGORRY
(ELEV 160M, POP 1475) 🏠 ⏣ ⬛ ⓒ ⬤ *i*
(80.5KM TO HENDAYE PLAGE)
Fountains and WCs near church and tourism office. The 11th-century church features
a Baroque retablo that portrays the stoning
of St Etienne and preserves its old Cagot
door. The elegant, 11th-century Romanesque
bridge is just to the left as the GR10 enters
town.

⌂ Gite Karrikan Do Pr Dr R Gr W S Z, 5/28,
€18.50/-/66/-, DP, gitospit@orange.fr,
0559374704, open Apr–Nov, reservation
required, no wifi

⌂ Hotel Arcé Pr Dr R Gr W S Z,
€-/185/195/280, DP58, contact@hotel-
arce.com, 0559374014, open Apr–Nov

Make sure you have plenty of water and
snacks before setting out. This is the most challenging day on the GR10 and there are no services
along the way. **Climb to Pic de Buztanzelhay**
(**7.5km**, 1030m). Descend through a wooded
hillside, passing the turn-off for a seasonal spring
(**1.9km**). Ascend to a stunning walk along a border
ridge, leading to **Pic d'Iparla** (**2.3km**, 1045m). A
long, rocky descent follows.

273

18KM BIDARRAY (ELEV 145M, POP 675) 🍴 ⊕ ⛺ ◉ (62.5KM TO HENDAYE PLAGE)

Fountain by church, WC in *mairie*. The Pont d'Enfer, a Romanesque bridge, is also known as the 'Bridge of Hell;' legend holds that witches built it deep at night. Another legend claims the nearby Harpeko Saindua cave has healing waters that can cure eczema, among other things.

▲ **Gite Aire Zabal** ⓄⓄⓄⓄ ⓀⓇⓌⓈⓏ, 6/31, €17/-/34/-, DP18, Rue de la Poste, mayie.irrinoa@yahoo.fr, 0559377292, camping €6/person, no wifi

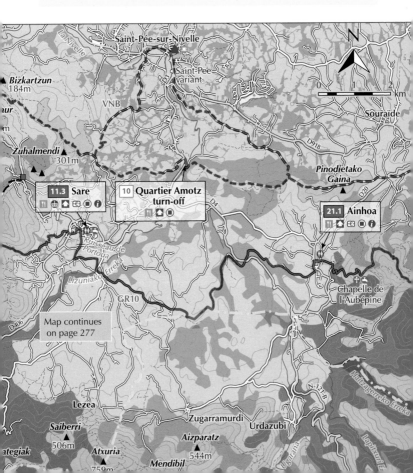

Leave Bidarray the way you entered. Climb – hands necessary at some points – to **Col de Méhatché** (7.9km, 720m), then pass through the very welcoming ⬥ Ferme Esteben Borda ◉ Ⅾⓞ Ⅾⓡ Ⓡ, 0559298272, restaurant (**2.5km**). Descend past **Chapelle de l'Aubépine** (8.6km, fountain).

21.1KM AINHOA (ELEV 120M, POP 670) ⓘⓘ ⬥ Ⓔ ◉ ❶ **(41.4KM TO HENDAYE PLAGE)**
WC below church. A border town in the 13th century under King Henry III of England's authority, known for collecting tolls from pilgrims. Ainhoa was destroyed in the Thirty Years' War (1618–48); only the church and the Machitorénéa House survived.

⬥ ▲ Camping-Gite Harazpy Ⅾⓞ Ⓚ Ⓡ Ⓦ, 1/12, €18.5/-/-/-, 0559298938 or 0675580485, camping €18/tent, open Mar–early Nov

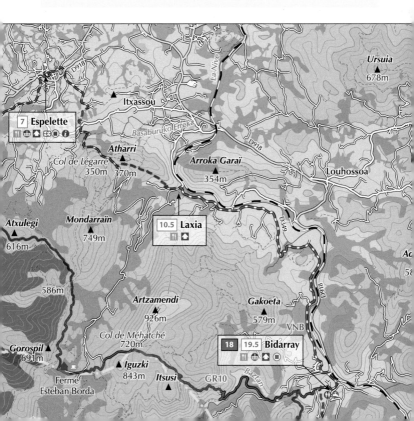

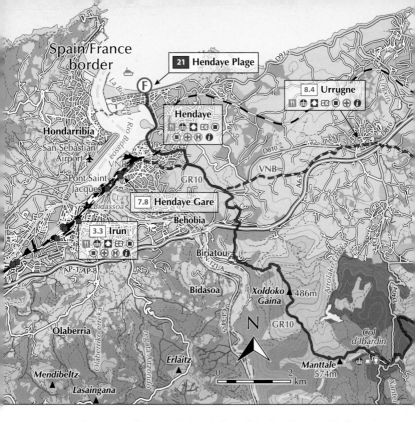

An uncharacteristically easy and relatively flat walk leads to the beautiful village of

11.3KM SARE (ELEV 80M, POP 2650) 🍴 ⊕ 🏠 🏧 ◉ 𝒾 (30.1KM TO HENDAYE PLAGE)

Bronze Age remains have been found in the area, particularly funereal caves. It was loyal to the Church during the Revolution and suffered incredibly as a result. In 1794, the entire town was deported to Gascony. Later, the region became popular with celebrities, including Napoleon III (who stayed in the Chapel of St Catherine), Ho Chi-Minh, Orson Wells, Winston Churchill, and Charles de Gaulle.

🏠 ▲ **Camping de la Petite Rhune** ◎ 🅳◎ 🅺 🆁 🆆 🆂, 4/20, €18/-/-/-, contact@ lapetiterhune.com, 0615293638 or 0559542397, campsites in summer only, breakfast €6

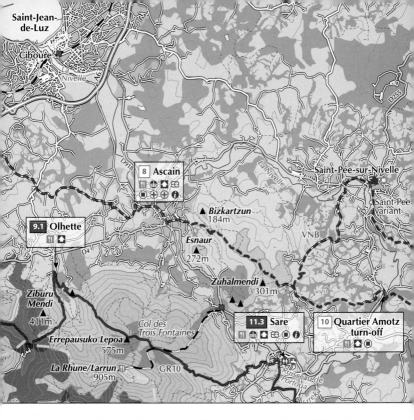

Climb to the **Col des Trois Fontaines/Errepausuko Lepoa** (**5.6km**, 575m). It is possible to summit La Rhune (905m) and access two bar/restaurants by detouring left at this point, following green arrows 1.8km (350m ascent).

9.1KM OLHETTE (ELEV 90M) 🍴 🏠 (21KM TO HENDAYE PLAGE)
All services off-route.

- 🏠 🏠 **Trapero Baïta** Do Pr Dr R S, 3/14, €25/-/70/-, DP20, 80 Chemin de Manttu Baïram, leteich@hotmail.fr, 0559544259, open mid Apr–Oct, camping €10/person

- 🏠 Hotel Trabenia Pr Dr R Gr S, €-/69/82/105, hotel.trabenia@orange.fr, 0559540191, closed Feb, bar/restaurant, breakfast €10

Pass through **Col d'Ibardin**, a shopping area lining the border between France and Spain, with grocery stores, restaurants, and lots of alcohol (**6.8km**). Climb to two final mini-peaks, **Manttale** (**1.2km**, 574m) and **Xoldoko Gaina** (**3.1km**, 486m). Descend to the outskirts of **Biriatou** (**2.3km**), where it's possible to fork left into the village (fountain) or fork right, bypassing it.

The GR10 and Voie Nive Bidassoa briefly overlap, before splitting near the outskirts of Hendaye (**4.3km**). Follow the VNB if your goal is to travel directly to Irún and the Camino del Norte. Turn right and stick with the GR10 if you would prefer to first complete the GR10 at the Atlantic Ocean, continuing to

---

21KM HENDAYE PLAGE (ELEV 10M, POP 16,330) 🍴 ⊕ 🏠 🄬 🄬 🄗 ⊕ 🛈
821.2KM TO SANTIAGO DE COMPOSTELA
Like Irún, Hendaye has suffered as a border town for much of its history, experiencing damage in the Franco-Spanish War and the Napoleonic Wars, in particular. The arrival of the railroad in 1863 changed things dramatically; almost overnight, the city became a prominent resort center.

🏠 🏠 Bella Vista Guest Center Pays Basque 🄳🄾 🄳🄻 🄱🄻 🅁 🄲🄻 🅆 🅂 🅉, 48/142, €44.5/-/-/-, incl DP, Rue Goyara, contact@cbe-horizon.fr, 0559705851, open Apr–Nov, swimming pool

---

If continuing from Hendaye, you can either backtrack to the train station and pick up the walking route into Spain (and the Voie Nive Bidassoa) from there or – in July–August – head south to Hendaye's ferry dock (0.9km), catching the boat across to Hondarribia, Spain. From there, you can continue directly on the Camino del Norte.

The GR10 is so strenuous, you'll sleep well at the end of each day's walk

THE VOIE NIVE BIDASSOA

Start	Pilgrim Office, Saint-Jean-Pied-de-Port, France
Finish	Albergue de Peregrinos, Irún, Spain
Distance	77.2km
Total ascent	1850m
Total descent	2040m
Difficulty	Moderate
Time	3–4 days
Percentage paved	76%
Gîtes	Bidarray 22.2km, Espelette 39.7km, Saint-Pée-sur-Nivelle 45.7+5.8km, Irún 77.2km

Shorter, flatter (although definitely not flat), and paved – but still a pleasant walk through Basque Country and its lovely villages. This route is waymarked with scallop-shell stickers and yellow, white, and blue blazes on traffic posts. While it overlaps for a stretch with the GR8, bringing back the red-and-white blazes, don't be led astray by these.

2.7KM LASSE (ELEV 210M, POP 330) 🛏 (74.5KM TO IRÚN)
WC and fountain next to Auberge.

🔺 Auberge Etchoinia 🇵🇹 🇩🇷 🇰 🇷 🇨🇷 🇼 🇸 🇿, €-/-/70/-, DP21, aubergeetchoinia@sfr.fr, 0559370157, open May–Oct, bar/restaurant

The Voie Nive Bidassoa splits from the GR10 (**2.1km**). Walk through **Anhaux** (**2.5km**) and **Irouléguy** (**1.3km**, fountain by church), then pass Hotel-Restaurant **Manexenea** (**5.8km**).

19.5KM BIDARRAY (ELEV 145M, POP 675) 🔳 🌐 🛏 ◉ (55KM TO IRÚN)
Fountain by church, WC in *mairie*. The Pont d'Enfer, a Romanesque bridge, is also known as the 'Bridge of Hell;' legend holds that witches built it deep at night. Another legend claims the nearby Harpeko Saindua cave has healing waters that can cure eczema, among other things.

🔺 Gîte Aire Zabal 🇴 🇩🇴 🇵🇹 🇩🇷 🇰 🇷 🇼 🇸 🇿, 6/31, €17/-/34/-, DP18, Rue de la Poste, mayie.irrinoa@yahoo.fr, 0559377292, camping €6/person

Follow D349 all the way to

10.5KM LAXIA (ELEV 110M) 🍴 ⛺ **(44.5KM TO IRÚN)**
Fountain at trailhead.

⛺ Apartments Ondoria 🅾 🅿️ 🅳🆁 🅺 🆁 🅶 🆆 🆂, €-/-/80/80, contact@ondoria.fr, 0559297539 or 0645469561, bar/restaurant

Ascend a footpath to **Col de Légarré** (**2.6km**), merge with the GR8 (**2.3km**), then split from it soon after (**0.3km**).

7KM ESPELETTE (ELEV 115M, POP 2025) 🍴 ⊕ ⛺ 🅾 🅲 🛈 **(37.5KM TO IRÚN)**
Famous for its *piment d'Espelette*, a red pepper that is generally dried and used as a key seasoning in Basque cooking – and in a locally produced dark chocolate.

⛺ Gîte Le Jeu de Paume 🅳🅾 🅺 🆁 🆆 🆉, 1/6, €20/-/-/-, 47 Place du Jeu de Paume, ithurriamarie@gmail.com, 0601406080, open Apr–Oct, washing machine included

The walk to Ascain is the most strenuous part of the VBN. Rejoin the GR8 (**3.1km**) while ascending to **Pinodietako Gaina** (**1.2km**, 275m). Pass the turn-off to detour to Saint-Pée-sur-Nivelle (**1.7km**). (This waymarked variant leads 5.8km to the town and its gîte, ⛺ Gîte des Pèlerins 🅾 🅳🅾 🅺 🆁, 1/12, €10/-/-/-, Place de l'Église, jakobia.senpere@gmail.com, 0614125122, and then returns to the VNB 3.2km after the Quartier Amotz turn-off, 5km later. All told, this adds 6.8km to the VNB.) Go right back down to the Nivelle River, then turn right on **D3**. Turn left soon after.

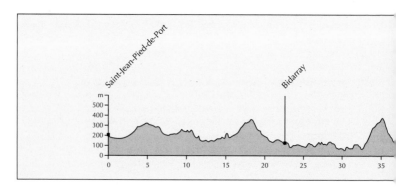

10KM TURN-OFF TO QUARTIER AMOTZ (ELEV 32M) 🍴 △ ◉ **(27.5KM TO IRÚN)**
Alternately, continue straight on D3 for 0.6km to access WC, bar/restaurants, cheese/sausage vending machine, and accommodations.

🏠 Hôtel Trinquet ◎ Pr Dr R Cr S, €-/-/50/60, DP24, hotel.trinquet@gmail.com, 0559541490

🏠 Hotel Mendionde ◎ Pr Dr R Cr S Z, €-/65/80/-, DP24, mendionde@gmail.com, 0559541490

Climb right back up. Split with GR8 (**3.8km**), which continues onto Sare, then reach the **Col de Zuhalmendi** (**0.2km**, 301m). Go all the way back down.

8KM ASCAIN (ELEV 65M, POP 4195) 🍴 ⊕ △ ◉ Ⓒ ⊕ ⊕ **ⓘ** **(19.5KM TO IRÚN)**
A commission of inquiry oversaw the burning of Ascain's bishop in 1609, for behavior linked to demonic sorcery. Like other towns in the area, including Espelette, Ascain was targeted in the French Revolution, with many of its Basque residents deported.

Follow minor paved roads all the way to

8.4KM URRUGNE (ELEV 55M, POP 9674) 🍴 ⊕ △ ◉ Ⓒ ⊕ **ⓘ** **(11.1KM TO IRÚN)**
Its Renaissance-style Église Saint-Vincent features heavy fortifications and three floors of galleries.

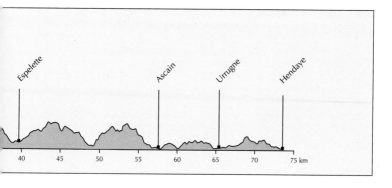

Horses are often your only companions in the Pyrenean hills

The Voie Nive Bidassoa merges with the Voie de la Côte, another branch of the Chemin Saint-Jacques, in Urrugne. It then also merges briefly with the **GR10** (**5.3km**), before splitting soon after (**0.2km**). After navigating through urban sprawl, pass near the Hendaye Gare (train stations, SNCF and Euskotren).

7.8KM HENDAYE (ELEV 10M, POP 16,330) ⊞ ⊕ 🅐 🅒 ⊚ ⊚ 🅗 ⊕ **ⓘ** (3.3KM TO IRÚN)
See the GR10 description for info.

⌂ ⌂ Bella Vista Guest Center Pays Basque 🄳🄾 🄳🄿 🄱🄿 🅁 🄲🄵 🅆 🅂 🅉, 48/142, €44.5/-/-/-, incl DP, Rue Goyara, contact@cbe-horizon.fr, 0559705851, open Apr–Nov, swimming pool

Proceed to the **Pont Saint-Jacques**, which leads into Spain and the Camino del Norte. Yellow arrows begin on the Spanish side, leading to the Albergue de Peregrinos in the town center.

3.3KM IRÚN (ELEV 10M, POP 16,330) ⊞ ⊕ 🅐 🅒 ⊚ ⊚ 🅗 ⊕ **ⓘ** 819.7KM TO SANTIAGO DE COMPOSTELA
Irún lies across the Río Bidasoa from French Hendaye. As a border town, it has been a frequent site of diplomatic wrangling. Franco and Hitler met across the river at Hendaye rail station. In exchange for Spanish support, Franco demanded significant territorial promises, none of which Hitler was willing to concede. Hitler was bored by the general and skeptical of Spanish military capability; Spain thus remained neutral throughout World War II. However, the dissolution of Franco and Hitler's relationship came too late for Irún, which had seen its historic core obliterated by German bombers (at Franco's behest) during the Spanish Civil War. Because of this, most of today's Irún is modern.

⌂ Albergue de Peregrinos Jakobi 🄳🄾 🄱🄿 🄺 🅂 🅉, 3/60, €Donation, c/Lesaka 1, irunsantiago@yahoo.es, 640 361 640, open Mar–Oct

282

APPENDIX A

Stage planning tables

		GR65			
Book stage	Location	Distance from start	Distance from previous point	Distance, book stages	My itinerary
1	Le Puy-en-Velay	0.0	0.0	16.7	
	Montbonnet	16.7	16.7		
2	Saint-Privat-d'Allier	23.3	6.6	26.1	
	Monistrol-d'Allier	30.6	7.3		
	Saugues	42.8	12.2		
3	Le Clauze	50.3	7.5	19.3	
	Chanaleilles	56.7	6.4		
	Domaine du Sauvage	62.1	5.4		
4	Saint-Alban-sur-Limagnole	75.3	13.2	28.2	
	Aumont-Aubrac	90.3	15		
5	Les Quatre Chemins	101	10.7	27.3	
	Finieyrols	106.4	5.4		
	Nasbinals	117.6	11.2		
6	Aubrac	126.6	9	32.7	
	Saint-Chély-d'Aubrac	134	7.4		
	Saint-Côme-d'Olt	150.3	16.3		
7	Espalion	158.1	7.8	21.3	
	Estaing	171.6	13.5		
8	Campuac (via GR6)	183.1	11.5	35.3	
	(Golinhac (via GR65))	(185.7)	(14.1)		
	Le Soulié	192.1	9 (6)		
	Sénergues	197.5	5.4		
	Conques	206.9	9.4		
9	Noailhac	213.6	6.7	24.3	
	Decazeville	225.8	12.2		
	Livinhac-le-Haut	231.2	5.4		

Book stage	Location	Distance from start	Distance from previous point	Distance, book stages	My itinerary
10	Montredon	236.6	5.4	23.2	
	Saint-Félix	245.8	9.2		
	Figeac	254.4	8.6		
11	Faycelles	261.8	7.4	30.8	
	Gréalou	274.5	12.7		
	Cajarc	285.2	10.7		
12	Saint-Jean-de-Laur turn-off	295.6	10.4	27.5	
	Limogne-en-Quercy	304.3	8.7		
	Varaire	312.7	8.4		
13	Bach	318.3	5.6	32.5	
	Mas de Vers	327	8.7		
	Cahors	345.2	18.2		
14	Labastide-Marnhac	357.3	12.1	23.8	
	Lascabanes	369	11.7		
15	Montcuq	378.4	9.4	23.7	
	Lauzerte	392.7	14.3		
16	Durfort-Lacapelette	404.7	12	27.8	
	Moissac	420.5	15.8		
17	Malause turn-off	431.7	11.2	19.8	
	Espalais	439.2	7.5		
	Auvillar	440.3	1.1		
18	Saint-Antoine	448.7	8.4	32.8	
	Flamarens	453.3	4.6		
	Miradoux	457.4	4.1		
	Castet-Arrouy	462.1	4.7		
	Lectoure	473.1	11		
19	Marsolan	481.9	8.8	32.1	
	La Romieu	491.7	9.8		
	Castelnau-sur-l'Auvignon	496.5	4.8		
	Condom	505.2	8.7		

Book stage	Location	Distance from start	Distance from previous point	Distance, book stages	My itinerary
20	Larressingle turn-off	510.5	5.3	33.8	
	Montréal-du-Gers	521.5	11		
	Lamothe	531	9.5		
	Éauze	539	8		
21	Manciet	550	11	21	
	Nogaro	560	10		
22	Lanne-Soubiran	568.1	8.1	27.6	
	Lelin-Lapujolle	575.4	7.3		
	Barcelonne-du-Gers	585	9.6		
	Aire-sur-l'Adour	587.6	2.6		
23	Miramont-Sensacq	605.3	17.7	33.8	
	Pimbo	614.4	9.1		
	Arzacq-Arraziguet	621.4	7		
24	Larreule	633.7	12.3	30.2	
	Uzan	637.7	4		
	Pomps	642.2	4.5		
	Arthez-de-Béarn	651.6	9.4		
25	Maslacq	661.1	9.5	31.6	
	Sauvelade	669.3	8.2		
	Navarrenx	683.2	13.9		
26	Castetnau-Camblong	685.2	2	19.5	
	Lichos	697.5	12.3		
	Aroue	702.7	5.2		
27	Larribar-Sorhapuru	717.4	14.7	24	
	(Saint-Palais)	(722)	(19.3)		
	Ostabat-Asme	726.7	9.3 (11.3)		
28	Larceveau	730.4	3.7	22.2	
	Gamarthe	736.4	6		
	Saint-Jean-Pied-de-Port	748.9	12.5		

Book stage	Location	Distance from start	Distance from previous point	Distance, book stages	My itinerary
	GR651/CÉLÉ VALLEY VARIANT				
1	Figeac	0.0	0.0	25.7	
	Béduer	12.3	12.3		
	Corn	19	6.7		
	Espagnac-Sainte-Eulalie	25.7	6.7		
2	Brengues	29.7	4	15.9	
	Saint-Sulpice	34.1	4.4		
	Marcilhac-sur-Célé	41.6	7.5		
3	Sauliac-sur-Célé	50	8.4	18.3	
	Cabrerets	59.9	9.9		
4	Bouziès	66.8	6.9	10.7	
	Saint-Cirq-Lapopie	70.6	3.8		
5	Pasturat	85.8	15.2	33.2	
	Vers turn-off	89.6	3.8		
	Cahors	103.8	14.2		

Book stage	Location	Distance from start	Distance from previous point	Distance, book stages	My itinerary
	ROCAMADOUR VARIANT				
1	Figeac	0.0	0.0	22.8	
	Cardaillac	10.4	10.4		
	Lacapelle-Marival	22.8	12.4		
2	Thémines	33.4	10.6	24	
	Gramat	46.8	13.4		
3	Rocamadour	59.2	12.4	12.4	
4	Montfaucon	79.3	20.1	25.5	
	Labastide-Murat	84.7	5.4		
5	Cras	95.7	11	24.2	
	Vers	108.9	13.2		
6	Cahors	125.2	16.3	16.3	

APPENDIX B
Useful sources of information

Updated information on accommodation

Gronze
The top site for accommodation info on the pilgrim roads, although it's still developing its French coverage
www.gronze.com

ACIR
A reliable resource for information on all the French *chemins*
https://chemins-compostelle.com/hebergeur/voie/10

Miam Miam Dodo
The French guidebook, updated annually, has a thorough collection of accommodation profiles
http://chemindecompostelle.com/Selection/CarteFrance.html

In addition, the Camino Forum (www.caminodesantiago.me/community) has lots of experienced pilgrims with expertise to share.

Transport

For additional information see 'Getting there and back' in the Introduction. Before exploring more specific bus and train sites below, it's worth making an initial search on Rome2Rio (www.rome2rio.com).

Bus

Compostel'Bus
(service between Le Puy and Conques)
www.bus-chemin-compostelle.com

La Malle Postale
(service between Le Puy and Moissac)
www.lamallepostale.com/en

Transports Claudine
(service between Saint-Jean-Pied-de-Port and Conques)
https://claudine32.com

Migratour
(service in the Haute-Loire département)
www.autocars-migratour.fr

LIO
(service throughout the Occitan region – covers Saint-Chely-d'Apcher to Barcelonne-du-Gers)
https://lio.laregion.fr/transport-interurbain

La Région Nouvelle-Aquitaine
(service in the Nouvelle-Aquitaine department)
https://transports.nouvelle-aquitaine.fr

Txik Txak
(service between Aire-sur-l'Adour and Saint-Jean-Pied-de-Port)
www.txiktxak.fr

Train

SNCF
www.sncf.com/en

TGV
https://en.oui.sncf/en/tgv
(while TGV is part of SNCF, sometimes discounts can be found through this site)

Trainline
www.thetrainline.com
(a good option for purchasing tickets if SNCF isn't working)

Air

Air France
www.airfrance.com

British Airways
www.ba.com

RyanAir
www.ryanair.com

EasyJet
www.easyjet.com

Baggage transport

La Malle Postale
(provides service on the GR65 between Le Puy and Moissac, as well as the Célé Valley and Rocamadour variants)
www.lamallepostale.com/en

Transports Claudine
(ships packs between Conques and Saint-Jean-Pied-de-Port, and on the Célé Valley variant)
https://claudine32.com

Creánciale (pilgrim passport)

Before departure, you can obtain the *creánciale* from Camino-related groups including:

Confraternity of Saint James (CSJ)
www.csj.org.uk

American Pilgrims
http://americanpilgrims.org

Canadian Company of Pilgrims
www.santiago.ca

Camino Society Ireland
www.caminosociety.com

Once in France, the *creánciale* can be obtained from the cathedrals in Le Puy-en-Velay and Cahors, and in most tourism offices along the way.

Emergency services

General emergency: tel 112

Medical emergency: tel 15

Police: tel 17

Fire service: tel 18

APPENDIX C
English–French glossary

Note: for non-French speakers, it is quite common on the Via Podiensis to have your host each night phone ahead to reserve the next night's accommodation. Should you wish to request this, ask/show your host: *Je voudrais faire une réservation pour demain soir à __* (insert gîte/hotel/town name). *Pourriez-vous les appeler pour moi?*

English	French	English	French
altarpiece	le retable	close the gate	ferme la porte
backpack/rucksack	le sac à dos	closed	fermé
		clothesline	la corde à linge
baggage transport	transport de bagages	corner	le coin
		cross	la croix
bakery	la boulangerie/pâtisserie	detour	le deviation
bathroom	WC/la toilette/cabinets	doctor	le docteur/médecin
beware of dog	attention au chien	donation	la donation
bill (in a restaurant)	la facture/note	door, gate	la porte
		dovecote	le pigeonnier
blister	l'ampoule	dryer (clothes)	la sèche-linge
bridge	le pont	far	loin
bull ring	les arènes	food	les aliments
bus station	la gare du bus	fountain	la fontaine
butcher's shop	la boucherie	goodbye	adieu/au revoir
castle	le château	good evening	bonsoir
cathedral	la cathédrale	good morning	bonjour
cave	la grotte	good night	bonne nuit
central plaza	la place centrale	grocery store	l'épicerie
chapel	la chapelle	guesthouse/B&B	la chambre d'hôtes
cheese	le fromage		
church	l'église	help	aide

English	French
here	ici
hermitage	l'ermitage
highway	l'autoroute
hill	la colline
hospital	l'hôpital
hotel	l'hôtel
how much is it	combien ça coûte
hunting preserve	la réserve de chasse
inn	l'auberge
intersection	le carrefour
left	gauche
limestone plateau	le causse
livestock-shoeing station	le métier/travail a ferrer
mass	la masse
mill	la mouline
monastery	le monastère
near	près
neighborhood	le quartier
no	non
open	ouvert
pain	la douleur
path	le chemin
pilgrim	la pèlerin
pilgrim hostel	le gîte d'étape (not a literal translation)
pilgrim passport	la créanciale
please	s'il vous plaît

English	French
post office	la poste
refreshment booth	le buvette
restaurant	le restaurant
right	droite
river	la rivière/fleuve
shoes	les chaussures
sports center	le centre sportif
stamp (pilgrim passport)	le tampon
stamp (postage)	le timbre
straight	tout droit
street	la rue/voie/route
supermarket	le supermarché
telephone	le téléphone
time	les temps
thank you	merci
tourist office	l'office de tourisme
town	la ville/commune
town hall	la mairie
train station	la gare
valley	la vallée
washing machine	la machine à laver
water (drinkable)	l'eau (potable)
where is/are	où est/sont
yes	oui
youth hostel	l'auberge de jeunesse

APPENDIX D
Further reading

Other guidebooks and resources

The long-time guide-of-choice to the Via Podiensis is *Miam Miam Dodo* (www.levieuxcrayon.com), although you potentially need three separate books to get you through (*GR65 – Le Puy to Cahors, GR65 – Cahors to Saint-Jean-Pied-de-Port*, and the *Célé and Rocamadour variants*). While the guides are in French, they are easily decoded, and also available in app form.

Angelynn Meya, *The Lightfoot Guide to the Via Podiensis*, Eurl Pilgrimage Publications, 2017. An English-language guidebook to the Via Podiensis.

Melinda Lusmore, *I Love Walking in France* (series), self-published, 2020. A series of ebooks focused on the Via Podiensis.

Helen Martin, *Lot: Travels Through a Limestone Landscape in Southwest France*, Wiltshire, UK: Moho Books, 2008. An exceptional resource, invaluable to the background research conducted for this guide.

Books on pilgrimage and Santiago de Compostela

Edwin Mullins, *The Four Roads to Heaven: France and the Santiago Pilgrimage*, Oxford: Signal Books, 2017. The best English-language primer on the pilgrim roads through France. Mullins' *Cluny: In Search of God's Lost Empire* is also important historical context.

Beth Jusino, *Walking to the End of the World: A Thousand Miles on the Camino de Santiago*, Seattle: Mountaineers Books, 2018. While many pilgrim journals describe the Camino Francés, Jusino's account begins in Le Puy.

Jonathan Sumption, *The Age of Pilgrimage: The Medieval Journey to God*, Mahwah: HiddenSpring, 2003. A detailed survey of the pilgrimage boom in the medieval Christian world.

Phil Cousineau, *The Art of Pilgrimage*, San Francisco: Canari Press, 2012. A multi-faceted look at pilgrimage and the pilgrim experience.

Adam Hopkins, *Camino: Pilgrims to Paradise, the Road to Santiago, Then and Now*, Movement Publishing, 2020. An excellent survey of the history of the camino, focused primarily on its Spanish section.

Books on French history and culture

On the construction of French identity: Graham Robb, *The Discovery of France*, New York: Norton, 2007 and David Bell, *The Cult of the Nation in France*, Cambridge: Harvard UP, 2003

On Gallo-Romanic history: Bijan Omrani, *Caesar's Footprints: A Cultural Excursion to Ancient France: Journeys Through Roman Gaul*, New York: Pegasus, 2017

On the Albigensian Crusade: Jonathan Sumption, *The Albigensian Crusade*, London: Faber & Faber, 2000 and Stephen O'Shea, *The Perfect Heresy*, London: Gardners, 2001

On the Hundred Years' War: Desmond Seward, *A Brief History of the Hundred Years War*, London: Constable & Robinson, 2003

On the Wars of Religion: Mack Holt, *The French Wars of Religion, 1562–1629*, Cambridge UP, 2005

On the French Revolution: Jeremy Popkin, *A New World Begins: The History of the French Revolution*, New York: Basic Books, 2019 and Simon Schama, *Citizens: A Chronicle of the French Revolution*, New York: Vintage, 1990

On modern French history: Jonathan Fenby, *The History of Modern France*, New York: Simon & Schuster, 2016

On the Beast of Gévaudan: Jay Smith, *Monsters of the Gévaudan: The Making of a Beast*, Cambridge: Harvard UP, 2011

On Basque history and culture: Mark Kurlansky, *The Basque History of the World*, New York: Penguin, 2001

APPENDIX E
Major festivals along the way

A very partial list of festivals along the Via Podiensis follows, but keep in mind that many other smaller, local festivals take place throughout the year.

May

Transhumance Aubrac
(Aubrac Region)
www.transhumanceaubrac.fr

Festival de Bandas
(Condom)
www.festivaldebandas.fr

June

Les Médiévales de Saint-Cirq Lapopie
(Saint-Cirq-Lapopie)

July

Cahors Blues Festival
(Cahors)
www.cahorsbluesfestival.com

Africajarc
(Cajarc)
www.africajarc.com

Festival Galop Romain
(Éauze)

Fête de la Saint-Fleuret
(Estaing)

Festival de Théâtre
(Figeac)
https://festivaltheatre-figeac.com

La Fête du Saumon
(Navarrenx)

August

Festival du Film
(Espalion)

Les Rencontres Musicales de Figeac
(Figeac)
https://en.festivaldefigeac.com

Festival de Rocamadour – Musique Sacrée
(Rocamadour)
www.rocamadourfestival.com

Festival Celte en Gévaudan
(Saugues)
https://festivalengevaudan.com

September

Roi de L'Oiseau Renaissance Festival
(Le Puy-en-Velay)
www.roideloiseau.com

La Rue des Enfants
(Montcuq)
www.laruedesenfants.org

Montgolfiades (hot-air balloon festival)
(Rocamadour)

October

Festivités de la Sainte-Foy
(Conques)

DOWNLOAD THE ROUTES
IN GPX FORMAT

All the routes in this guide are available for download from:

www.cicerone.co.uk/1102/GPX

as standard format GPX files. You should be able to load them into most online GPX systems and mobile devices, whether GPS or smartphone. You may need to convert the file into your preferred format using a conversion programme such as gpsvisualizer.com or one of the many other such websites and programmes.

When you follow this link, you will be asked for your email address and where you purchased the guidebook, and have the option to subscribe to the Cicerone e-newsletter.

www.cicerone.co.uk

CICERONE

Trust Cicerone to guide your next adventure, wherever it may be around the world...

Discover guides for hiking, mountain walking, backpacking, trekking, trail running, cycling and mountain biking, ski touring, climbing and scrambling in Britain, Europe and worldwide.

Connect with Cicerone online and find inspiration.

- buy books and ebooks
- articles, advice and trip reports
- podcasts and live events
- GPX files and updates
- regular newsletter

cicerone.co.uk